'I loved this memoir – centurie̲ ̲ ̲ ̲ ̲ ̲ ̲ ̲ ̲ ̲ ̲ ̲ ̲ ̲ ̲old through the prism of one life'
— Raynor Winn,
author of *The Salt Path* and *Landlines*

'The pace is pleasantly unhurried. Simmons observes the natural world with precision and affection from the modest summit of Ditchling Beacon to the sopping lowland of the Weald'
— *Times Literary Supplement*

'This is a brilliantly modern take on one of the oldest of literary genres – the pilgrimage narrative. Gail Simmons walks a long-forgotten trail, and along the way encounters places, people and a myriad of obstacles, for who walks so far in today's car-obsessed world? But this is no ordinary walk, but one with a purpose: to discover the meaning of what it means to be British in these troubled and disjointed times'
— Stephen Moss, author of *Ten Birds That Changed The World*

'As she follows a long-lost pilgrimage route, Gail Simmons finds a whole new way of looking at a familiar landscape. Every footstep is steeped in history, every path is imbued with the traces of all those who came before'
— Neil Ansell, author of *The Circling Sky*

'Few books change the way you see familiar landscapes: this is one of them. A sacred, humble and rewarding journey, like the pilgrimage itself'
— Ben Rawlence, author of *The Treeline* and *City of Thorns*

'A stunningly evoked, sensitively drawn journey into a part of England that feels both ancient and entirely new. Such is the subtle power and lightly-worn erudition of Simmons' writing'
— Sophy Roberts,
author of *The Lost Pianos of Siberia*

'An old route for pilgrims is given new and vivid life through Gail Simmons as a solo woman walking. A compelling blend of history and nature writing that is a gift to all of us who love this iconic stretch of chalk cliffs and downland'
— Tanya Shadrick,
author of *The Cure for Sleep*

'This is a book for the modern pilgrim, as well as nature and history lovers'
— Helen Moat, BBC *Countryfile*

'Through four pagan seasons, following the ancient Gough Map and the Old Way, Gail Simmons pioneers a very modern pilgrimage, but finds that the past is not so far away . . . walking becomes an act of faith again – but also, it becomes an act of vulnerability and strength, loneliness and connection, peril, exposure and joyful epiphany. Gail makes a compelling journey over iconic chalk country – between the sea and what once was the sea, to a homecoming we can all aspire to'
— Nicola Chester, author of *On Gallows Down*

'Wandering the Old Way across 386km of the UK's south coast allows Simmons ample room to touch on history, folklore and modern politics. Along the way she also delves into what long walks, such as the old pilgrim trails, mean to us today and why being a woman walking alone still feels like a radical act' — *Wanderlust*, Stanfords' Staff Picks

'An absorbing tale of pilgrims, peasants, knights, kings and history on our doorstep' — *Country Walking*

'A lively and well-informed companion that makes you – pilgrim or walker – want to see the places for yourself. It brings to life the world of pilgrimage, whether with its ancient focus on the goal, or the modern focus on the journey' — *Church Times*

'[Simmons] is an engaging companion, bringing to life the places and people she meets en route and offering thoughtful reflections on what it means to travel – especially as a lone woman. Delightful'
— *Country Life*

'Such a joy to read . . . the author makes a great walking companion, sharing opinion, nostalgia and wit in warm tones. The Old Way deserves hikers' attention and love; we are lucky to have a chronicler as companionable as Simmons to tell its story' — Andy Wasley, *The Great Outdoors*

'Simmons is a veteran travel journalist, and she conveys a sense of place deftly . . . a welcome addition to the ever-growing library of British walking literature' — *Resurgence & Ecologist*

Author, academic and broadcaster Gail Simmons is a 'walking writer'. Her previous book, *The Country of Larks*, was shortlisted for the Edward Stanford Travel Writing Awards 2020, and she has contributed to the *Times*, *Telegraph*, *Independent*, *Wanderlust* and *TIME* magazine as well as appearing on the BBC's 'From Our Own Correspondent' and 'Woman's Hour'. Gail has an MA in Medieval History and a PhD in Creative Writing, and teaches at Bath Spa University on their MA in Nature and Travel Writing.

Also by Gail Simmons

The Country of Larks: A Chiltern Journey

Gail Simmons

BETWEEN THE CHALK AND THE SEA

A pilgrim's path along the south coast

HEADLINE

First published in 2023 by
HEADLINE PUBLISHING GROUP

First published in paperback in 2024 by
HEADLINE PUBLISHING GROUP

7

Cataloguing in Publication Data is available from the British Library.

ISBN: 978 1 4722 8030 5

Southwick Ampule © Alice Pattullo/centralillustration.com
Map of author's route © Martin Lubikowski, ML Design
Chanctonbury Ring, etching by Alex Buckels, c.1935. National Galleries Scotland,
Purchased 1980. © Estate of the Artist.
Celtic Wheel of the Year © littlepaw/iSTOCK
German Woodcut of Pilgrims in Europe © World History Archive/Alamy

Designed and typeset by EM&EN
Printed and bound in Great Britain by Clays Ltd, Elcograf S.p.A.

HEADLINE PUBLISHING GROUP
An Hachette UK Company
Carmelite House
50 Victoria Embankment
London EC4Y 0DZ

The authorised representative in the EEA is Hachette Ireland, 8 Castlecourt
Centre, Dublin 15, D15 XTP3, Ireland (email: info@hbgi.ie)

www.headline.co.uk
www.hachette.co.uk

For Alice of Southwick,
my companion on the Old Way

Thirteenth-century pilgrim ampule
of St Thomas Becket, found in the house of
Richard of Southwick, Southampton.

The Old Way

SURRE

HAMPSHIRE

Titchfield

Chichester

WEST
SUSSEX

Chanctonbury
Ring

Southampton

Havant

Steyning

Test

Itchen

Hamble

Meon

Arun

Adur

ISLE OF
WIGHT

Arundel

Boxgrove
Priory

ENGLISH CH

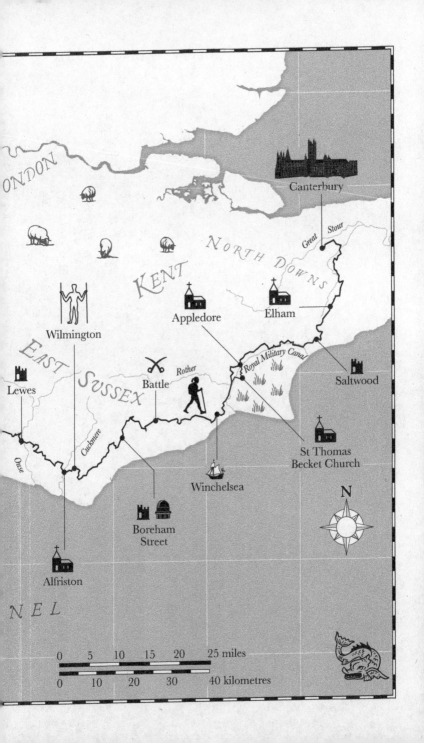

Chanctonbury Ring, West Sussex, by Alec Buckels (1892–1972).

Contents

Author's Note

The medieval texts quoted in this book have been transcribed from the originals by the author, except for Wynkyn de Worde's *Informacion for pylgrymes*, which was transcribed by William Connor.

To protect the privacy of individuals, some names in this book have been changed.

Bedrock

For the Ancient Greeks, it was *chalix*. In Latin, it's *calx*. In Old English, *cealc*. For twenty-first century geologists, it's calcium carbonate. These are a few of the aliases for a soft, sedimentary limestone composed of the mineral calcite, formed deep under the oceans by the compression of billions of microscopic plankton. We mortals know it as chalk, and it is the bedrock of my life.

Chalk's porcelain whiteness, gleaming through its fragile skin of turf, raises the spirits in all seasons.

Winter strips chalk downland to its most stark and elemental, the hilltops frosted and sculptural, the beech woods leafless and skeletal. Spring is when hares streak over bare hills, blackthorn trees are snowed with blossom and drifts of bluebells shimmer in beechwoods. Cowslips and violets nudge through warming earth as the first skylarks soar above sheep-shorn turf. Then summer arrives, bringing wheat fields glowing gold, the grassland braided with wildflowers. In autumn, ploughed fields turn tawny, and soil glints with upturned flint.

Chalk downland is unique, and supports one of the richest habitats for flora and fauna in Western Europe.

I grew up in chalk country, and I've lived on or near chalk hills much of my life – from the Chilterns of my childhood home via the Berkshire Downs near Oxford, to the Yorkshire Wolds not far from where I now live.

Not far, but far enough for someone shaped, sculpted and smoothed by chalk.

Half a century has passed since I first set foot on chalk – a tiny splinter of time in its 145-million-year existence. Now, following an old way buried under history, my feet would once again anchor themselves into ancient, white rock.

IMBOLC

'An ancient Celtic festival associated with the goddess Brigid, celebrating the beginning of spring and held on or around 1 February'

Late afternoon in early February. Outside, dusk settled on pastures yellowed by lingering winter. The earth lay dormant. In the Celtic Wheel of the Year this is Imbolc, a festival that heralds the first stirrings of spring. Imbolc, from the Old Irish 'in the belly', marks the onset of lambing when the ewes start lactating. Midway between the winter solstice, or Yule in the Celtic calendar, and the spring equinox at Ostara, it augurs the quickening of the year, when the northern hemisphere stirs from its sleep, bringing promise of renewal. Imbolc is a time for hope, and for new beginnings.

There were few stirrings of spring that February day as I gazed through my study window. Spring arrives late in North Yorkshire, and I knew that soon the yellowed grass would green, the curlew would return, splitting the skies with its hypnotic call, and silent fields would resound with the thin bleat of lambs.

I turned my eyes back to my desk. Spread out on the desktop was a map – a life-size poster reproduction of the original Gough Map, now kept in Oxford's Bodleian Library. I'd bought the poster on a visit to the Bodleian the previous summer. Following a Sunday newspaper commission, I was researching a feature on 'walks with meaning' and discovered the map was on rare public display, so I crossed the country to see it. Dated to around 1360, and measuring roughly two feet by four, the Gough Map is possibly an updated copy of one made as early as 1280, during the reign of Edward I. Reputedly the most accurate map of Britain prior to the sixteenth century, you can almost overlay it with a modern map, except that Britain – following the convention where maps (like churches) were orientated towards the east – is tilted on its side.

This version of the Gough Map might be over 600 years old, but studying the poster I made out the rivers Severn and Thames, the Humber and the Wear. The New Forest and Sherwood Forest were identifiable, and, on the border with Scotland, Hadrian's Wall is distinctly marked (called by its old Latin name, *murus pictorum*: the Picts' Wall). Most curious of all was the matrix of overland routes, depicted in red pigment and connecting towns and villages familiar to us today. The antiquarian Richard Gough, who owned the map and bequeathed it to the Bodleian Library in 1809, called these red lines 'roads'. Recently, historians have questioned their purpose, as many more obvious roads, such as Roman Watling Street, are omitted from the map. What is clear is that these lines represent itineraries of some kind, with their distances meticulously recorded.

One of these itineraries runs in a gentle curve, parallel to the coastline between Southampton and Canterbury. Roman numerals mark the distances between the intervening settlements – Havant to Chichester, Arundel and Bramber to Lewes, Boreham Street to Battle and Winchelsea, Rye and Appledore to Canterbury. Picturesque towns on England's south coast, now attracting retirees and tourists, London commuters and young professionals, and whose former significance as seaports, defensive settlements, market towns or religious centres is embedded in centuries of often turbulent history.

Historians have not paid much attention to this particular red line, buried in the top-right corner of a medieval map. It doesn't lead to or from London, as several other lines do, and although Canterbury had been a major religious centre since Henry II incited the murder of Thomas Becket two centuries earlier, Southampton in 1360 was then best known for its shipbuilding industry and as a commercial port. It was only when Will Parsons, co-founder of the British Pilgrimage Trust, studied the map afresh in 2016 that he concluded that, because Canterbury's significance has always been chiefly spiritual, this was a lost pilgrimage route from Southampton, where pilgrims from Europe landed before travelling on to Becket's shrine in Canterbury. Before arriving in Southampton, these pilgrims crossed the English Channel from France, just as others scaled the Alps on their way to Rome, or tramped over the Pyrenees en route to Santiago de Compostela.

For the past few years the British Pilgrimage Trust, a charity dedicated to renewing pilgrimage in Britain, has been researching the history of this route, retracing and reviving what is thought to be the first pilgrim itinerary marked on a map of England. When I interviewed him for my article on meaningful walks, Will Parsons talked passionately about a recent 'groundswell of interest' in pilgrimage, with latter-day pilgrims wanting to connect with those who had trodden identical paths for centuries. 'Knowing that others have gone the same way, by the same track, under the same trees', as he put it. As a keen walker and amateur historian myself, I could only agree. We might be living ever more secular lives in the West, but at the same time we are increasingly eager to reconnect to the landscape, to nature and to our built heritage, as it disappears before our eyes. For Will Parsons, a chance discovery on an obscure medieval map dovetailed with a rising awareness of our ancient and sacred routes, and the Old Way was born.

Mindful of Hilaire Belloc's 1904 classic *The Old Road*, which describes a possible pilgrimage route from Winchester to Canterbury (better known today as the Pilgrim's Way), the British Pilgrimage Trust named their rediscovered route the Old Way.

Crossing some 240 miles of countryside, it avoids busy main routes and instead follows a meandering network of paths, drovers' tracks, riverbanks, beaches, lanes and foot-worn holloways, tracing the uplands that contour the southeast coast of England. Punctuated by ruined monasteries, isolated churches and holy wells, it's a natural and built topography reassuringly familiar to pilgrims throughout the Middle Ages.

Starting in Southampton's medieval port, where Henry II began his own pilgrimage of repentance to the site of Thomas Becket's murder, the Old Way meanders along four sea-skirting counties: Hampshire, West and East Sussex, and Kent. It traverses, for the most part, chalk upland shaped over 80 million years into steep, secretive valleys and smoothed hills where horizons stretch for miles. The oldest fossilised remains of humans in Britain were found here, and the landscape is scored with prehistoric monuments, testament to the importance of chalk to our ancestors. And all along the route, there's the constant, shape-shifting presence of the sea – sometimes visible, sometimes just out of reach – framed by the white chalk cliffs that so define this island's history.

Chalk has defined my history too, and has made me who I am. Like that most pliable of rocks, my life has been shaped by the elements, and moulded by events, but my home was always close to chalk. After many years living and working in Oxford, where we'd regularly drive to the Berkshire Downs to plant our boots on chalk, I moved to North Yorkshire with my husband, Richard, and two energetic cats. The weather was colder, the Dales landscape, to eyes accustomed to the benevolent Downs or Cotswold hills, harsher. It was a shock.

For the first two winters, I escaped. As a travel journalist, I had the perfect excuse. I took off from Manchester and flew through monochrome skies, touching down a few hours later amidst the colour, noise and warmth of the Caribbean. In Santo Domingo, the capital of the Dominican Republic, I rented an apartment and wrenched my Italian into Spanish. I made friends, got tipsy on Brugal rum and danced the *bachata* to the sentimental strains of Antony Santos. Whenever I could procure a car I explored Hispaniola, the island shared between the Dominican Republic and Haiti, researching the story of Christopher Columbus's journeys to the land he named 'Little Spain' and penning articles for UK newspapers to fund my stay.

Later, I swung east, travelling to and writing about the Arab nations of Jordan, Syria, Lebanon, Oman, Tunisia and Libya. Then, in 2010, the Arab Spring set the region alight and my travel journalism dried up. No one except war correspondents were going there now, and no travel supplement wanted my stories on the Arab world. So I began writing about, and rediscovering, my homeland, meanwhile studying for a PhD and teaching creative writing.

Life as a writer and teacher was busy and interesting, and over the years I've grown to love the landscape of the Yorkshire Dales. The burnished heather moors, blooming briefly purple in summer. Empty valleys, where often all you hear are sheep, their bleats lifted on a barbed wind. Lone thorn trees, twisted on rain-scrubbed hilltops.

Our Pennine farmhouse, its metre-thick walls hewn from local millstone grit glittered on unforeseen sunny days, and held steadfast in gales that scour the winter fells, causing the pair of sycamore trees in an adjoining field to bend and moan. It was sturdy, safe. Yet still it didn't feel like home and my life, unlike the gritstone under our house, lacked permanence. In spring, summer and autumn, the habitual restlessness could be assuaged by walking. On sharp winter days when out on foot, my spirits would lift and brighten like chalk.

This was not one of those days. Looking out again at the drab panorama beyond my window, I craved the radiance of chalk once again. I glanced back at the reproduction Gough Map laid out on my desk, its colours a little faded after some 600 years. It had been rolled up in its cardboard tube for the past few months, and I had to weigh down each end with books to study it properly. This was the first time I'd looked at it since my research the previous summer, when I'd heard about the Old Way from Will Parsons. Another long-distance path to add to my ever-expanding bucket list.

We are lucky in Britain. The country is latticed by long-distance paths and national trails. Offa's Dyke, the Ridgeway, the Icknield Way – all of these were on my agenda. Apart from the Cotswold Way, which Richard and I had walked in our early twenties, and even with my decades-long love of walking, I hadn't completed any other long-distance path in Britain. Maybe it was guilt at taking so much time off, a guilt I didn't feel when Richard and I walked the 100 miles of the Cotswold Way. We carried our own luggage and didn't book accommodation ahead, trusting in providence as the summer days lengthened before us.

A few years later, working as a guide for a hiking holiday company, I walked alone from the Tuscan coast to Orvieto in Umbria. I set off with trepidation and a small rucksack, knowing I'd be alone for a fortnight in a country where my command of the Italian language was still rudimentary. But as the days passed, and I walked on through an ethereal land of Etruscan ruins, sunken roads and hilltop villages, I didn't want it to end.

Nearly three decades had passed since that lone walk through the Etruscan hills, and the time for another prolonged walk felt right. Perhaps it was something to do with my age, and the nagging sense of life contracting more rapidly than I would wish. In a world that seems to be moving ever faster, days passing in a whirl of work and domesticity, walking compels us to slow down. Deliberately slowing to a walking pace, refusing to hurry to someone else's agenda, is an act of resistance. There was a reason the Jarrow March of 1936 was so powerful: walking makes a statement. It's visible. It shows integrity and thoroughness of intent. It's putting your feet where your mouth is.

When walking, time's strictures loosen. The lengthier the walk, the further time unravels. On a long-distance walk, over many days, weeks or months, time feels infinite. Walking can also be a liberation. You can switch off your mobile phone and put your everyday life into airplane mode. Unlike your family, friends and colleagues, the ground, as you place one foot in front of the other, expects nothing from you. Neither does the sky arching over your head, nor the air you inhale, nor the sun and wind and rain on your skin. As the days pass, you become at one with the path beneath your feet. As you walk on, you lose – or temporarily mislay – your identity in the immensity of the landscape. The spent carapace of your normal life sloughs away, and you rediscover the chrysalis of your essential self.

Like many others, including several friends and acquaintances over the years, I'd thought about walking the Camino de Santiago. Not only is it the long-distance walk *par excellence*, it's also a historic route of pilgrimage. It has a purpose beyond the sheer enjoyment of putting one foot in front of the other over hundreds of miles.

The Camino might be the most famous pilgrim route in Europe, but it's not the world's only one. The globe is overlaid with them, from the *Haj* to Mecca in Saudi Arabia, and the Kumano Kodo in Japan. For me though, the Camino's popularity was off-putting and, in an era of *flygskam*, or flight shame, travelling across the continent for a walk felt unnecessary. So instead of taking a long-distance walk I flung myself into my work as a freelance travel journalist, and domestic life with my husband and pets, taking shorter walks in the countryside when time allowed.

In the months following my article research, my mind often returned to the Old Way. The route crosses a long stretch of chalk landscape I hardly knew, including the South Downs of Sussex and the North Downs of Kent. I'd been meaning to walk the South Downs Way for years, but could never find the time, or the justification, to commit to it. As a graduate of medieval history, the scholar in me was captivated by the notion of a medieval pilgrimage route. As a middle-aged adult with a strong sense of the sacred, though not adhering to any formal religion in spite of my Church of England upbringing, I wanted to explore whether a traditional pilgrimage had any resonance with my busy, largely secular, twenty-first century life.

No longer young or carefree, I wanted to put my feet where my words were, and put into practice what I'd written about in my newspaper feature about walks with meaning. Not only was the Old Way geographically nearer to home than the Camino de Santiago, but it was emotionally closer, too. It had been too long since I'd felt the crunch of chalk under my boots and followed white paths ribboning across open turf, drawing me onwards over ice-carved hills. Geologically and spiritually, the Old Way delivered.

Just like Geoffrey Chaucer's fictional pilgrims, I would begin my own pilgrimage in spring. I would witness the season's unfurling over England's chalkland. Chalk down (from the Celtic word *dūn*, or 'hill') and its grasslands are truly exceptional. Britain has half the world's surviving chalk downland, but even so it's now one of our rarest and most threatened landscapes. Before the Second World War this fragile and flower-rich calcareous grassland was widespread, but 80 per cent of lowland chalk and limestone grassland has now disappeared, largely under the plough, depriving plants and wildlife of one of the richest habitats in Western Europe. For thousands of years chalk down has been a precious habitat for people too. Prehistoric burial mounds, ancient stone circles, enigmatic carved figures and imposing Iron Age hillforts scatter England's chalk hills, evidence of our deep connection to this most supple of terrains.

Unlike Chaucer's ninety-mile route from London to Canterbury, the Old Way is 240 miles long, and would take around a month to walk in one go. Yes, I would see spring unspool, but I would not experience chalk down in its other seasonal guises. I might see the bluebells in the beechwoods, but I would miss the flower-flecked pastures of summer, the flinty furrowed fields of autumn and the stark shapes and monochrome palettes of winter. So why rush it? Why not walk the Old Way in sections, and savour it over all four seasons of the year?

Medieval pilgrims did not only walk in spring. Sometimes, their journeys would take months, or even years. Chaucer's fictional characters may have been on a spring jolly, but for many pilgrims the journey was a serious, and often perilous, affair. Although not compulsory, going on pilgrimage was encouraged by the Church, and it wasn't meant to be easy. Nor was pilgrimage purely a late-medieval activity, though this was when the majority of pilgrim accounts were written. When St Augustine arrived in Canterbury in 597, he introduced Roman Christianity to England – the version that endured for almost 1,000 years until Henry VIII broke with Rome in 1534. But Christianity, and pilgrimage, had existed in the British Isles since at least the fourth century, and was still thriving in the Celtic north and west when Augustine stepped ashore on the Kent coast to proselytise the Anglo-Saxons under the direction of Pope Gregory 'the Great'.

Both Christian belief systems, Roman and Celtic, superimposed their festivals on pagan traditions and feasts, ones that had existed for millennia. Pope Gregory, when he sent Augustine to England, decreed that the newly converted Anglo-Saxons should build places of worship on pagan sites, and adapt pagan celebrations to Christian ones. Yule became Christmas, Ostara was transformed into Easter, Samhain metamorphosed into All Saints' Day and Halloween. Other important Christian festivals, such as St Valentine's Day in February, St John's Day in midsummer and Lammas Day in early August also co-opted their pagan predecessors Imbolc, Litha and Lughnasa. Other pagan-cum-Christian festivals marked the solstices and equinoxes.

Following the Old Way in all seasons, then, would be much more than a long-distance walk. It would be a meaningful journey through the strata of English history from prehistoric times to the twenty-first century, and through our pagan, as well as Christian, past. Just like digging down through layer upon layer of soft, white sedimentary rock.

Walking across this sliver of southern England, I wanted to discover what such a journey on foot meant today. At a time when the nation recalibrates its place within Europe, what might a medieval pilgrimage reveal about modern Britain? And what, if anything, would it reveal about me as I approached Mabon – my own autumnal equinox?

I rolled up the poster of the Gough Map and turned on my laptop. There were plans to be made, accommodation to be booked, and all the other organisation that goes into preparing for a journey on foot. No matter. This was Imbolc after all, the time for hope and new beginnings. Soon I would be on the path, striding out across southern English uplands so familiar from my Chiltern childhood. Walking the Old Way, between the chalk and the sea.

It would be like going home.

Informacion for pylgrymes

Wynkyn de Worde *c.*1498

Wynkyn de Worde (died c.1534) was a German immigrant to London who worked with William Caxton before setting up his own printing press. In 1498, de Worde published a guide for pilgrims visiting the Holy Land, which included the following advice for travellers departing from Venice.

Also I counsel you to have with you out of Venyse [Venice] Confeccons Confortatives Laxatives Restrictives Grenegynger [fresh ginger] Almondes Ryce Fygges Reysons grete & smalle. whyche shall doo you grete ease by the waye. And Pepyr Saffron Cloves & Maces a fewe as ye thynke need. and loof sugre [loaf sugar] also.

Also take with you a lytyll caudron. a fryenge panne. dysshes. Platers. Sawcers of tre [treen, i.e wood] cuppes of glasse. A grater for brede. & suche necessaryes. Also ye shall bye you a bed beside saynt Markys churche in Venyse where ye shal have fether bed. A matrasse. A pylowe. Two payre shetes and a quylte. & ye shall pay but thre dukates [gold coins]. And whan ye come again bring the same bed again and ye shall have a dukate & an half for it agayne though it be broke and woren. And marke his hous & his name that ye boughte it of ayenst ye come to Venyse.

OSTARA

'A pagan and Wiccan holiday celebrating the spring equinox, sometimes also called Eostre or Easter'

SOUTHAMPTON TO TITCHFIELD

I

Sunlight bouncing off water. Gulls squabbling overhead. Seaweed marinating in diesel. An imagining of shores beyond these shores. The promise of fresh horizons that has, over centuries, drawn the *Mayflower*'s pilgrims, the *Titanic*'s passengers and Carnival's leisure cruisers to this port city to set sail across oceans. A promise that has now drawn me to set foot across the chalk uplands of southern England.

I couldn't see it yet. But coming from the Yorkshire Dales, where deep valleys and heathered hills absorb the light like blotting paper, I knew the moment I stepped off the train at Southampton that here, at last, was the sea.

The year was approaching the spring equinox, the point of equilibrium between day and night, light and dark. In the Celtic calendar, this was the feast of Ostara, which takes its name from Eostre, the Saxon goddess of spring symbolising rebirth and renewal. Her legacy lives on today in oestrogen, a hormone essential to female fertility.

It was an auspicious moment to begin my journey along the Old Way – or so it then seemed. The red line on the Gough Map showed the first stage taking me from *hampton*, as it was known in the Middle Ages, as far as the old Roman settlement of *houentre*: the market town of Havant, near Portsmouth. The Gough Map measures the distance as twenty-two (XXII) miles, though the Bodleian's Map Librarian, Nick Millea, writes in his book *The Gough Map: The Earliest Road Map of Great Britain?* that these were possibly medieval French miles, each measuring around two kilometres. Modern miles of 1,760 yards, standardised in 1675, are much closer to the Roman mile, the noun arising from *mille passus*, or '1,000 paces' in Latin. To confuse matters further, a Roman pace was measured as two steps – roughly five feet. For the sake of my sanity I ignored the Gough Map measurements, and any attempts to wrap my head around French or Roman mile conversions. Instead, I went by the Old Way online guide, which estimates the walk to be around thirty-six modern miles, a journey that would thread together ruined monasteries, forgotten pilgrim churches, hidden sanctuaries and holy wells.

My original idea had been to carry on to Arundel – the end of the third stage on the Gough Map's itinerary, and a week's walk away. Pilgrim-style, I would carry my belongings with me, and stay in accommodation most closely resembling that which medieval pilgrims would have chosen. Matters of authenticity aside, my budget was also a constraint, just as it was for pilgrims throughout history. This meant staying in cheap hotels, bed and breakfasts and, where possible, holy sites such as churches or monasteries. Providing shelter for pilgrims and other needy travellers was the charitable duty of medieval religious houses, and many parish churches are now offering 'champing', or sanctuary, accommodation. That was the plan, anyhow. To paraphrase the poet Robert Burns, the best-laid plans of mice and women oft go awry – and so it turned out.

Before setting off on the first leg of my journey along the shingle shore of Southampton Water to Hamble, a walk of around ten miles, I wanted to spend a day exploring old Southampton. I'd read that its medieval city walls were largely extant, and although I knew the famous fortifications of York and Chester, I had never visited Southampton's. For the architectural historian Nikolaus Pevsner there were 'few, if any, examples of medieval urban defences as impressive as those in Southampton'. Although the city was badly bombed during the Second World War, and further blighted by post-war development, there were many fine monuments to discover.

Bargate, guarded by a pair of magnificently rampant lions, was my entry to medieval Southampton. Dating from the twelfth century, Bargate pierces the oldest section of the city walls and remains the most impressive medieval gate in Southampton, albeit in its current amputated form. For seven centuries Bargate bridged the walls defending the city's northern boundary, with photos from the 1920s showing trams trundling through its central archway. Then, in the 1930s, Bargate's adjacent walls were bulldozed to make way for new roads – heralding both the age of the car, and the end of an era.

Once you tread, though, between the leonine sentries into Bargate's atmospheric archway, the rumble of traffic fades, and your boots echo on stone pavements worn down by eight centuries of feet, hooves and wheels. Antiquity enshrouds you like a dawn mist, and the inimitable thrill of entering a great medieval city on foot quickens your step. A thrill that must also have quickened the step of untold generations of pedestrian travellers before me. The majority of people in the Middle Ages, when Bargate was built, had little opportunity to travel. Some of those that did – the merchants and pedlars, the soldiers and lawyers, the royals and their commissioners, the vagabonds and outlaws, the peasants and pilgrims – once walked through this archway too.

And perhaps, like me that early spring afternoon, those generations of travellers were greeted by music. No minstrel with a mandolin serenaded this twenty-first century pilgrim. Instead, a beanie-hatted busker belting out *Wonderwall* on his guitar was my welcome. Half a millennium may have passed since pilgrimage was banned by Henry VIII, but some things haven't changed for the stranger entering Southampton on foot.

Countless such strangers have arrived, and departed, over these many centuries. In the late Middle Ages, Southampton's port was the third most important in the country, after London and Bristol. Southampton's merchants mainly exported wool, then the prime commodity of the English economy, to mainland Europe. Accompanying the sacks of wool aboard the merchant vessels departing from Southampton were pilgrims, many of them en route to the continent's second religious destination after Rome: Santiago de Compostela. In turn, wine was imported into Southampton from France and Spain, and silk from Italy. Disembarking with the barrels of wine and bales of silk were pilgrims, many arriving from southwest France and Spain on their way to England's top pilgrimage destination – the shrine of St Thomas Becket in Canterbury.

These voyages were no pleasure cruises, as today's passengers sailing from Southampton might expect. Merchant ships required a licence to carry pilgrims, though this in no way guaranteed a comfortable voyage, as medieval accounts of sea-faring pilgrims reveal. Seasickness, overcrowding, foul smells and maltreatment by the crew, along with the possibility of shipwreck, were the hazards facing seaborne pilgrims. Understandably then, both merchants and their passengers took the shortest maritime route to their chosen country, and from much of Western Europe the shortest route to southern England was across the Channel and up Solent Water, to Southampton.

Dover may be geographically closer to cities like London and Canterbury, but its port did not surpass Southampton's until the advent of motorised shipping. Like Bristol, Southampton lies in a sheltered estuary and the city's unusual 'double high water' grants it a generous seventeen hours of rising water each day, doubling the number of boats that could sail into the city. As late as 1914 – just two years after the *Titanic* famously and fatally steamed away from its docks – Southampton was still the south coast's main port, with Dover playing catch-up. While Kent was closer for pilgrims from northern France travelling to Canterbury, Southampton was the landing point for pilgrims from much of mainland Europe. And it's the route from Southampton to Canterbury, not Dover to Canterbury, that is marked in the Gough Map.

From Southampton, pilgrims disembarked and continued on foot or horseback to Canterbury, visiting local shrines and other holy places along the way, just as I would. As Chaucer's motley band proved, not all pilgrims came from overseas. One home-grown pilgrim was Richard of Southwick, a wealthy merchant and burgess of Southampton who died *c*.1290 – around the time the original Gough Map is thought to have been designed. Archaeo-logical evidence recovered in 1966 from the cesspit in Richard's lost house in Cuckoo Lane included – among the wine jugs from France, glass from Venice, silk from Persia and the bones of a Barbary ape – a pair of pewter St Thomas ampules of holy water (mixed with a little of the saint's miraculous blood) from Canter-bury. The Old Way eastwards would have led him there.

Today, Southampton's trade is in tourists, who congregate from all corners of Europe for their 'cruise of a lifetime', and in students, the town being home to two universities. After a gap of 500 years few pilgrims now arrive here, booted and backpacked as I was that day, eager for the journey inland. Along with this surge of anticipation, one shared by all departing travellers, a tide of despondency sluiced over me as I drifted through the city streets. A familiar sensation, and one I've experienced throughout my life arriving for the first time in a new place. Perhaps it stemmed from childhood when, as the daughter of a nomadic army family, we'd move houses – and sometimes countries – every year or so. This meant new schools every year or so also, and the hollow feeling in the pit of my stomach as I again became the 'new girl', the outsider.

Back then, I had no say in the decision-making of my parents. As an adult, this peripatetic existence was a choice. I even made a living – sort of – from it. For the first few years, I revelled in my rootlessness. Richard was uncomplaining and, as the domestic linchpin and chief cook in our home, perfectly able to carry on without me as I ran off on my jaunts across the globe. Yet, that evening, alone in an unknown city, I couldn't help tormenting myself. Even now, in my sixth decade I was forcing myself to become the outsider, deliberately placing myself many hundreds of miles from the security and comfort of home with all the vulnerability and loneliness this entailed.

Every pilgrim throughout history must have felt the same misgivings, embarking on a long and often perilous journey far from family and friends, aware they would not see home again for many weeks, or even months. For some, making a pilgrimage may not even have been a choice, with those deemed guilty of sin, such as Henry II following the murder of Thomas Becket, expected to undertake penitential pilgrimages. Journeying to sacred places was already well established in Anglo-Saxon England, with many

Who was Thomas Becket?

This is the story of how a 'low-born clerk' came to befriend and serve a king; how he followed his political appointment as Archbishop of Canterbury by taking holy orders and shifting his allegiance to a different lord and master; how this led to his shocking 'murder in the cathedral'; how, following his martyrdom, he became England's most famous saint.

Thomas Becket remains a well-known story, despite attempts to silence the cult of the saint by Henry VIII. It's a story of power and of fame, and of the triumph of life over death.

Becket was martyred on 29 December 1170, and we're still talking about him over 850 years later. He brought wealth to Canterbury Cathedral by attracting pilgrims from all over Europe. One such group of pilgrims was commemorated in Chaucer's *The Canterbury Tales*; centuries later T. S. Eliot revisited the martyrdom in his 1930s drama *Murder in the Cathedral*.

saints such as Cuthbert in Durham the focus of mass devotion, and only grew in popularity in the centuries after the Norman Conquest. With the added attraction of Indulgences – the remission of sins through holy acts – Europe in the Middle Ages was a continent traversed by pilgrims in their multitudes.

As *The Canterbury Tales* so vividly illustrates, medieval pilgrims came from all echelons of society. Safety was in numbers, and you would find yourself falling into step with earls, friars, messengers, jugglers, troubadours, peasants, bishops, or merchants such as Southampton's Richard of Southwick. The elderly and infirm were discouraged from going on pilgrimage, and if you were wealthy you could hire someone else to undertake one on your behalf, such as the London merchant who in 1352 paid £20 (around £12,000 today – equivalent to a luxury holiday in the Maldives) for a proxy to travel to Mount Sinai. Pilgrimage was one of the few endeavours where people from all walks of life would meet, and interact. Once on the road, pilgrims would then encounter other disparate wayfarers – from beggars in their rags to kings with their retinues. *The Canterbury Tales* might be the best-known example, but, as narratives from John Bunyan's *The Pilgrim's Progress* to Rachel Joyce's *The Unlikely Pilgrimage of Harold Fry* show, pilgrimage has long been a pretext for experience and discovery outside the strictures of everyday life.

Making such a pilgrimage, especially one to a foreign land, was no small undertaking. A journey across unfamiliar country would be fraught with danger, and it was common for pilgrims never to return. For many, pilgrimage was indeed a sacred act, and although not everyone could make a longer journey to large centres such as Canterbury, Walsingham, Rome, Santiago de Compostela or Jerusalem, most people would make shorter pilgrimages to their local shrines. Many folk would also have a favourite saint who they would ask to intercede on their behalf, to cure them of various ailments, or help them become pregnant. Others, as we see from real-life pilgrim Margery Kempe's account, travelled as much for social reasons as religious ones.

Before setting out, pilgrims were required to pay off their debts, provide for their families in their absence and make a will. Customarily, the will would be enacted if the traveller did not return home within a year and a day. After this period had elapsed the pilgrim would be assumed dead, and their spouse free to marry again. By tradition the pilgrim was clothed in a rough tunic (sclavein) and bore a stout wooden staff with metal tip and soft leather pouch (scrip) tied around the waist – a 'uniform' (*habitus peregrinorum*) also adopted by thieves and vagabonds who disguised themselves as pilgrims to commit their nefarious deeds. With the blessing of the parish priest the pilgrim set forth. Once embarked on the journey he or she would need somewhere to stay overnight, and religious institutions such as monasteries offered accommodation to pilgrims as part of their sacred duty.

Wealthier and more important pilgrims, such as royalty, aristocracy and the higher ranks of the clergy, were offered lodgings as guests of the abbots at religious houses along the way. In towns like Southampton, those who could afford it stayed in inns, while lowlier pilgrims lodged in hospices, which catered for poor travellers in what we would today call a hostel. Accommodation at medieval hospices would have been basic, crowded and flea-ridden. No such establishments survive in Southampton today, so instead I found hospitality at the Ibis Budget hotel, a few hundred metres from the old city centre.

On the edge of a retail park, and adjacent to a noisy road, the Ibis Budget hotel felt a little soulless as I unpacked my rucksack that evening, the homesickness setting in like fog rolling in off the Solent. An IKEA superstore, a few minutes' walk down the road, supplied some Scandinavian cheer, warmth and – dare I say it – *hygge*. I bought a vanilla-scented candle to light in my room and warm my spirits, and tucked into a bargain plateful of fish and chips at the store's restaurant. As it turned out, the rules of the hotel forbade lighting candles, so I had to make do with my reading lamp to thaw the atmosphere.

This somewhat spartan start to my journey felt appropriate, for while some pilgrims were wealthy like our merchant Richard of Southwick, many were ordinary people with little money. Pilgrimage, after all, was not supposed to be luxurious. It was meant to be a test of devotion, and of character.

Tomorrow, I knew, would be better. The Old Way would lead me out of the modern city and onto paths along shingle beaches with vistas of chalk hills soaring beyond.

As I lay in my hotel bed trying to sleep in a new city with its metropolitan sounds of car horns, revving motorbikes and police sirens, I thought of Richard of Southwick. This successful merchant, who ran a large household very close to my hotel, would surely have had a wife. This unnamed wife may well have accompanied Richard to Canterbury. After all, we know from Chaucer's fictional characters, as well as real pilgrims whose testaments survive, that women went on pilgrimage too. In 1498 Wynkyn de Worde, a Flemish assistant to William Caxton who later set up on his own, published *Informacion for pylgrymes unto the Holy Londe* – perhaps the first guidebook in English, offering helpful tips to pilgrims intending to travel to Palestine. There's no evidence that Richard of Southwick or his wife ventured that far afield.

Assuming then that Richard of Southwick's wife did go on pilgrimage to Canterbury, what might she have worn, and how did she travel? What possessions did she take with her? What did she eat and drink on the way? As the wife (or widow) of a wealthy merchant she probably travelled on horseback, like Chaucer's Wife of Bath. As I lay there, the thrum of traffic ebbing as the clock ticked towards midnight, Richard's wife began to take shape in my mind as a real person – one with whom I could imagine travelling along the Old Way, despite our differences in status. She lived at the time the first version of the Gough Map was made, in around 1280, so made a fitting companion for the purpose of this pilgrimage. Now she just needed a name. The Wife of Bath was called Alisoun, so what about Alice? This was, after all, the second most popular female name in late thirteenth-century England (Matilda was the first), around the time that Richard and his family lived in Cuckoo Lane. 'Alice of Southwick' had a nice ring to it. So I drifted into sleep contemplating Alice, my fellow traveller along the Old Way to Canterbury.

The following morning, reinforced by a cooked vegetarian breakfast at IKEA and heartened by thoughts of Alice, I ventured onto West Quay. In the Middle Ages this was the busiest commercial quay in the city, where vessels docked, goods were loaded and unloaded, and passengers embarked and disembarked. Today, it's a humming shopping centre where modern pilgrims come to venerate at the shrine of consumerism. I was hoping for inspiration at West Quay, to absorb the atmosphere of a once-great medieval port, but it did not inspire me that morning. I was about to walk away when I found myself face to face with some of the most impressive medieval walls in England. Here another archway, less grand than Bargate's, punctured the walls. This was the Westgate, from where Henry V's army sailed on his way to victory at Agincourt in 1415. Two centuries later, the *Mayflower* docked here on her way to Plymouth before carrying the Pilgrim Fathers across the Atlantic to begin new lives in the New World.

The moment you pass through the Westgate, built following the French raid of 1338, the ambience alters. It quietens, thickens. All images of West Quay Retail Park erased, you enter the realm of a bygone traveller.

Once through the gate you follow the old layout of the city inside its circle of fortifications, perceptible even after the destruction of the medieval port by the Luftwaffe and post-war city planners. Within its web of sinuous streets you unearth fragments of the past, such as the thirteenth-century Medieval Merchant's House, now faithfully restored as a tourist attraction. Exploring its rooms, I imagined Alice of Southwick, bustling around her own house in nearby Cuckoo Lane, packing for her pilgrimage to Canterbury. Nearly demolished as a slum in the 1930s, the Medieval Merchant's House now teeters alongside the block of flats that, in the Sixties, replaced the rest of this terrace of timber-framed houses. Off Westgate Street is Cuckoo Lane, where other wealthy merchants, and the Southwicks themselves, lived in waterfront houses during the thirteenth century. Following the 1338 raid, these houses were torn down and great ramparts built in their place, though Cuckoo Lane itself survives.

Everywhere, jostling with these survivors, were reminders of the devastation of the Second World War. During the Blitz, hundreds of Southampton's citizens were killed. Over 4,000 houses were destroyed, and 11,000 seriously damaged. Only one church within the city walls, St Michael's, escaped harm. Dating from around 1070, immediately after the Norman Conquest, it's the oldest church in Southampton, though now dismally surrounded by post-war development. Nearby is Holy Rood, founded in the 1320s and once the church of sailors, a roofless shell after the bombardment of 30 November 1940. Today, it's dedicated to the sailors who served in the Merchant Navy, and to those who lost their lives at sea.

Along with these remnants of its medieval architecture, and much of its original plan, Southampton's streets retain many of their former names. Bugle Street, from the Latin *buculus* (bull) was once the hub of the commercial city. French Street is named after the population that settled here after the Norman Conquest, while English Street (now called High Street), together with East Street, was where the Saxons lived. Native and immigrant populations still live side by side in this city, just as they have done for almost 1,000 years.

Today, these medieval thoroughfares are colonised with the Superdrugs, Burger Kings, Tesco Expresses and Costa Coffees common to most British high streets, and the city's ramparts couldn't keep out the familiar whine of an ambulance siren. Like its counterparts throughout the land, medieval Southampton would also have been noisy. Walking those frayed streets I heard the past din of everyday life: the squawk of chickens, the bellow of traders, the profanities of sailors, the gossip of fishwives, the yelping of street dogs and, above all, the ringing of church bells punctuating every hour of the medieval day. It would have been a smelly town as well, though in place of the stench of rotting food, raw sewage and unwashed bodies, the modern city has its own distinct town-centre aroma of frying chips, steaming coffee and diesel fumes.

Several hours of strolling Southampton's streets later I found myself once again at its most imposing medieval monument, Bargate. The road leading north from Bargate, out of town, is called Above Bar Street and in the thirteenth century grew into a separate suburb. No traces of the original neighbourhood remain today, obliterated by twentieth-century development. It was here that medieval travellers – and perhaps pilgrims – could seek accommodation and sustenance if they found themselves locked out of the city at curfew.

A chill dusk was falling as I stood between the twin lions standing sentinel at Bargate. They seemed to herald my curfew too, so I turned around and retraced my steps through the old city streets. Ahead lay West Quay Retail Park, my pilgrim hostel at the Ibis and my last night in Southampton before I set out the following morning, along the Old Way to Canterbury.

II

'Most curious and ancient' was the description of a rare medieval map on its sale to the eighteenth-century antiquarian Richard Gough, who, bequeathing it to Oxford's Bodleian Library, also lent the map its present name. Compared to its contemporaries, the Gough Map is remarkably accurate. Drawn on two stitched-together sheepskins, and measuring just under two feet by four, it's not a large object, but one full of curiosities. Among these are its vignettes – enchanting sea monsters, shipwrecks, churches, fortified towns, towers and castles. London appears as two fairy-tale fortresses with crenellated towers, a gate with portcullis and four church spires picked out in gold leaf. The port of Southampton, or Hampton as it was called in the fourteenth century (from the Old English *hamm*, 'river-meadow' + *ton*, 'settlement'), didn't merit the gold-leaf treatment. Of lesser importance than the capital, it's depicted as two buildings with a spired church and is perched lopsidedly on the wrong bank of the River Itchen.

In 1611, around 250 years after the Gough Map was made, and some seventy years after pilgrimage was outlawed by Henry VIII, the historian and cartographer John Speed also drafted a map of Southampton. His gave far greater consideration to a lifelike portrayal of the city, with streets, churches and gates all drawn with precision. As with the Gough Map there are illustrations, although these are realistic rather than symbolic. Rendered in three dimensions, and hand-coloured in pastel shades, Southampton's ramparts, the castle atop its motte, the churches and friaries are all shown. There are even half a dozen masted ships, including a galleon in billowing sail skimming the choppy waters of West Quay.

To the east of the city there are orchards, salt marshes and meadows, now long buried under tarmac. Look closely, and you can spot God's House, and to the right is God's House Gate, appearing just as it does today. Founded in 1197 as an almshouse by Gervase le Riche, God's House would also have hosted passing pilgrims, as did most religious houses. A possession since the fourteenth century of The Queen's College, Oxford, it narrowly escaped Henry VIII's commissioners as university institutions were excluded from the 1530s Acts of Suppression.

Look even closer and you can make out a figure with ballooning breeches, a hat and a staff striding purposefully away from the God's House Gate across the meadow (labelled by Speed as God's House Grene). Some have interpreted the figure to be a traveller, suggesting that he may have been heading east along the Old Way, although a more prosaic version has him off to play a game of bowls on the green next to the former hospital.

That purposeful figure could also have been me as I left Southampton that Monday morning to begin my pilgrimage, down to the hat, staff and loose-fitting trousers. I'd become quite fond of the Ibis Budget over the two nights I'd spent there, but wanted to begin the journey from where many of my medieval forebears and John Speed's traveller set out – God's House Gate. Retracing my steps of the day before, I walked the pavements of West Quay, past the retail park and IKEA. Sooted city trees were in bud, and just discernible above the diesel a spring softness sweetened the air.

From God's House Gate I was hoping to pick up the Solent Way, a long-distance footpath hugging sixty miles of the Hampshire coast, as far as Hamble. On the way I would visit Netley Abbey, a few minutes' walk from Southampton Water, just as my medieval forebears would have. Where possible, the modern Old Way uses and connects such established routes, in the same way that pilgrims would once have followed pre-existing roads across country. Although, in the Middle Ages, these were not roads at all. Medieval roads did not exist in the way we understand them today, as specific entities traversing the landscape. Unlike Roman roads, engineered to ease the moving of troops, or modern asphalted roads built to carry traffic, medieval roads did not have defined boundaries. Instead, they were corridors of multiple, unpaved tracks, up to a mile wide that emerged by habitual use to become 'easements' – what we might today call legal rights of way – between one place and another.

Often, additional routes would deviate from the main trajectory depending on the season, the terrain and the potential dangers. The Icknield Way, a 5,000-year-old trackway linking Wiltshire and East Anglia, is a case in point. On the chalk escarpment of the Chilterns, a more direct lower track was used in summer when the weather was drier. In winter, travellers preferred the upper route over the hills, which was less boggy underfoot.

For medieval pilgrims, soggy feet were the least of their troubles. Brigands lying in wait, injury and disease, hunger and thirst, wolves and wild boar beset the unwary traveller. I'd yet to encounter any such perils on my pilgrimage, though attempting to cross the A33 dual carriageway was proving almost as hazardous. Southampton may not today be the great trading centre it once was, but the ferry terminal on the other side of the A33 proved that it's still a major port, still sending passengers on their way to Europe and beyond, on modern pilgrimages to the world's tourism hotspots.

The ferry terminals were conspicuous that morning, though the Solent Way was proving elusive. Finding your way in towns – especially those in which the original layout has been carved up by modern ring roads and bypasses – is always harder than in the countryside, when your path stretches visibly ahead. With my rucksack and boots I felt out of place as I marched alongside the dual carriageway in search of the Solent Way, passing further ferry terminals fenced off with razor wire. I met no one and doubted whether the drivers of the cars and lorries that rumbled past even noticed me, a lone walker in a city of wheels.

A swathe of grass and trees opened out ahead, fringed to the north by a row of slim, stuccoed buildings. All bow windows and delicate fanlights, Queen's Terrace lingers elegantly on, a survival of Southampton's Regency past when visitors such as Jane Austen lodged in this fashionable resort, bathing in the therapeutic waters.

Like much of modern Southampton, Queen's Terrace is a little run down these days, its pastel colours fading, plaster flaking, though its occupants still enjoy views over Queen's Park, as the green swathe is called. This was once marshland known as Porter's Mead, named from when Southampton's porters, carrying goods to and from merchant ships, grazed their horses here. Following the Marsh Act of 1844, Porter's Mead was drained to make way for the docks from where the *Titanic* sailed in 1912. It was across Porter's Mead that John Speed's baggy-trousered traveller marched and where, 400 years later, I followed in his footsteps. As I strode through Queen's Park, longing to be out of the city, birdsong floated from the nascent leaf canopy and the radiant spring anthems spurred me on.

The Old Way crosses the River Itchen via a modern toll bridge, built in the 1970s to replace the former ferry. On the bank nearby stands the site of the Cross House, which offered shelter to medieval travellers using the ferry, and may well have been where Alice of Southwick crossed the Itchen on her way to Canterbury. Happily the bridge is gratis for walkers, proving that there are still some advantages to being on foot in the age of the car. The day was overcast, as drab as the bridge. Not the best conditions for embarking on a long journey when you wish for the weather to fill you with hope and optimism, as it did Chaucer's pilgrims as they rode out from Southwark six centuries earlier.

Then, bang in the middle of the bridge, my first waymark of the Solent Way. A pea-green arrow on a lamppost, in its centre the silhouette of a flying tern, the bird known to generations of sailors as the sea-swallow. The first encouraging sign that I was on a reliable long-distance path that would take me, via other reliable long-distance paths, the 240 miles to Canterbury. I was on a concrete bridge under a concrete sky, stranded amid Southampton's expanding metropolis, but the gloom of a few moments ago lifted and my pace accelerated. I felt as if my walk had truly begun, although I couldn't help noticing, alongside the green arrows, discreet signs on the parapet advertising the Samaritans.

Green arrows drew me on and over the bridge, towards the opposite shore. On the other side the waymarks petered out. It all seemed a little half-hearted, as if Hampshire County Council didn't quite believe that people would use this path. My map was no help either, so I did what people have done for centuries, and followed my nose.

My nose led me close to the water's edge, and it soon became clear why the green arrows had run out. Ahead was Woolston Waterside, a new development of apartment blocks truncating the path along the shore. The path that ordinary folk, making their way to and from Southampton, have used since Roman times when this port was called *Clausentum*. A billboard outside the marketing suite invited potential purchasers to 'eat, drink, live by the water', but there were no people eating or drinking by the water that Monday morning. Even if there had been, would I find someone who knew where the Old Way lay, entombed beneath concrete?

I longed to escape this gleaming high-rise maze and find the paths that would take me to Canterbury. I wanted to shake off the claustrophobia of this swollen city, stride out across shingle beaches and open hills, empty sky above my head and chalk crumbling beneath my feet. Walking can set you free, liberate you from the bonds of work, domesticity, even your personality if you so wish. I felt anything but free that morning, lost in the labyrinth of Woolston Waterside.

I was about to give up and head back over the Itchen Bridge when a signpost materialised, pointing towards Netley. This was promising. Netley Abbey was on the Old Way, so in the absence of any further green arrows I followed this road, leading me past rows of pleasant semi-detached houses, where I chanced upon a youth of around fourteen years old. Tracksuited, hair shaved around the sides of his head, he was fiddling with a BMX bike.

'Hello – can you tell me if this road will take me to the seashore?' I hazarded, not expecting much of a response from this bike-absorbed lad. Still, nothing ventured, nothing gained.

'Yes.' He didn't look up from his bike, but at least I knew I was heading in the right direction. I thanked him and turned to walk away. The teenager looked up, wiping his hands on a grubby rag.

'Go all the way down the road, and you'll see the football cages on your left. Then if you go straight on down Victoria Road . . .'

'The what cages?'

'Football cages. And then if you keep going straight on, you'll find the path to the waterfront.'

In my other, more bucolic and isolated life, our paths may never have crossed. Certainly not at home. Here, my weekend walks took me deep into rural Nidderdale, where I rarely met anyone at all – just sheep, lapwings and curlews. Even on my daily circuits around the local reservoir in pursuit of those despotic 10,000 steps my companions were mostly dogs dragging their owners, joggers plugged into headphones or hikers brandishing Nordic walking poles. My helpful teenage guide went back to tinkering with his bike and I, thanking him, walked on.

As I neared the sea, my thoughts turned to the egalitarianism of walking. It has not always been so. Before the late eighteenth century most people walked only because they had to, or if they were on pilgrimage. Walking was the preserve of the horseless poor. With the rise of the Romantic movement came the idea of walking for pleasure, prompting such poets as Wordsworth to pen some of their finest works after traipsing the countryside on foot. It took the mass trespass of Derbyshire's Kinder Scout in 1932, and the campaign that followed, to ensure universal access to the countryside.

Now, nearly a century later, we have become a nation of walkers. Our landmass may be modest in size, but it's fretted with 140,000 miles of public footpaths, bridleways and byways, and exploring them is one of our favourite pastimes. In the countryside certainly, but also in towns, along canals, railways, alleyways. In Britain you can walk out of your front door and find yourself near a public footpath, one that has been in use for centuries.

But here, on Southampton's easternmost fringes, I was not merely going for a walk. I was going on a pilgrimage, and that made all the difference. 'Going for a walk' means you're in control of your destiny. You can choose which path to take, which territory to explore, and which to avoid. On pilgrimage, if you wish to reach your destination, you have to follow a prescribed path. And if you need help to find your way, you have to engage with anyone you encounter along that path. The term 'pilgrim' comes from the Latin *peregrinus*, meaning foreigner, stranger. When you venture into the unknown, you become that stranger, throw off your safety net. You are dependent on the help, the hospitality, of others. You may not even speak the same language, but somehow you manage to communicate, to understand one another. This was as true in suburban Southampton today as it was in medieval France, Spain or Italy.

Just as my teenage BMX enthusiast had promised, Victoria Road led me straight to the waterfront and into a familiar sea-side edgeland of peeling playgrounds, scrubby bushes, doting dog walkers, multi-coloured joggers, eager weekend sailors. And my first close-up, that day, of the sea. Technically, Southampton Water is an estuary, fed by the three tidal rivers that converge here: the Itchen, the Hamble and the Test. But it looked like the sea, it sounded like the sea and above all it smelled like the sea. I guzzled great lungfuls of ozone-rich air as the estuary spread out before me, gleaming like beaten pewter. Kaleidoscopic dinghies gyrated in the water as if this were Salcombe not Southampton, yet it wasn't picture-postcard seaside. All around was evidence that Southampton is, as it always has been, a working port. Soundless container ships slid by, ghostly leviathans from faraway shores. Across the estuary, a metropolis of slender towers breathed vapour beneath a sliver of lemon sky. My map told me these were the chimneys of Fawley Oil Refinery, but at that moment they might have been the minarets of Damascus at sunset, viewed from Jabal Qasioun overlooking the ancient city.

Weston Shore, where I now found myself, is now South-ampton's only natural coastline. Originally a separate fishing community, it's been sucked into the maw of greater Southamp-ton. To my left, a row of Sixties tower blocks rose behind reeds that hissed in the wind. To my right stood Art Deco beach shelters, forlorn vestiges of this former resort, the grandly named Weston Parade. From here jubilant crowds waved off the *Titanic* as she set out on her first and last Atlantic voyage. Now, Weston Parade is largely patronised by pugs, labradoodles and cockapoos – city dogs and their proud parents, who stop to coo over each other's pets as other folk fuss over babies in prams.

As so often in communal spaces such as this, the coastal path was accented by wooden benches, many dedicated to lost loved ones. I'd passed a handful already that morning, but the one before me now was draped with a bouquet of scarlet berries like a medieval shrine adorned with votive offerings. Henry VIII, in his crusade against the established Church, did his best to suppress the archaic habit of shrine-visiting. In 1538 he decreed that Thomas Becket's shrine in Canterbury, for over three centuries the third most important European pilgrimage destination after Rome and Santiago, be demolished and the saint's bones burnt.

Henry VIII could not so easily demolish the human spirit, the need we all share to find solace and inspiration in visiting places imbued with special significance, whether religious or secular. That longing to make a physical connection with someone or something no longer here, and perhaps take something of that person or entity away with us – just as medieval pilgrims took home souvenirs from the shrines they visited: badges, crosses, phials and other such trinkets. In the Middle Ages, shrines of major saints like Thomas Becket drew many thousands of pilgrims a year. Today, it's Graceland, Anfield or the battlefields of Flanders that draw the masses, while benches such as this, overlooking the sea at Weston Shore, are not unlike the hundreds of shrines dedicated to minor-league saints strewn across the medieval landscape.

I rested for a moment on the bench and gazed out over South-ampton Water. A seashell tied to the bouquet, its inside painted with a striped lighthouse, surf and herring gulls, bore the words: 'It is okay to live a life others do not understand'. I took these words as an augury, for ahead lay the sea and, beyond, the high chalk hills that formed the bedrock of my life and whose promise lured me on like the tune of the Pied Piper.

I was a couple of hours into my walk, had barely left Southamp-ton, when a buzz from the fitness tracker on my wrist told me I'd already reached my 10,000 daily steps. Steps that are so hard to accomplish during a typical day sitting at my desk. Being static, sedentary, depresses me. It always has. As a schoolgirl I'd stare out through classroom windows, counting down the hours and years, dreaming of escape. Later stints in 'proper' jobs didn't cure me of my restlessness, and I never settled down to office work, always resigning after a few months. As a freelance writer I was less fettered now than in those barely remembered school days, but still I was mostly desk-bound. Even when I did find time to walk, on days crammed with work and domesticity, my walks never seemed long enough. Often, I'd finish a walk wanting to carry on – for another day, another week, forever. Now, I had a week's walking ahead of me. Not forever maybe, but long enough.

A few moments after the triumphant buzz on the wrist an urgent stab of pain in my foot brought me up short. I'd hoped, after sessions with the physio over the previous few months, that my plantar fasciitis – that tediously middle-aged ailment — had healed. I'd been a keen walker all my adult life, always been pretty fit. Now, only half a day into my 240-mile pilgrimage, this was a portent of impending mortality – or at least an undignified slide into a crumbling old age. Perhaps I couldn't walk on forever, after all.

A metal detectorist, head bowed in concentration, scoured the shoreline. Behind him, a pair of crows sifted through shingle. Scavengers, human and avian, side by side yet existing in parallel realms. The path now coiled through trees. Here, at Weston Wood Nature Reserve, among the birds and the buds, the wind and the rushes, I finally left the city behind and entered a portal into the natural world. Southampton Water opened out further, a foreshadowing of oceans stretching to far continents.

Shingle crunched underfoot. Gorse, egg-yolk yellow and coconut-scented, brushed my sleeve. Waxy-leaved holm oak, flexed by the prevailing wind, darkened the sky. And along with the ache in my foot, a pang of nostalgia for northern trees. For silver birches, Scots pines, stately sycamores, tangled oaks. Although I'd been born in Northumberland we only stayed there three months and I wasn't a Northerner by upbringing; soft chalk hills of beech and ash were my childhood habitat. Now I was standing on the familiar soil of southern England, missing the austere drama of the northern landscape, its rocks and moors and trees. Perhaps, like many a long-time ex-pat, I would never feel entirely at home in either landscape.

I was heading to Netley Abbey, for my medieval forebears the first religious waypoint on the Old Way. A path cut up from the shore and through a recreation park to the ruins, where a noticeboard at its entrance declared that Netley Abbey, founded in 1238, is the most complete Cistercian monastery in southern England. I knew something of the Cistercians from the great abbeys near my home in North Yorkshire – Fountains, Rievaulx, Byland, Jervaulx – and understood that the monks craved isolation and separation from the tumult of the outside world. This wooded corner would have been perfect for them. The Rule of St Benedict stipulated that monks were obliged to welcome guests 'as if they were Christ', and pilgrims like Alice of Southwick were offered hospitality at Netley. It is said that in medieval England you were never more than half a day's walk from an abbey, so finding a place to stay would not have been difficult.

After the suppression of the monasteries, and three centuries following its foundation, Netley Abbey fell into disrepair. They were demolishing it for building materials, so the story goes, when a worker on site was killed, and demolition halted. Over the following century it was abandoned and overgrown with trees and ivy – just the sort of romantic spectacle to attract artists and poets such as John Constable, Thomas Gray and Jane Austen, all of whom found inspiration here.

I found inspiration too, sitting amid the peaceful ruins, eating my picnic. Above the faint noise of traffic, muted by the surrounding trees, rose the insistent, syncopated song of a great tit. In that moment I sensed the peace and seclusion that the Cistercian monks longed for when they first made their home here beside the sea. I got up to leave, and spotted something lying on the grass in the middle of the cloister. A shell. What was a shell doing here, in the abbey ruins? In the Middle Ages pilgrims on the Camino de Santiago wore a cockleshell, the emblem of St James, pinned to their tunics like a badge. This one was an oyster shell, probably dropped by a gull after swallowing its contents. St Thomas Becket's emblem was not a shell but an ampule, usually made of lead or tin and filled with 'Canterbury Water' like those found in the house of Richard of Southwick.

That afternoon in Netley Abbey, on the first day of my pilgrimage along the Old Way, the oyster shell felt like a good luck charm, a sign that I would indeed reach Canterbury. So I picked it up, slipped it into my trouser pocket, and went on my way.

Back on the foreshore I glimpsed through soaring pines and under brightening skies the three tributaries of Southampton Water that convene here. This is a landscape where water regulates life, and livelihoods. The saline waters of the tidal estuary have, for millennia, brought prosperity to these islands, yet even more essential was the fresh water flowing from the land itself such as in Westfield Common. Here, signs pointed to Caddick Well, a holy spring long revered for its medicinal qualities, which, a noticeboard informed me, caused bottles of it to be sent 'as far afield as Surrey'. A photo on the board showed a Victorian-looking canopy with a cross, which bore the inscription, 'Let him that thirsteth drink this water'. Vessels anchored offshore also once filled their casks from this spring, its place marked on a maritime map of 1783. I found no trace of the spring, although the noticeboard assured me that its waters can still be seen running across the nearby beach.

I walked on, thinking about water. How, in England, it pours so abundantly from the sky and spouts so generously from our taps that we have forgotten its value. How water is life, both for passing travellers and for our ancestors who sought out springs so they could build their communities. How holy springs are found wherever in the world people have chosen to settle, like the one at the Ottoman village of Dana, balanced on a mountain above Jordan's Wadi Araba in one of the driest, most barren regions on earth. I visited Dana one early April a few years ago. It was a Friday – a weekend in Muslim culture. The spring, which for centuries has irrigated Dana's terraced gardens, gushed from a crack in the mountainside. In an arid country such as Jordan fresh water is a miracle, and milling around the spring were villagers of all ages enjoying their Friday off. Picnicking parents with play-ful kids, and old shepherds in *keffiyehs* squatting on stone walls. Young men strumming ouds, showing off to girls with hijabs and kohl-lined eyes, chattering on mobile phones. An ancient, inno-cent, universal celebration of precious, life-giving water.

Much closer to home, on the edge of Port Meadow in Oxford where I lived for over two decades, lies the hamlet of Binsey – a scattering of stone and thatch buildings on the banks of the River Thames, not far from the ruins of Godstow Nunnery. Here, in the garden of the lonely church of St Margaret of Antioch, is a holy well dedicated to Oxford's patron saint, the Mercian princess St Frideswide. It's not much to look at these days. Just a low wall, edged with daffodils in spring. An arch is carved into the Oxfordshire limestone, and if you squint underneath into the darkness you can just make out a pool of stagnant water. Stagnant holy water.

Above the arch is an inscription in Latin dated 1874, though the well itself dates back many centuries, and perhaps even to pre-Christian times, when springs like this were venerated. During the Middle Ages this well water was said to possess healing properties, and Binsey became a place of pilgrimage with priests appointed by St Frideswide's Priory in Oxford (now the college chapel of Christ Church) to administer to the crowds. So keen were pilgrims to imbibe its healing waters that a stone hut with locked doors was built over the well to protect it, and the crutches of cured pilgrims festooned the adjacent church.

After the Reformation, when such superstitions were discouraged, the habit of visiting holy wells died away – overtly at least – and by the mid-nineteenth century Binsey's well lay in ruins: 'overgrowne with nettles and other weeds, and harbouring frogs, snails, and vermin', prompting its late-Victorian restoration. Since then it's best known as the 'treacle well' in Lewis Carroll's *Alice in Wonderland*, 'treacle' being a medieval term for a healing fluid. And, in literary circles, for these lines in Gerard Manley Hopkins's poem:

> *My aspens dear, whose airy cages quelled,*
> *Quelled or quenched in leaves the leaping sun,*
> *All felled, felled, are all felled . . .*
> ('Binsey Poplars', felled 1879)

These days there are no joyous young men with guitars, picnicking families or laughing kids at St Margaret's Well in Binsey as there were at Dana, where water still means life. The connection to our ancestral traditions, and our reverence of water, has largely been forgotten. Yet people still come to Binsey, solitary pilgrims who leave votive offerings – posies of flowers and other small objects placed there by careful hands and hopeful hearts. Adherents of the 'old religion' perhaps, or just New Agers tuning in to the mystical vibe of this solitary spot.

My feet sank into shingle as I walked from Westfield Common along a ribbon of beach trimmed with woodland, light suburbia to my left, heavy industry to my right. Not the most idyllic of shoreline walks, but Southampton Water has been a working channel where merchant ships have plied their trade since at least the Middle Ages. Though today they are more likely carrying barrels of crude oil rather than vats of fine Malmsey wine.

The shingle led me past the BP oil terminal to a promontory of Hamble Common behind which shelters the village of Hamble-le-Rice. Named after the crooked river in which it sits (OE *hamel + ae)* and the brushwood that surrounds it (OE *hrís)* it's now one of the county's foremost yachting towns and famed for its century-old annual regatta. Hamble has always been a boating town. In 1439, Henry V's flagship, the *Grace Dieu*, was struck by lightning when moored here, and sank to the bottom of the river, where it remains. A century later the common was the site of a fort, St Andrew's Castle, built in the reign of Henry VIII when England was threatened by invasion from France and the European territories known as the Holy Roman Empire. Four hundred years on, a new menace from continental Europe led to Hamble Airfield becoming the home to the flying school where Spitfire pilots honed their skills in readiness for the Battle of Britain.

St Andrew's Castle was decommissioned in 1642, during the English Civil War, and has since largely been lost to coastal erosion. On the promontory, where I now walked towards the village, are the remains of an even earlier structure, an Iron Age hillfort now buried under Hamble Common. During the Middle Ages, when this land belonged to the nearby St Andrew's Priory, pigs were allowed to feed on fallen acorns in autumn and winter, a tradition known as pannage. Now a tangle of gorse and scrub, this is one of the few remaining coastal heathland sites in Hampshire, a place of antiquity and peace, and a fitting end to the day's walk.

III

Since at least 1493 a ferry has crossed the Hamble, linking the port cities of Southampton and Portsmouth. Pilgrims, who perhaps rested overnight at St Andrew's Priory, would have used the ferry, though the Gough Map shows the red line vaulting the river. I pictured a small wooden boat rowing pilgrims across, like the ferries that plied passengers over the Thames in medieval London. These pilgrims – perhaps Alice of Southwick among them – didn't envisage the bubblegum-pink boats that convey today's holidaymakers, cyclists and ramblers to Warsash on the river's eastern bank. One of these boats, *Emily*, ferried me across to the Hamble the next morning, depositing me at the Hook-with-Warsash Nature Reserve. A feeding ground for many species of wading birds and wildfowl, it's also a habitat for birders, who hide among the reedbeds armed with powerful telescopes and high-end binoculars.

Flotillas of dinghies rotated on flickering waters as I followed a coast path wisped with tamarisk trees and streaked with yellow gorse. Ahead, perhaps only five miles away, rose the vaporous silhouette of the Isle of Wight, emerging from the water like a hallucination.

The colour of the sea shifted as I left land behind, the estuary-grey now tinted with aquamarine, hues melding where the water touched the skies, way out in the open seas. I was gazing into the offing, in old nautical parlance a far-off area of sea visible from land yet beyond anchoring grounds. In modern idiom 'in the offing' means a possibility rather than a reality, and as I trudged along the shingle, where every step felt like two as my boots sank into the pebbles, it was a metaphor for my own solitary voyage. My journey's end was still over 200 miles away, a possibility rather than a certainty. Only two days into my pilgrimage, and I was well beyond my anchoring grounds.

Now in the Mabon of my life, I still wasn't sure what my anchoring grounds were. As a family we'd moved from England to Canada and back, and from England to Germany and back, before my father left army life and we settled in Buckinghamshire's commuter belt. By the age of ten I'd lived in thirteen different houses and been to six different schools, igniting in me a restlessness that has never left. After university, and uncertain what career I wanted, I took on various jobs – a live-in assistant in a West Cumbrian castle, listing historic buildings for English Heritage, a hiking guide in Tuscany and Umbria, a freelance travel writer. Wandering the world, I was searching for a place to drop anchor.

The search for somewhere to belong did not confine itself to foreign parts. It was as if a centrifugal force was pulling me away, only for a centripetal one to yank me back again. Back from my travels to the Middle East and Hispaniola, I looked for connections in the Yorkshire landscape that would bind me to it, make it home. After almost twenty years of living there, I still wasn't sure I'd succeeded.

A kestrel hovered above the cliff, head fixed and immobile before it swooped, aim true as a missile. Taking my cue from the kestrel I climbed onto the cliff, hoping the going would be easier, and followed a path between hedgerows of holly, blackthorn and elder, buckled by westerly winds. The path led to Meon Shore, where beach huts fronted the shingle, each set within its own fenced domain. Evolving from the wheeled bathing machines that protected the modesty of Victorian women, the huts were originally used as 'holiday homes for the toiling classes'. With their retro seaside glamour, they're now highly desirable beach-front properties changing hands for the price of a small, terraced house in many parts of the country.

I turned inland to follow the River Meon, heading for the chalk hills and bidding farewell – for now – to the sea. The morning's mizzle had turned to rain as I followed a track along the Titchfield Canal, one of England's oldest man-made waterways. My destination was Titchfield Abbey, around eight miles from Hamble, and a suitable ending to the day's walk.

Mud, mixed with last autumn's leaf fall, slowed my pace along the canal. The walk became a slog, as it was for medieval pilgrims when roads were largely unpaved. Not a single main road was built between the Roman period and the turnpikes, or toll roads, in the eighteenth century. Heavy goods were delivered by sea or river. Until the introduction of toll roads, which funded much-needed improvements, the feet and legs of pilgrims were sheathed in mud. At least I had a pair of stout waterproof boots, unlike my medieval forebears who waded through the mud wearing hose and porous leather shoes. Women, in their floor-length gowns (or kirtles), fared even worse. As a wealthy merchant's wife, Alice of Southwick may have dressed for her journey in a fur-lined mantle, or cloak, with the wimple covering her head topped by a wide-brimmed hat to protect her from the worst of the elements. No wonder those who could afford to – perhaps Alice herself – travelled by horse.

On the shingle I had been sinking. Here, I was sliding in mud. Because I was sliding I couldn't find my rhythm, and walking is all about rhythm. It's about finding a pace that feels right for your body, striding out and letting your thoughts soar free. It's about solving the world's problems, and your own, as your legs propel you across the landscape. It shouldn't be about concentrating on every step to avoid skidding into a ditch. The mud was so distracting, my eyes cast so downward, that I nearly didn't notice the waterway itself. Lined with reeds, rushes and willows, effervescent with spring buds, everything shimmered green.

Southampton was behind me, and Fareham lay ahead. Between them was the village of Titchfield, where I now emerged from the mud. Founded by Jutes in the sixth century, its name derives from the Old English *Ticcenfeld*, meaning the pasture where young goats are kept. No goats roamed that day among the pastel-painted, russet-roofed cottages, or grazed in the yard of Titchfield's grand flint church. One of the oldest in Hampshire, St Peter's is of Saxon origin and retains its fine Norman doorway of carved sandstone and its medieval spire, tiled with wooden shingles. These are fortunate survivors of the Victorian restoration, which did not spare the church's interior.

Except, that is, for the South Chapel, which houses the marble and alabaster monument to the Wriothesley family, whose lives were entwined with the history of England. Thomas Wriothesley, 1st Earl of Southampton who served as Lord Chancellor under Henry VIII, was notorious for the torture of Anne Askew. Anne was later burnt at the stake, a horrific end to a remarkable life.

Born in Lincolnshire in 1521, Anne, a staunch Protestant, was married aged fifteen to local Catholic squire Thomas Kyme. The couple did not see eye to eye on spiritual matters and the marriage was an unhappy one. After bearing two children and being thrown out by Kyme she petitioned for divorce – allegedly the first Englishwoman to do so – reverting to her maiden name of Askew. It was Anne's own husband who accused her of heresy, an accusation that eventually led to her execution in 1546. England at this time still adhered to the Catholic Church, and although Henry VIII might now be remembered as the king who broke with Rome, he was also a Catholic. His piety was so conspicuous that in 1521, after penning an attack on Martin Luther, he was awarded the title of Defender of the Faith by Pope Leo X. The title was later revoked by Pope Paul III, but has since been used by Henry's successors, including our current monarch.

Henry remained a Catholic all his life, which makes his decision in 1536 to dissolve England's monastic houses, including the next waypoint on my own pilgrimage, all the more abhorrent. Today, Titchfield Abbey lies to the north of the village, across the

A27. I walked towards the abbey, the traffic from the road fading as I passed its great fifteenth-century tithe barn.

Founded in 1222 by Peter des Roches, Bishop of Winchester, Titchfield Abbey was home to the Premonstratensian, or White, Canons. Premonstratensians were renowned for their scholarship, and over the centuries created a vast library at the abbey. Containing 224 volumes, each comprising several books, Titchfield's library is thought to have been among the largest in England, second only to that of Reading Abbey. It was when studying surviving manuscripts from Titchfield's library that Will Parsons determined the probable route of the Old Way, finding evidence that its canons travelled from here as far as the priory of St Pancras at Lewes – some sixty-five miles as the crow flies, though significantly longer as the monk walked.

When the canons of Titchfield weren't praying, studying, writing manuscripts or walking to Lewes they offered hospitality to travellers and pilgrims, hosting such royal luminaries as Henry V, who in 1415 stopped here on his way to Southampton to launch the invasion of France. When his descendant Henry VIII shut down the monasteries he not only deprived 14,000 monks, nuns and friars of their homes and livelihoods, he dispossessed the communities of their local hospital, the poor of their alms, the girls of their education, the travellers of their shelter. Historians have noted that, after the Dissolution of the Monasteries (1536–9), social problems and criminality in England increased considerably. Vagrancy became rife. Henry VIII had already clamped down on 'beggars and vagabonds' with the Vagabonds Act of 1532. Almost overnight, the poor had lost one of their primary means of support.

Titchfield's abbot seems to have colluded in the abbey's eventual demise, selling off its treasures and livestock, securing a pension and ending his career as Treasurer of Salisbury Cathedral. Or perhaps he knew the game was up and took the shrewdest course of action both for himself and for his canons. In any case, he fared better than some of his contemporaries – men like Richard Whiting, the elderly Abbot of Glastonbury who, along with two of his monks, was hanged, drawn and quartered on Glastonbury Tor for refusing to surrender his abbey to Henry's commissioners.

It was raining by the time I arrived at Titchfield Abbey that early spring afternoon. Its function as lodgings for pilgrims was over, the now roofless building granting me little shelter. Like so many others, it was converted into a private residence – in this case for Henry's loyal servant Thomas Wriothesley, who now lies entombed in St Peter's Church along with his grandson, Sir Henry Wriothesley, the 'Fair Youth' of Shakespeare's sonnets.

Today Titchfield is a peaceful spot, with its orchard, walled garden and tall Tudor gatehouse bisecting the nave of the Premonstratensian church. As I huddled under one of the abbey's remaining arches, alone and taking refuge from the strengthening rain, it was hard to imagine this place as a backdrop to such tumultuous times. Yet our own times are not without tumult, our relationship with Europe as fraught as Henry's once was. Four years on from Britain's seismic decision to leave the European Union, still the arguments and counter-arguments raged, dividing families and friends.

I put these thoughts out of my mind, and looked up. I was two days into my walk along the Old Way and now, over the mellow-bricked garden wall, through the veil of mist and rain, lay the chalk hills of the South Downs rising gently, seductively ahead.

I didn't know it then, but it would be months, rather than hours, until I would set eyes on them again.

Margaret Paston to her husband, John

28 September 1443

The Pastons, a family of Norfolk gentry, are renowned for the Paston Letters — the largest surviving collection of fifteenth-century correspondence in English. In this missive, Margaret Paston (c.1422–84) is writing to her husband, John (1421–66), who was away in London, where he worked as a lawyer.

To my rygth worchepful husbond, John Paston, dwellyng in the Inner Temple at London, in hast.

RYTH worchipful hosbon, I recomande me to yow, desyryng hertely to her of yowr wilfar, thanckyng God of yowr a mendyng of the grete dysese that ye have hade; and I thancke yow for the letter that ye sent me, for be my trowthe my moder and I wer nowth in hertys es fro the tyme that we woste of yowr sekenesse, tyl we woste verely of your a mendyng. My moder be hestyd a nodyr ymmage of wax of the weytte of yow to oyer Lady of Walsyngham, and sche sent iiij. nobelys to the iiij. Orderys of Frerys at Norweche to pray for yow, and I have be hestyd to gon on pylgreymmays to Walsingham, and to Sent Levenardys for yow;

Modern translation:

To my right worshipful husband, John Paston,
dwelling in the Inner Temple at London, in haste.

Right worshipful husband, I recommend myself to you,
desiring heartily to hear of your welfare, thanking
God of your mending of the great disease that
you have had; and I thank you for the letter that
you sent me, for by my troth my mother and I were
not in heart's ease for the time we learned of
your sickness, till we learned verily of your
mending. My mother behested another image
of wax of the weight of you to our Lady of
Walsingham, and she sent four nobles [gold coins]
to the four Orders of Friars at Norwich to pray for you,
and I have behested to go on pilgrimage to
Walsingham, and to St Leonard's for you;

LUGHNASA

'The third quarter-day in the Celtic year, closely related to the British Lammas and celebrated on 1 August'

TITCHFIELD TO ARUNDEL

IV

As I sheltered from the rain at Titchfield Abbey that early spring afternoon, summer was no more than a whispered promise. Now, in late July, it was trumpeting its presence, assailing me with its colours, pummelling me with its sounds and scents. It was disorientating, like waking from a coma to find I'd missed four months of my life. Which, in a way, I had. We all had. From the outbreak of Covid in late March 2020, until early July 2020 when lockdown restrictions were eased, our normal lives had been on hold. Unable to complete my spring walk to Arundel, I'd made the decision to resume my pilgrimage when it was next safe, and travel permitted.

The interlude, while difficult in many ways, had its upsides. Like so many others confined to home those spring months I'd relished the season, observing more closely than ever the transformations taking place in my immediate surroundings.

They happen slowly, those early portents of spring. You count them off, one by one. First, the snowdrops of January, then the crocuses of February. In March come the daffodils, in April the bluebells. You grasp at each morsel until, in May, you're presented with a feast. Snowy blackthorn blossoms on leafless branches, wood anemones shimmer in the wind, hares lope across open fields. So much abundance, so much fecundity, that it overwhelms. Then, in late June, the tender green of early summer thickens and darkens. Before you know it, before you've truly had a chance to grasp it with both hands, the landscape ripens into the maturity of high summer, and early middle age. A parable for life, perhaps.

High summer was when I returned to Titchfield Abbey. Surrounded by yellowing summer grasses whirring with crickets and flickering with butterflies I sat beneath an old apple tree, a vestige of the orchard that once supplied the abbey. Somewhere above my head came the thrilling, trilling song of a skylark – along with the curlew and lapwing, one of my favourite birds and an affirmation of the season. Nearby, families newly out of lockdown picnicked under velvet skies stitched with soft, downy cloud. I'd only experienced two days of the Old Way in early spring. Now, I embraced the remainder of this stretch as a summer walk, planning to return next spring for the journey to Canterbury, just as Chaucer's pilgrims did.

In the Celtic calendar, this was Lughnasa. Unlike the Anglo-Saxons, who chiefly venerated the solstices and equinoxes, the Celts celebrated the cusp between seasons. The end of July is almost halfway between the summer solstice and autumn equinox when summer turns on its axis, shifting to autumn. For ancient Britons, Lughnasa, or Lugh's Gathering, was a time to give thanks for the fruit and the grain. Taking place on the threshold of harvest, this was a time of feasting and festivals of fire. For Christians, quick to embrace pagan rituals to placate the incumbent population, it became Lammas (loaf mass), or First Harvest. Traditionally celebrated on 1 August, Lammas was now only a few days away. Ripening apples dangled above my head, waiting to be picked. I longed to sit there all day, under the apple tree, listening to the larks and watching the butterflies, the sun warming my back. But, like every pilgrim before me, I had a bed to reach that night. Wickham was my destination, and a few days later I would arrive in Arundel, so completing stage three of the Gough Map's itinerary.

Munching on a fallen apple I left the serene confines of Titchfield Abbey and re-entered the twenty-first century, dodging cars and Lycra-clad cyclists ringing their angry bells. I crossed the River Meon via Stony Bridge, also known as Anjou Bridge for its association with the marriage of Henry VI and Margaret of Anjou at the abbey in 1445. The current narrow bridge replaced the medieval structure in the seventeenth century, its builders careful to add a small, triangular refuge for pedestrians – still handy today when you have to leap aside to allow traffic to pass. Cars and bicycle bells, the rush of the river beneath, Stony Bridge today is a mix of old and new, of peaceful and noisy.

It was a relief to get off the road and onto the bridleway leading alongside the stream, and feel my feet crunching the gravel once again. I was walking along a shaded track, lined with oaks and flanked by paddocks of horses swishing tails and nuzzling one another's necks. Scenes so familiar from my Chilterns childhood they clutched at my heart. Like many girls on the cusp of adolescence, I'd learned to ride a pony. Several of my friends in the village where I grew up had their own horse, and so I begged my parents for one too, adding 'and a pony' to the end of my mother's scribbled shopping lists. Pancho, a wilful Palomino, eventually arrived to live in the field behind our house, and was fed, ridden and loved for a couple of years until my interests turned to boys and pop music, and Pancho was sold on to the next horse-mad girl.

These days, I prefer walking to riding, but climbing this hill I envied Alice of Southwick and her mount. Saddlebags carried her personal possessions, her Bible or other devotional aid and a change of clothes, though she may well also have had a pack-horse with her for heavier items such as bedding. Archaeological explorations of Richard of Southwick's house in Southampton uncovered personalised wooden bowls, suggesting that these were portable items that might have been used in a communal space, such as a refectory or alehouse, while the owner was on the road. Pilgrims travelling on foot wore a leather scrip tied around their waist, containing a small number of essential belongings: money, documents and some food, and probably a bowl as well. Like the scrip, the staff of a walking pilgrim was blessed by the priest before departure. My own version of the wooden staff, a telescopic aluminium hiking pole, was back home in Yorkshire.

On I went, under a Victorian brick railway bridge from where exhaled the hoot of a train, never as intrusive as the roar of a car engine. As I walked further from the coast the track climbed, and the weight of my rucksack bore down. After so many months of not carrying anything on my back it felt like an excrescence, yet the promise of chalk hills pulled me onwards and upwards.

I was faintly aware of fringing a town now, but the tree-lined lane, the paddocks and horses, the bracken and the birdsong, lulled me into believing I was alone in deepest countryside. Almost. The discarded water bottles and crisp packets, the messy presence of humanity as I neared the town gave the lie. Medieval pilgrims, as they passed the outskirts of towns, would have been similarly plagued with detritus. Not plastic bottles and foil pack-ets, but the rotting animal carcasses, the heaps of bones and the piles of human waste typically dumped outside town walls. In the Middle Ages, before council collections, natural scavengers like the red kite helped clean up discarded human rubbish. Protected by royal decree, their slaughter was a capital offence, yet by the nineteenth century kites were largely driven to extinction. In 1989 they were successfully reintroduced into southern England and now share the Hampshire airspace with fellow birds of prey, such as buzzards. Unlike buzzards, kites prefer carrion to live prey and the two species mostly co-exist, only sometimes locking talons over a scrap of contested food.

I was fluctuating between past and present, the eternal and the non-biodegradable, as I walked along that bridleway. Horse manure alternated with plastic wrapping, birdsong with rusty cans, soft summer winds with exhaust fumes. Now, as I approached the M27, it was the twenty-first century that took precedence, drilling itself into my consciousness. In the darkness of the underpass I stopped to rest, and to read the graffiti. '*To the Fareham Massive – Big Love*'. Then '*World Peace – give love a chance, Man – we owe it to ourselves*'. And my favourite:

> *I'm still in love with Sorcha*
> *More than all the sand in Persia –*
> *3rd December '15.*

Who says romance is dead?

And then out again onto an earth-beaten track, beeches and birches bowing overhead. The track narrowed, the woodland clotted, the birdsong intensified, the traffic quietened. I walked along a thin path through shrubs and bushes very like the dense hedgerows around my childhood home where my brother and I would make dens, crawling inside deep-gouged tunnels. At that young age I didn't know that our hedgy playground was probably very old indeed. The first hedges were planted in the Bronze Age as humans moved from hunter-gathering to farming, with some 95,000 miles of ancient hedgerows still existing today. One of these, the Black Hedge at Monks Risborough a few miles from where we lived, is mentioned in a charter of the tenth century. In those Buckinghamshire fields we would pretend we were pioneers in the Wild West. For a few hours, before our mother called us in for supper, we would 'go bush' – as far as this was possible in the English Home Counties.

I was now walking through Dean Copse: 'an important area of ancient woodland where a rich variety of wildlife can be discovered throughout the seasons', announced the notice at the exit of the wood. My OS (Ordnance Survey) map, on the other hand, told me I was on the outskirts of Knowle. I was lost, squinting at the map in the full glare of the afternoon sun, flummoxed by the crescents and the closes of these residential streets that led nowhere. Knowle was a pleasant enough place, but I ached to extricate myself and return to the open country where my feet knew which way to go.

Disorientated and hot after twenty minutes roaming the streets of Knowle, I sat under a hazel tree on a roundabout at the edge of the village and recovered my bearings. A serendipitous place to pause as straight ahead was the path, marching through a field of seared wheat. I walked on through the wheat towards Fiddlers Green Wood, dark with late July foliage. Summer in southern England is all rich golds and deep greens. Even the smell is golden. It's sunshine stored, waiting to be reaped. The scent of ripened grain, of Lughnasa, of Lammastide. For the pre-Christian Celts, the warrior god Lugh represented sun and light, and 'Lughnasa' was the festival of Lugh. Early Christian writers, keen to appropriate popular pagan traditions, transformed him into the Archangel Michael, while in Ireland, where the cult of Lugh was strongest, he metamorphosed into the leprechaun of Irish folklore.

In Fiddlers Green Wood at the end of the field, I found a forest of oak and Scots pine, birch and beech, the ground splashed with sunlight. Beneath my feet, the familiar grind of chalk. I was far from the Chilterns but this was the same geology, the same landscape, the same beech trees above my head, the same chalky crunch beneath my feet. I half expected to turn a corner and find myself back at my childhood home, dad mowing the lawn and mum washing up at the kitchen sink.

The road into Wickham, although a country lane, hummed with traffic. My map showed a path on the other side of the River Meon at the bottom of the valley, but no obvious way across. A woman in sleek jogging gear with a panting dog was resting beside the entrance to Fiddlers Green Wood.

'Hello, is there any way I can cross the river near here?' I asked her. 'I want to avoid walking along the road if at all possible.' Mapless medieval pilgrims navigated the route between towns and monasteries by asking local people to recommend the best, driest and safest routes. I was walking in the twenty-first century, armed with a 1:25,000 map and GPS on my phone, yet there's still nothing to beat local knowledge.

'Sorry, I don't think there is.' The dog-jogger had confirmed my fears. The only sensible way into Wickham was along the lane.

Never mind – the lane was leafy, overhung with oak and ash, hedged with dog-rose and blackberry flowers becoming fruit. Hedgerows, so familiar from my childhood, are exotic to me now. My current Yorkshire habitat is one of mossy stone walls – climbing up fells and plunging down dales, strutting across the landscape with northern grit. Hampshire hedgerows are soft-edged, gentle, pliable. And eye-achingly colourful underneath: deep pink willowherb, pale-purple thistle, rich amethyst vetch and all the hot, gaudy colours of a late July day laced the verges. Seizing their final chance to bloom this summer, they were throwing caution to the wind in a last, joyful hurrah.

Hounded out of the fields and meadows by intensive agriculture, verges are where wildflowers thrive now, with over 700 species growing alongside Britain's roads. Along with the wildflowers comes the wildlife: butterflies and bees, insects that pollinate our plants, and feed our birds. In recent years, the organisation Plantlife has discouraged the spring and early summer mowing of verges, inviting councils and landowners to leave mowing until August, when the flowers have seeded. Commuters, idling in traffic jams, can now enjoy the spectacle from their car windows, as can walking pilgrims, such as myself.

In the centre of Wickham I found the church of St Nicholas, as much the Chilterns as Hampshire with its knapped flint walls, stone dressings and carved, re-set Norman doorway. On the door was a note advising that the church was open for private prayer during the pandemic, from eleven to one. It was late afternoon now, and the door firmly locked, so I sat in the churchyard on a bench dedicated to Reg and Thelma Amey 'who loved Wickham'. The church is on a busy crossroad, yet retains its medieval tranquillity in spite of its Victorian restoration. I didn't need the building to be open to feel at peace. Sitting in God's Acre among toppling tombstones, birds hopping between the graves, was my own private prayer.

Wickham, the A334 cutting through its middle, is a village of tottering timber-framed cottages and smart Georgian facades arranged around a square as spacious and well-proportioned as a Roman forum. The *Dictionary of British Place Names* gives Wickham's meaning as a homestead (the Saxon word *ham*) associated with a *vicus* (a Romano-British settlement adjacent to a Roman military installation). Such a Romano-British settlement was discovered in 2018, alongside the Roman road which ran from Chichester to Winchester, whose course still exists heading northwest and southeast from the modern village. Archaeologists have described the settlement, which seemed to have reached its heyday in the first and second centuries AD, as a 'kind of Roman service-station'.

Banishing from my mind the image of a Roman Roadchef, I explored the village centre that afternoon. The sixteenth-century poet and antiquary John Leland described Wickham as a 'pretty townlet', and it still is, having been named Hampshire Village of the Year in 2007. After its demise as a Roman service station it flourished as a market town, from the Middle Ages holding a three-day May fair. The fair bolstered Wickham's status, and although its inhabitants today are mainly commuters and retirees, its agricultural past clings on in the gypsy horse fair held every May in the village square. Most famously, Wickham was the birthplace in 1320 of William of Wykeham, Bishop of Winchester and Chancellor of England. Rising from fairly modest beginnings to become one of the wealthiest men in the land, he is best known today as the founder of both nearby Winchester College and New College, Oxford. Not bad for a grammar-school boy from rural Hampshire.

It's not always easy for the modern pilgrim to find somewhere to sleep since monasteries, and the accommodation they offered, were abolished some 500 years ago. Not by nature an extrovert I usually prefer the anonymity of a hotel or inn to staying in the homes of strangers, especially after a day of walking, alone with my thoughts. But I was not just walking. I was on pilgrimage, and pilgrims wandering through the countryside depend on strangers for hospitality. A mile north of Wickham I found it, at a farmhouse B&B.

A hot shower to sluice away the sweat, and I was soon sitting with my hostess in the garden where she'd laid a table for an impromptu supper to save me walking back into Wickham. Noticing my bulging rucksack, she offered to move it on to my next stop at Havant. After spraining my ankle the previous summer, and with the plantar fasciitis nagging my other foot, its weight was becoming a problem so I happily accepted. My earlier misanthropy forgotten, we chatted over a chilled glass of Sauvignon Blanc, our conversation ranging from beef cattle to buzzards to Brexit.

V

An English summer's day, even one in a July heatwave, starts cool and fresh. There was a crispness to the air as I crossed the A32 the following morning, dodging the torrent of cars heading towards the coastal conurbations. That night I would reach Havant, the end of stage one of the Gough Map and a walk of around fifteen miles. My hosts had mentioned over breakfast how peaceful life had been during lockdown when the road was empty, and how they'd noticed more wildlife around their farm. The previous evening I'd spotted a young buzzard swooping over the pasture before landing on a fencepost, and early that morning had heard perhaps the year's last dawn chorus resounding from the woodland before being engulfed by the hum of engines.

Once I'd made it across the A32 and entered the woodland, the birdsong resumed. I walked from bright sunshine into stippled semi-darkness, the trees stretching towards the sky, diffusing daylight. It felt good to be on a pilgrim trail again, although it wasn't the Old Way I was now following. To avoid retracing my steps back into Wickham to pick up the Old Way I would walk the Pilgrims' Trail for a few miles before rejoining the main route later. This was another long-distance path I'd seen on my map when planning the day's walk. Running from Winchester to Normandy, the Pilgrims' Trail follows the route of the *Miquelots*, pilgrims who crossed the Channel from Portsmouth to worship at the abbey of Mont-Saint-Michel. Converging on the island from northern France, Germany and Scandinavia many *Miquelots* then travelled south to the Continent's second-greatest pilgrim destination, Santiago de Compostela in Spain.

I too was travelling south that morning. The Pilgrims' Trail passes through the Forest of Bere, an ancient hunting ground, or 'chase'. Bere, from the Old English *bær*, means wood or grove, while 'forest' comes from the Norman French for land set aside for hunting. Whether or not a forest was populated with trees was incidental. As it happened, this particular forest was populated with trees, through which my path passed peacefully. Blackbirds scuttled in the undergrowth, and chirped in the leaf canopy. The bracken had yet to turn bronze, and everything was a thick, dark green. This was a summer morning in late July, yet I seemed to have the whole forest to myself. No dog walkers, no joggers, no cyclists. Just the faint pop of a shotgun from far away, and the crunch of my boots on the path.

Unlike the Old Way, the Pilgrims' Trail is waymarked, and it was a respite not having to look at my map and just follow the trail's signage. But it didn't feel authentic. After all, medieval pilgrims had no signage to help them on their way.

My first choice of accommodation in Wickham had been Park Place, a community of Indian Franciscan nuns who run a pastoral centre for those interested in spiritual matters, but they were not accepting guests due to the pandemic. If they had, I might have felt more like a genuine medieval pilgrim seeking shelter at a local monastery. Though I would not have found my welcoming farmhouse B&B, or the Pilgrims' Trail with its dark green arrows leading me onwards through the ancient Forest of Bere. Serendipity is the pilgrim's reward.

I was thankful that day for those dark green arrows, and for not getting lost in the forest. Although this was leafy Hampshire, and I was surrounded by the sounds of civilisation – the murmur of traffic on the A32 and the popping of the distant shotgun – there was still that atavistic fear of the woods, a fear that tormented my forebears for whom terrain such as this was often dangerous. Wolves still roamed the forests of England in the Middle Ages, only becoming extinct in the reign of Henry VII (1485–1509), and bandits were undeniably a menace. Robbing a pilgrim may have been regarded as an abomination, but that didn't mean it was uncommon.

Or perhaps it is that fear that women uniquely experience. For centuries women were not supposed to venture 'abroad' (i.e. outside) without a male chaperone. In the early Middle Ages, pilgrimage was deemed inappropriate for women, with the Saxon

St Boniface (*c*.675–754) warning that female pilgrims risked forfeiting their virtue. Later, women often went on pilgrimage without their families, though married women had to obtain permission from their husbands to venture away from home. Even so, like Chaucer's famous female pilgrim Alisoun, the Wife of Bath, they typically travelled in groups for safety and companionship. A contemporary of the fictional Alisoun was the very real Margery Kempe, who lived from *c*.1373 to *c*.1440, around a century later than Alice of Southwick. Born into a merchant family in Bishop's (now King's) Lynn in Norfolk, Margery found fame, and a certain notoriety, as a mystic and a pilgrim. Like most ordinary people she was unable to write, so dictated *The Book of Margery Kempe* – the first autobiography in the English language – which described her pilgrimages to the Holy Land, Rome, Santiago de Compostela and, of course, Canterbury.

Margery enjoyed an eventful and controversial existence. Married at twenty, she bore fourteen children before embarking on a life of pilgrimage and spiritual quest. Her devotion expressed itself in marital celibacy, a refusal to eat meat and in 'abundant weeping' and shrieking, behaviour which often upset and annoyed her fellow pilgrims. For centuries lost, *The Book of Margery Kempe* was rediscovered in 1934, and offers a unique insight into the life of a female pilgrim in the later Middle Ages. Referring to herself in the third person, or in her words 'this creature', Margery describes how she at first 'set off on her travels with her husband, for he was always a good and easy-going man'. Later she would travel with her maidservant or an escort, often in a party of fellow pilgrims, sometimes alone. Her companions it seems, did not always enjoy the company of this pious vegetarian, and in Germany, on the way to Jerusalem in 1413, they tried to shake her off:

The fellowship [party of pilgrims] made great complaint about this creature to the legate, and said utterly that she could no longer be in their company, unless he would command her to eat flesh as they did, and leave off her weeping, and that she should not talk so much of holiness.

(*The Book of Margery Kempe*, c.1440)

Evidently, the sobbing Margery Kempe was proving a bit of a party pooper. Once the pilgrims reached Bologna, there was an attempt at a rapprochement:

When they heard say she was come to Bologna before them, they had great wonder and one of the fellowship came to her saying to her to go to his fellowship and ask if they would receive her again into their fellowship and so she did. If you will go in our fellowship, you must make a new covenant [promise]: you shall not speak of the gospel but sit still and make merry as we do at supper. She consented and was received back into their fellowship.

In Venice, they tried losing her again:

Also this fellowship, which had excluded the said creature from their table so that she should no longer eat amongst them, arranged a ship for themselves to sail in. They bought containers for their wine and arranged bedding for themselves, but nothing for her.

How much, though, was her fellow pilgrims' disapproval explained by her status as a woman travelling without her husband, determined to go her own way? In Rome, Margery had a run-in with a priest, one of her own countrymen, who 'stirred many people against her and said much evil of her'. Margery dismisses his spitefulness, writing that the 'cause of his malice was that she would not obey him'. Strong, independent-minded women like Margery have always been accused of disobedience, hysteria – or worse. As she herself says:

> As soon as she perceived that she would cry, she would keep it in as much as she could so people would not hear it and be annoyed. For some said it was a wicked spirit vexed her; some said it was a sickness; some said she had drunk too much wine; some cursed her; some wished she had been in the harbour; some wished she had been in the sea in a bottomless boat.

Today, walking alone is still a radical act for women. It's also a liberation: from work, family and domesticity. While men often walk to conquer: a mountain, a desert, a geographical pole, women usually walk to discover something – perhaps themselves – and to be free. With freedom comes danger, and like many women walking alone I was keenly attuned to what was going on around me in the Forest of Bere, wary not to lose myself too deeply in daydreams.

Norman royal hunting forests such as this are found throughout England. Some, like the New Forest in Hampshire, the Forest of Dean in Gloucestershire, Sherwood Forest in Nottinghamshire and Epping Forest in Essex, still survive – if not at their original size. Others, like Wychwood Forest in Oxfordshire and Knaresborough Forest in North Yorkshire largely exist as remnants, or in name only. Often, their previous incarnations as royal hunting grounds are echoed in the suffix 'chase' (from the French *la chasse*, 'the hunt'), as in Cannock Chase in Staffordshire, Malvern Chase in Worcestershire and Cranborne Chase in Dorset and

Wiltshire. Forests and chases were for the exclusive use of kings and their retinue, and local nobility who might be granted a royal licence to hunt in them.

Commoners who happened to live in the forest might also be given permission to use them in a limited way. Pannage, the right to pasture swine, who gorged on fallen beechmast, acorns and chestnuts, was permitted. In the New Forest it still is, and for sixty days each year 600 pigs are released to eat the acorns, poisonous to the forest's more famous equine inhabitants. In the Middle Ages commoners might also be permitted to collect firewood or cut turf for fuel, and allowed some other rights of pasture. If they poached animals reserved for hunting they could be punished for trespass against the *venison*, a term used not only for deer but for the meat of any game animal. Likewise, if they cleared the land for agriculture without permission, a procedure known as *assarting*, it was considered trespass against the *vert* (vegetation). Whether the commoner and his family were destitute, and at risk of starving, was immaterial.

Today, such rules seem barbaric. Yet beyond the Forest of Bere, on the leafy road heading south, hidden driveways led to secluded residences which, I presumed, were occupied by today's elite. Twenty-first century commoners, the ordinary citizens of nearby Portsmouth or Havant, can visit the forest. They can walk their dogs, go jogging, have a picnic with their families. But no overnight camping is allowed except in designated parks, and dwelling in the forest is still the preserve of those with the means to live here. Notices warn the public, in the politest possible terms, to stay away. One reads, in large, red letters, 'PRIVATE ROAD – NO THROUGH ROAD – NO BRIDLEWAY – SPEED LIMIT 10 MPH'. An arrow at the bottom of the board directs today's commoners 'TO CAR PARK FOR FOREST WALK'.

Heaven forbid that I should trespass on private land. With its roots in the Latin verb *transpassare*, and the Old French *trespasser*, meaning 'to pass over', the word inveigled itself into Middle English around the turn of the fourteenth century. In the Middle Ages, most of the countryside was commonly, and communally, farmed and grazed. From the seventeenth century landlords began enclosing common land, a practice formalised by the Acts of Enclosure passed between 1720 and 1840. Between the early seventeenth and the early nineteenth centuries, nearly seven million acres of countryside were enclosed. The result of this legalised land grab was widespread rural poverty, and civil unrest, culminating in the Kinder Scout trespass of 1932 and the founding of the Ramblers Association three years later. Today, unless the current government implements its manifesto plans to make intentional trespass a criminal act in English law, it remains a civil offence only.

Earlier in the year, before setting out on my pilgrimage, I'd ordered a Pilgrim Passport from the Association of English Cathedrals. As part of the unhappily timed Year of Pilgrimage 2020, these passports were available in every Church of England cathedral, allowing holders to document their journeys by receiving a stamp at each cathedral visited. I didn't think producing mine would cut much ice here, but polite notices could not erase my entitlement to walk on a public right of way. So I followed the Pilgrims' Trail along a shady lane lined with rhododendron and overhung with chestnut and oak, and between meadows where ponies grazed the sparse pickings of dry summer grass. Crickets serenaded as I passed between the hedgerows, and through the gaps I glimpsed views of Hampshire hills. This path, linking two historic settlements, would once have been well trodden. Now that everyone travels between towns and villages by car, bypassing these ancient routes, it was closing in on itself. Brambles caught my arms as if trying to slow my progress, like a gossipy neighbour tugging at my sleeve, hoping for a chat. I shrugged off the brambles and continued on my way.

The weather had been dry for days, and in the open fields the earth had hardened and fractured. Here in Kiln Wood, another vestige of the Forest of Bere, the path remained muddy, trampled by horses and scored by mountain bikes. The light fell through the tree canopy and splashed onto the ground, raining sunshine. The verges spangled with wildflowers dressed in late-summer shades of rich purple and deep pink, and hidden among the summer flowers a few strands of creamy cow parsley, clinging on beyond its allotted season. Rather like me.

I was heading towards Southwick, where I planned to rejoin the Old Way after my detour on the Pilgrims' Trail. My map showed the course of the old Roman road from Chichester to Winchester traversing this lane, and, where the Roman road once crossed, a large and venerable oak cast its shade across the road. Trees like this have always marked crossroads, and offered succour to passing travellers, so I shrugged off my daypack and sat under its deep green umbrella. Around the oak, summer grasses rustled and swayed under late-July sun, but its circle of leafy shade was dark and cool.

Lichened walls lined the lane into Southwick, namesake of the wealthy Southampton merchant whose imaginary wife, Alice, was now accompanying me to Canterbury. It was an English dream: brick cottages in shades of rose, silver and blush, thatched roofs and tidy flowerbeds. A dream – or an illusion? One of the prettiest of the brick cottages, encased in a white picket fence with roses framing the door, warned passers-by of CCTV and guard dogs. Further on, in the centre of the village, the Cross of St George fluttered atop the church tower. On this hot day the church looked cool and inviting, but like so many that summer it was closed except for occasional private prayer. I made my way to the back of the building and sat among the tombstones. Salubrious Southwick, so idyllic, yet in spite (or perhaps as a consequence) of its beauty and prosperity, giving every impression that its villagers were living in fear: fear of strangers who may be burglars, fear of uninvited guests passing through.

Or perhaps I was just overheated, ill-tempered from my long morning's walk. I bought an ice cream from the village shop-cum-café, and found a bench outside. Sitting opposite me was an elderly man who said his name was Tom. He was slender and tanned, white bearded, his blue eyes pale and cloudy. He'd come down to Southwick in March from his home in Derbyshire. Just for a short holiday, to visit his son who lived in the village. Then lockdown happened, and he'd been stranded here ever since. Not that he minded; the climate was better than in Derbyshire. His wife had already gone home, but he had an appointment with the local hospital to attend before he could follow her.

'I've got trouble with me bladder. Got to have a scan,' Tom told me as I ate my ice cream. We discussed our respective ailments for a few minutes, then seeing I was on foot he asked where I was headed. I told him about my medieval-style pilgrimage.

'There's a lot of history around these parts,' Tom said. 'The Normandy thing. Monty was here – I was in the army, and I met

Monty a few times. He was in the same regiment as me. Of course, he's dead now.' I told Tom that my father had been in the army, in the Royal Artillery. Tom's father had also been in the Royal Artillery. He'd volunteered in the 1930s and had only been in the army for six months before he was invalided out.

'Rather a bad rupture. He'd be in his hundreds if he was alive now. Got family yourself? Any kids?'

'I've got a husband, and cats. They're far less trouble than children.' I got up to leave. 'Or so people tell me.'

'Might bump into you again sometime,' Tom said as I wriggled back into my backpack. We couldn't shake hands so I waved him goodbye, my good mood restored. I'd arrived in Southwick an hour ago, hot and bothered, feeling unwelcome amid the picture-perfect cottages and thatched roofs. The CCTV signs, the locked church door, the sheer loveliness of the place had peeved me. Now I'd talked with a stranger, made a human connection, learned something of someone else's life and troubles. And I was a better, cheerier person for it.

Tom had been right about the 'Normandy thing'. Southwick was the centre of Operation Overlord, where the D-Day Landings were planned. Dwight Eisenhower and General Montgomery (Monty) lodged at Southwick House in the spring of 1944, when the momentous decision was taken to commit 300,000 people and 7,000 vessels to an operation decisive to the outcome of the Second World War. Momentous days indeed, but it wasn't all hard work. The Golden Lion pub, which I passed as I left the village, became the unofficial Mess, where officers unwound over a pint or two. In 2019 the Red Lion hosted the seventy-fifth anniversary of Operation Overlord. A 1940s shuttle bus took visitors to Southwick House, where the famous D-Day wall map is still preserved, and an exhibition of wartime village life was staged in the church – the Peculiar of St James Without-the-Priory Gate, to give it its full title. No doubt plenty of pints were downed that day as well.

The Second World War, the Battle of Britain, the Blitz and the D-Day Landings are events that still loom large in our collective psyche. When we speak of 'the War' it is invariably the Second World War we mean, when plucky Britain stood up to the might of Hitler's army. These southern counties were, after all, the 'threshold of England', and it's on England's chalky fringes, where you feel you can reach out and touch France, that its spectre still looms largest.

I walked down the hill, and out of the village. My map showed the remains of a priory here – the same priory that St James's Church is 'without'. First founded in 1133 by Augustinian canons within Portchester Castle, it was relocated to Southwick in the middle of the twelfth century over fears of seaborne Viking raids. The priory soon became renowned as a centre of pilgrimage, and Henry VIII is said to have visited Our Lady of Southwick, as it was then called, in 1510. Twenty-eight years later this devout Catholic, who had venerated Thomas Becket's shrine on at least five occasions, dissolved the priory, along with the remainder of England and Wales's religious houses. Like so many of these abandoned and despoiled buildings, it was converted into a private residence. Southwick House was its Victorian replacement, requisitioned by the Royal Navy in 1941 to become home of Operation Overlord, and now reincarnated as a golf club. From Augustinian priory to golf club in less than 500 years. How the mighty are fallen.

Not much of the original priory remains, which was a pity as I would love to have stayed here like my medieval predecessors. Instead, I would have to walk on to Havant before finding a bed that night. I continued along the edge of the priory, its roof peeping over the brick-buttressed wall. Verges bloomed with brazen summer flowers: wild chicory, a powder-blue flower that opens in the morning and follows the sun, closing at noon when the sun is at its zenith. Oxeye daisies, also known as moon or dog daisies, attract a large range of pollinating insects, particularly bees and butterflies. And chalk-loving carline thistles, mecca for a wide variety of butterflies, including the rare large blue. Declared extinct in England in 1979, the large (actually quite small) blue butterfly has now been reintroduced to Somerset and Gloucestershire, where it is doing rather well at a handful of sites.

I love these hot summer afternoons, fissured earth beneath my feet, hot wind crackling the grass, crickets rasping, blue skies streaked with cirrus. Placing one foot in front of the other, relishing the shade of trees where I happened upon it, air cooling abruptly like opening a fridge, emerging again into wind perfumed like the crust of fresh-baked bread. In the Yorkshire Dales much of the land is pasture, staying green and damp throughout the summer months, and I'd almost forgotten the aroma of an arable late July, so familiar from my Chiltern childhood. Now meadow brown butterflies, their dull wings splashed with orange, danced ahead as I walked, living out their brief lives in the fullness of the summer sunshine. As was I.

Just when it was becoming too hot I found myself diving headlong into the dark chill of Sawyer's Wood. I was still in the Forest of Bere, though this particular scrap of woodland is named after the men who earned their living cutting timber, the word stemming from the Middle English *saghier*, to saw. Now belonging to the Southwick Estate, these woods were traditionally managed by local people for their timber.

The same was true of the next woods I passed. Broomground Coppice, Greathunt Coppice, Potwell Coppice, Newlandsmoor

Coppice: all named after the practice of cutting back trees to their stumps to stimulate growth, thus providing firewood or timber. Tell-tale signs of this past management can still be seen in the thin stems growing from short trunks, or 'stools'. It's been decades since these woods were coppiced, and those once-thin stems are now fully grown trees. In those forgotten coppices I found the first sloes of the season. Fruit of the blackthorn tree, fat and purple, sloes look as sweet as grapes but are wincingly bitter on the tongue. Steeped in a mixture of gin and sugar, strained and decanted, by Christmas they are the flavour of summer just before it slips into autumn. The taste of Lughnasa.

Christmas still felt a long way off as I passed through open, light-filled fields, pasture and deep-shaded woodland, where last year's leaves mulched under my boots. I was walking in warm winds across purring fields of tawny grasses and thistles. Ahead were the red roofs and chimney pots of Purbrook, the town seeping into the valleys at Purbrook Heath. My feet were beginning to ache now, not only because of the distance I'd covered that day but because I was walking on tarmac, which jolted through my sprained ankle and amplified the heat.

A moment of peace and calm as I entered woodland again. This was Gundymoor Wood, a last vestige of the Forest of Bere before Havant and the sea, and I was heading down the ominously named Scratchface Lane.

Scratchface Lane runs alongside the remains of a villa that once stood by the Roman road from Chichester to Bitterne, or *Clausentum*, as the Roman settlement of Southampton was called. Known by historians as Route 421, this series of interconnected Roman routes stretched along the south coast from Kent to near Land's End, and was probably later used by medieval pilgrims. It also passed through Wickham, where it joined Route 420 to Winchester, and I'd been criss-crossing it all day as it morphed from a faint line on the OS map to a busy trunk road, and back again.

Now under the management of Hampshire County Council Countryside Services, Scratchface Lane didn't live up to its name that afternoon. The A3 (M) roared, but I still found pools of silence and tranquillity as I followed this ancient track towards Havant. Bidding farewell to the peaceful interlude of Scratchface Lane with its old hedgerows, rowan trees hung with summer berries and meadows of bending grasses, I entered Havant along the Roman motorway, now buried under asphalt.

Like all Roman settlements Havant is laid out on a grid plan, its roads radiating to all four points of the compass. The Roman plan was overlaid by the later medieval settlement, yet I still sensed two millennia of history underfoot as I walked arrow-straight into the centre of town. I was heading for my hotel, an eighteenth-century coaching inn on East Street, the road that once led pilgrims east to Canterbury. The road that would, I hoped, lead me to Canterbury too.

Canterbury, still 200 miles distant, seemed impossibly far away as I flopped onto my bed at the inn. I was hot, sticky, my feet ached and I couldn't imagine walking another step, let alone another 200 miles. According to my fitness tracker, 10,000 steps was approximately four miles. I did a quick calculation on my phone. I had another half a million steps to go before I reached Canterbury.

My malaise was not assuaged by a conversation with a young waitress when I went down to the hotel restaurant for dinner that night.

'Just you?' the waitress asked as she showed me to a table in the corner of the restaurant and handed me a menu.

'Yes, just me.'

'Are you staying here on your own?'

I nodded.

'Oh, that's sad.'

'Well, if you've been married as long as I have, it's not so sad.' It was meant in jest, yet as the words emerged a twinge of melancholy twisted my gut. Perhaps she was right, and it was rather sad to be travelling alone, not to be sharing your supper and bed with a companion.

Or perhaps the twinge was merely a pang of hunger after the day's long walk. I ordered fish and chips, and thought about what the waitress had said. She hadn't meant to be unkind. Female pilgrims like Margery Kempe, and Alice of Southwick a century earlier, rarely stayed in inns unless accompanied by their husbands. Indomitable traveller that she was, Margery Kempe still feared for her safety when journeying alone. On the way to Aachen the men at the inn where she was lodging 'spoke many lewd words unto to her, giving her indecent looks . . . she had great fear for her chastity and was very anxious'. Even though two maids from the inn stayed with her overnight 'she dared not sleep for dread of defiling'. I didn't need any maids to stay with me, but was surprised that in this day and age it's viewed as unusual for a woman to be walking on her own, eating on her own, sleeping on her own.

VI

The morning sun exploding through the curtains rinsed clear the previous night's exhaustion, melancholy and homesickness. On a journey like this, with no obligation except to place one foot in front of the other across an uncharted landscape, each new day is a clean page, an unwritten story. Today I was setting forth on unfamiliar paths, yet reassured in the knowledge that I was treading in the footsteps (and hoof prints) of so many before me, from Roman legionaries and medieval pilgrims to the bewigged coach passengers, queens, presidents and prime ministers who once sojourned at this illustrious Georgian inn.

Taking it slowly in the heat, it would be a two-day walk to the cathedral city of Chichester. First, I would skirt Chichester Harbour with its saltmarsh, sand dunes and mudflats, passing through Warblington, Chidham (where I would stay), Bosham and Apuldram, now tranquil villages that played a pivotal part in English history. This was the closest I'd get to the sea since I'd left Southampton, and I yearned to see it again. Strange, perhaps, for someone who loves chalk landscapes, but I was born beside the sea. Not here on the south coast, but in the northeast, where the River Tyne empties into the flat grey expanse of the North Sea. My father had been posted to Tynemouth, and we left just three months after I was born. I don't have any memory of that time, but my passion for the sea is deep and life-long. And as a Home Counties girl who lived out her teenage years in the beechy Chiltern Hills far from the sea, I never understood why.

A few years ago, I returned to Tynemouth, now a seaside town some ten miles downstream of Newcastle. Its principal landmark is a ruined priory, and although the remaining structure is largely Gothic it stands on the site of an Anglo-Saxon monastery. Surrounded by the castle, the priory's skeleton now perches sombrely on the cliff edge, its sandstone smoothed by 1,000 years of wind and rain, its gravestones standing guard over it like battle-weary soldiers.

Tynemouth had become fashionable as a bathing resort in the eighteenth century, and in the nineteenth century Victorian engineers spent forty years building a breakwater and pier which stretches nearly half a mile into the North Sea. As you walk along the pier you can sense the force of the waves like a living thing as they surge against the stone walls. Did my mother push my pram along this pier when I was a baby all those decades ago, and did I imbibe the spirit of the sea as its salt-spray splashed over me?

On Havant's East Street I continued east, passing townhouses that had seen better times. The desirable residences of three centuries ago were today an assortment of offices and shops, a fair few of them shut up as if for good. Many of Havant's Georgian facades disguise buildings of much earlier origin, unsurprising in a city with two millennia of history. Archaeologists have found remains of Roman buildings beneath the church of St Faith, which stands on the crossroads of East, West, South and North Streets, and Anglo-Saxon pottery was discovered under East Street dating from when Havant was *Hamanfuntan* – *funta* (founts, or springs) belonging to Hama. The documentary record of the town goes back to 985, after King Æthelred granted the land to the monks of St Swithun's, Winchester.

My map found a path weaving between the townhouses. This path was called The Twittens, a Hampshire name for a town footpath, 'twittens' meaning betwixt and between in local dialect. East Street was probably a more direct route out of town, but unable to resist a twitten I wound my way betwixt and behind East Street. Another fine morning had dawned, and Havant's menfolk, dressed in knee-length shorts and bronzed with the year-round tan that you only get living by the coast, were out with their dogs. They paused to talk to their fellow dog walkers, voices wavering between a West Country burr and Estuary English – a commonplace accent within a 100-mile radius of the capital. For me, this was characteristic of the Hampshire I'd been walking through since Southampton. A county that borders West Country Dorset on one side, yet remains steadfastly within London's commuter belt. Hampshire felt an ambiguous betwixt and between sort of place, rather like the twitten that I was walking along.

Or perhaps it was me, a wayfaring stranger just passing through, who was ambiguous, unfixed, indistinct, never sure where was home. The softly moulded chalk hills, or the sea. The south of England, or the rain-sculpted landscapes of the north. As the long-suffering Richard once said, 'the problem is that you can't decide if you're a southern softie or a northern sprite.' He had a point, though perhaps I could be both. As a Pisces I'm a water sign, which, if you believe in such things, would explain my love of the sea. Chalk is sea made stone, and I loved chalk and sea equally. I also loved wildness, and however loudly you sing chalk's praises, wild it is not. The Yorkshire Dales are, as far as it's possible in England, wild. In the Dales you can get hopelessly lost and hypothermic, in need of the Mountain Rescue. You can explore its vast underground cave system, occasionally never to resurface. Compared with the Dales, the Downs are a walk in the park.

One twitten led to another, and to another, winding between the houses and businesses of Havant and towards the sea. Rather than meandering, as it first seemed, I was in fact walking in a straight line as it cut a swathe through the messy street plan of the modern town. This was an ancient path – medieval at least – leading directly out of Havant to the Saxon hamlet of Warblington. And although the route today is severed by the A27, the old paths and twittens always find a way through, and I soon found myself back in rural Hampshire, with its farms and paddocks of sleek, well-fed horses.

Warblington is one of those heart-achingly perfect little places that you find scattered throughout Anglo-Saxon England. Just a moated manor house, a medieval church and a cluster of cottages. Often, this patina of English village perfection hides a murkier history – in Warblington's case, the removal of its villagers in the fifteenth century to create a private deer park for Richard Neville (the 'Kingmaker), and the ghost of previous inhabitant Lady Margaret Pole, Countess of Salisbury, beheaded in 1541 by Henry VIII. The church, all flint and stone and tiled roofs sloping nearly to the ground, is dedicated to St Thomas à Becket, sometimes referred to as St Thomas of Canterbury's Church, and the first I'd found named for the saint on my pilgrimage. Interestingly, medieval documents referred to it as the church of Our Lady, it only assuming its current dedication (with the archaic and erroneous spelling of the saint's name) in 1796.

While not specifically built for pilgrims, churches such as Our Lady/St Thomas à Becket attracted pilgrims who wanted to pray for that particular saint's intercession, or to offer them thanks. This would be especially true if the church held a relic of the saint. And it would also have catered for its own parishioners, just as it does today.

A funeral of one of those parishioners was taking place inside the church, so I strolled around the churchyard with its trees planted in memory of the departed. One of these was an olive, just about thriving in this southern fringe of England, beneath which lay a pebble painted with an image of the church, its steeple topped with a cross. This was clearly a much-loved place, and sitting under the shade of its sheltering trees I could quite see why.

An aged and twisted yew leant across my path, one of several in the churchyard. Yew trees like this (*Taxus baccata*) are often senior to the churchyards they stand in. Among the oldest living things in Britain, around 330 yews predate the tenth century, with sixty of these 2,000 years old and counting. They are the earliest recorded tree, anywhere. One of the few native evergreens of Northern Europe, the yew's deep green branches were a symbol of

'A low-born clerk'

The Middle Ages were a time of hierarchy: there were lords and there were peasants. Even within the Church there was a hierarchy, with bishops and abbots at the top. This was a time of limited social mobility.

As a Londoner, Thomas Becket was born outside the feudal system, and his parents Gilbert and Matilda were also outsiders: merchants who'd emigrated from Normandy. He was born in Cheapside in the city of London around 1120 and sent to grammar school at a time when literacy was uncommon outside the clergy. He later studied at the universities of Paris and Bologna and he came to work for Theobald, Archbishop of Canterbury, where he was surrounded by learned men. He evidently stood out to his employer as, though not a full member of the clergy, he was appointed Archdeacon of Canterbury in 1154, a role that came with an enormous salary of £100 a year.

King Henry II was the image of a medieval monarch: fiercely ambitious, energetic and short-tempered. He set out to control the kingdom not through the barons but through an army of clerks, who were educated commoners (the basis of our civil service today). Among them was Thomas Becket, who was recommended to Henry by Theobald, and who was appointed royal chancellor, also in 1154. Henry and Thomas became friends, going on hunting expeditions together and becoming drinking buddies.

For the next eight years, Becket lived a privileged life of power and luxury at the royal court, amassing huge wealth. The Church was the one part of his realm that remained beyond Henry's control. Clergy could only be tried in ecclesiastical courts, however serious their crimes. The king could not touch them.

When Theobald died in 1162, Becket was appointed to succeed him as Archbishop of Canterbury. Henry supported his appointment, but had assumed Becket would continue as chancellor at the same time, conveniently allowing royal control of the ecclesiastical purse strings. Becket, who had other ideas, was hurriedly ordained as a priest just twenty-four hours before his consecration as archbishop, also resigning from his role as chancellor.

everlasting life, its boughs decorating churches on Palm Sunday – palm trees being in short supply in medieval England. Even before Christianity reached these shores yews were revered in Celtic mythology, a tradition that continues with today's Druids. Yew needles are highly poisonous to nearly all living creatures, which is why they are found in churchyards away from roaming livestock.

Musing on yews and Druids I parked myself beside the entrance to the church, where someone had placed a bowl of water for passing dogs. For passing pilgrims there was nothing that muggy morning. Nothing except peace, tranquillity and an impression of deep, deep age.

Sitting there, I contemplated the funeral taking place inside the church. This was, after all, the year of the pandemic, and I hoped the person whose life was being commemorated had not died of Covid. In the twenty-first century death, particularly in the West, is often hushed, hidden from view, almost embarrassing. Covid, with the daily news reports of casualty numbers, made death public once again, just as it was in the Middle Ages. In medieval

England, as in the rest of Europe, death was a visible part of daily life. As in many developing countries today, around one in four died in childhood. Pregnancy was the next danger point, when death in childbirth was common. Then there were the diseases, many of which are curable today by antibiotics. The most notorious of these was the Great Pestilence, the disease which ravaged Europe in 1347–51, killing two thirds of the population of Europe and which the Victorians in typically melodramatic fashion called the Black Death.

After a few minutes I got up to leave. A middle-aged man with sinewy forearms was leaning on the flint wall of the churchyard, his hands clasped. Wearing blue working trousers, heavy boots, a polo-shirt and baseball cap, he had the tanned, contented face of a man who had spent his life outside. He looked wholly at ease in his surroundings, as deeply rooted in the soil as the old yew. I said hello, and asked if he was working here – the churchyard gardener perhaps? He answered in an accent more West Country than Estuary English, telling me he was the gravedigger. Of course. Why else would he be standing there that day, leaning on the flint wall of the churchyard? Polo shirt and baseball cap notwithstanding, his was a profession as old as the chalk hills.

'What's the church like inside?' I asked. 'I can't see it because of the funeral.'

'Old,' the gravedigger replied. 'Just a normal, old church.'

None the wiser as to its architectural merits, I asked him if he knew the way to Emsworth.

'Just follow the path through the fields, and you'll reach Emsworth.' Of course, I again thought. To the gravedigger, for whom these paths were as familiar as the knotted veins on the back of his hands, the route to the neighbouring village was self-evident. I walked away, sorry to say goodbye to this 'normal, old church' without seeing inside but glad that such peaceful places, right on England's edge, survive. And glad too that men like Warblington's gravedigger still existed, men for whom this lovely old church was just part of the fabric of his life. Nothing special. Only those inhabiting very different, unrooted lives consider such a place remarkable.

As I left Warblington my thoughts turned from Hampshire to an encounter in Jordan, and a journey I'd made along the ancient King's Highway to Petra. Khirbet al-Dharih was the ruin of a Nabatean temple and village, unhurriedly crumbling back into the rock. Like so many of southern Jordan's ancient settlements, including the built structures of Petra itself, the town was largely destroyed by a catastrophic earthquake in 363. A Byzantine community re-inhabited the town, followed by early Islamic peoples.

Khirbet al-Dharih now stands forlorn against its backdrop of bare hills, bypassed by the coachloads of tourists on their way to the Nabatean capital of Petra. I was exploring the ruins with my archaeologist friend, Mahmoud, who pointed out the temple – reused by the Byzantines as a church – villas and public buildings. Evidently it was once quite the town. With its decaying columns, fallen lintels decorated with vases, vines and acanthus leaves as crisp as the day they were carved, fragments of pottery scattered at my feet, it felt as if it had been abandoned yesterday.

An elderly shepherd, his head wrapped in a checked *keffiyeh*, strolled by with his flock of scraggy goats. The dull chink of bells echoed around the hills, a sound unaltered since Khirbet al-Dharih's heyday two millennia ago. The shepherd, picking his way through the rubble in sandalled feet, barely looked up as he passed.

'What do you suppose the shepherd makes of these ruins?' I asked Mahmoud. 'Do you think he knows how special this place is?'

'For the local people, these are . . . just old stones,' Mahmoud replied. Perhaps the shepherd's was the more respectful way to remember this silent, windswept place. A great civilisation dissolving into the ground, overgrown by poppies and wild thyme, sinking beneath drifts of sand, untroubled by mass tourism. The little church of St Thomas à Becket may only be half its age but it shared with Khirbet al-Dharih its timelessness, its aura of having grown from the earth like a yew rather than being built from stones by the sinewy hands of men.

I walked on, following a path hemmed with willowherb, bindweed and ripening blackberries, light silvering as I neared the sea. My map told me that this track was the Wayfarer's Walk, a long-distance path from Inkpen Beacon in Berkshire which follows an old drovers' route seventy miles to Emsworth, from where cattle would be exported across the Channel. From the Middle English *weyfarere*, a wayfarer is one who travels, especially on foot, and this is exactly what I was doing that day – 'faring', or making, my way to the next stop on my pilgrimage.

That next stop was Emsworth, where the Wayfarer's Walk ended. The tide was out, and the air smelled of seaweed and salt. Children paddled in pools on the beach, some carrying buckets and spades just like I did many decades ago on the beaches of

Cornwall and Devon. Pretty Victorian and Edwardian villas fronted the sea, alongside modern urban housing. My way was not a bit urban, overrun with wild pink geranium and blackberry bushes, fading nettles, seeded thistles and bending marine grasses as the coastal flora spilled onto the path. Ahead shiny fibreglass dinghies undulated on the rippled waters of the harbour.

Emsworth might be a yachting paradise now, but its heritage is oyster-fishing. For centuries the town was famed for its oysters, the trade reaching its peak in the last decade of the nineteenth century. Then, in 1902, four dignitaries at a banquet died after eating Emsworth oysters from beds contaminated with raw sewage, and the industry went into freefall. New sewers were dug and the industry revived, although the oysters are now being contaminated once again – not by sewage this time, but with particles from the fibreglass yachts in Chichester Harbour.

Emsworth today earns its keep through sailing and tourism, but it's still at heart a fishing town, as a heart-breaking plaque on the wall beside the harbour reminds the passer-by.

In memory of Emsworth Fisherman
COLIN LOADER, 27
who tragically died on
2nd August 1987
while working on the fishing vessel
THE ANGELA

He was one of the most well liked
and respected people on the land
and on the sea, the place he loved

Sadly missed by all his friends
and the people of Emsworth.

Colin Loader, a young man when he drowned after his fishing vessel overturned in Chichester Harbour, would now have been sixty. He died at the height of summer, exactly the time of year I was there when all seemed calm and safe and settled. Life at sea is as hazardous now as it ever was. Under its veneer of seaside fun, its buckets, spades and bobbing yachts, Emsworth was until recently a working harbour where people risked their lives – and sometimes lost them.

Leaving the village centre to the sailors and the tourists, I found the old marina, where retired fishing boats and veteran sailing vessels are moored. This is a quiet, forgotten creek, well away from the holidaymakers with their freshly creased shorts and polished deck shoes. I sat down on a bench next to a hand-painted notice cautioning that this was a beauty spot, not a rubbish bin. Butterflies warmed their wings in the long grass, and a pair of swans sifted through the mud for tasty titbits. Across the creek in a shabby wooden-hulled boat a tanned and shirtless fisherman sat smoking, occasionally casting his rod into still waters.

The way from Emsworth led me past old Slipper Mill Pond, a saline lagoon where great crested grebes, kingfishers and little egrets feed, through fields of wheat woven with bindweed and spangled with poppies. The ground was as brittle as the wheat, summer wind crackling through the stems. To my left surged the

South Downs, their gold and green mantle obscuring the white chalk underneath. I was happy, walking the hinterland between rock and water, between the chalk and the sea.

At Prinsted, half a mile further on, I saw and smelled the sea once again. A discreet sign on the public footpath labelled this the Sussex Border Path. I'd left Hampshire, and I was entering the territory of the South Saxons. Until they were united under Æthelstan (894–939), the Anglo-Saxons were not one people. From the early fifth century, Angles, Saxons and Jutes settled in Celtic Britain, with the Britons being pushed to the west and north of the country. Angles settled in Mercia, Northumberland and Anglia, where they separated into the North Folk and South Folk. Jutes colonised Kent, while settlers from Saxony made their homes in the east, west and south of the country. These regions became the domains of the East Saxons, West Saxons and South Saxons: Essex, Wessex and Sussex.

Driving, you might pass road signs demarking county boundaries, displayed with the county's coat of arms. When you're walking, one county drifts into another, the terrain changing slowly, incrementally. England's smallness of scale, the subtle shifts in the landscape as you move through it, means you are never bored. There is always a stile to clamber, a gate to open, a stream to cross, a slope to climb, a wood to wander through, a church to visit, a pub or tea shop to stop at. There's wilderness if you want it, but it's the intimacy of the English countryside that appeals to many walkers. A permeable landscape, as porous as chalk. One you walk through, rather than over.

This was the edge of Chichester Harbour, a tidal estuary of saltmarsh, sand dunes and mudflats. Walking along its sea wall I passed what my map told me was Marsh Farm, now a residence of smoked glass and grey paintwork. The marsh had been drained, and with it the sense of wilderness that once prevailed here. A scrap of undrained marsh remained alongside the house, its reeds rustling in hot breezes. On my right, water slapped against the sea wall, with the rushes a symphony of countryside and sea.

The path skidded away from the sea again, through a field of scorched barley and parching winds towards Chidham. The earth was mosaiced underfoot, and the ears of barley bowed in the heat. Chidham is another of those perfect South Saxon places, with its manor house hidden by high walls, medieval church and pub, its mellow brick facade hung with flower baskets and strung with wisteria. The only clue I was in the twenty-first century came from the latter-day Saxon backdrop of a lawnmower, humming above the birdsong.

St Mary's Church was locked, but the porch was open so I pushed apart the doors and sat inside for a few moments. Pinned to the wall, and framed with poppies, was a banner with the roll of honour of the men of Chidham who lost their lives in the First and Second World Wars. Outside the porch, red-painted pebbles arranged in the shape of poppies lined the flagged path. The past feels exceptionally close here, in this quiet hamlet beside the brackish sea. Its isolation did not protect it against the ravages of war, and in 1944 a Wellington bomber crashed after an accidental mid-air collision with a Mosquito, killing the crew of both aircraft.

Not much else happened at Chidham in the preceding millennium, and you have to wind back thirteen centuries to its most significant event – the birth in 681 of the Saxon saint Cuthman. Starting out life as a shepherd, after his father's death he pulled his invalid mother in a wheelbarrow to Steyning on the South Downs, where he built a wooden church that grew into a monastery and became a major pilgrimage site. Medieval pilgrims also visited St Cuthman's birthplace here at Chidham, where a modern stained-glass window shows him pushing his mother along in her wheelbarrow. The fourteenth-century chapel built in St Cuthman's memory is still etched with graffiti and pilgrim crosses. When Henry VIII banned pilgrimages the loss of revenue caused the church to fall into neglect. Happily, it's now in a good state of repair, treasured by its parishioners and a destination for latter-day pilgrims such as me.

Etymologists believe Chidham acquired its name from the village's location on a pouch-shaped peninsula, *ceod* meaning a bag or pouch, and although facing the sea its villagers looked inland for their livelihoods. The susurrating wheat fields I had walked through earlier were the source of Chidham wheat, a prolific variety discovered in the late eighteenth century by local farmer Edmund Woods. He belonged to a long tradition of Chidham farmers, one that reaches back some four millennia report the archaeologists who, in 1980, discovered flint scrapers on the shore of the peninsula. Formed of silica, flints have been used since early Palaeolithic times to make weapons such as arrowheads and tools, and scrapers for cleaning animal hides.

Where there's chalk there are flints, their glassy nodules buried in the white rock like pearls inside an oyster. St Mary's Church, like most on the chain of chalk hills stretching from the Chilterns to the south coast, is built of flint. All this week I'd been walking over chalk and flint, knitting the country of my childhood with the landscape of my pilgrimage.

I left the cool sanctuary of the church porch and, after a drink at the mellow brick pub, walked on. Across the lagoon rose the shingled spire of Bosham church, under whose chancel Harold Godwinson, or King Harold, is supposedly buried. A coffin containing his likely remains was discovered in 1954.

As I skirted the harbour towards the church I sensed the oscillation between land and sea. To my left grains ripened in the fields, and larks warbled into warm afternoon skies. To my right oyster-catchers bobbed in the lagoon. Chichester Harbour is known as an important habitat for waders and wildfowl, with curlews, herons, cormorants and whimbrels either residents or visitors. This is a land that has been reclaimed from the marsh, but it's a land that will soon be reclaimed once again by the sea. Like opposing armies fighting for sovereignty over a scrap of terrain, there's a sense of everything shifting. The landscape and seascape are shifting. People's lives are shifting, unsettled by the twin ructions of politics and the pandemic. Fomented in this mercurial place was deep uncertainty, a sense that despite the apparent immortality of villages like Chidham nothing was guaranteed any more.

VII

After spending the night at an Airbnb on the Roman road, today the busy A259, I now approached Bosham along the edge of the creek. Skylarks acrobatted above the wheat like Spitfires, wind hissed through the reeds. Salt-stunted oaks clung to the banks, tilting over water. The spire of Holy Trinity Church was a beacon for sailors, and for me also as I wound my way around the creek towards the village, cottages clustering around its church like children around their mother. The tide was out that morning, the dinghies in the harbour stranded in the mud, so I chose a path along the water's edge, picking my way through the seaweed and bladderwrack, sea aster and sea lavender. Dinghies slept in the harbour, a lull before the weekend storm of holidaymakers and hobby sailors. Sea mingled into land, and it was hard to see where one ended and the other began.

Coastal erosion is a growing problem for the inhabitants of this tidal estuary, just as 1,000 years ago the coming of the tide proved problematic for King Cnut. Ruler of the Northern Empire, a region encompassing what is now Denmark, Norway and England, it was Cnut who famously set his throne on the seashore and commanded, in vain, the incoming tides to retreat. The conventional moral of the story is the vanity of kings, though like many such fables its truth has been distorted in the telling. Cnut, the alleged villain of the tale, is instead its hero and his purpose was to refute the supposed divine power of monarchs.

Whichever version you believe, legend tells us this event took place at Bosham, although similar claims have been made by Gainsborough in Lincolnshire and Leasowe in the Wirral. In another, possibly apocryphal, tale Cnut's eight-year-old daughter drowned in a local mill pond. Apocryphal or not, a small stone coffin containing the skeleton of a child was found in 1865 under the chancel of Holy Trinity Church.

As the Bayeux Tapestry depicts, Bosham was where Harold Godwinson set off across the Channel in 1064 to meet William, Duke of Normandy, to discuss who should succeed Edward the Confessor, king of the Anglo-Saxons. Harold and his retinue were shipwrecked off the coast of Normandy, and on finally meeting

William at Bonneville-sur-Touques, Harold swore an oath of fealty to the Norman Duke, supporting William's claim to the English throne. On the death of Edward the Confessor in January 1066 Harold claimed the throne for himself, triggering William's invasion. The rest, as they say, is history, and this small village on the edge of England was its epicentre.

I sat on a bench beside the churchyard wall, under the boughs of a sycamore tree, soaking up the deep history of the place. Rain was forecast for later that day, and although the skies were clear the air was freighted, foreboding.

Tracks through fields of green and gold studded with ragged robin, willowherb and all the spiced colours of Lughnasa led me away from the village and into an afternoon of warm stirring winds, gunmetal clouds pregnant with rain, flat fields, wide skies arching overhead. Summer in full bloom, mature yet not gone to seed. A year in the prime of its life.

I was walking through one of England's most crowded corners, along a coastline stringed by conurbation. Once you step away from the settlements, though, you're enveloped in a world of wind and birdsong and wildflowers. You can walk for what seems like hours and not meet another soul. You're left alone with your footsteps, your thoughts and your daydreams. It is slow travel at its slowest. In an age that seems to be moving ever faster, slowing down is liberating. In a world that is ever more complex, putting one foot in front of the other is an act of meditation. Walking unlocks the landscape like no other form of movement, priming your senses. You are acutely aware of the sights, sounds, smells, textures of the landscape, yoking you to the earth beneath your feet and the sky above your head. Rather than being separated from the natural world, you fuse with it. When walking, you and the landscape become one.

Paths and tracks draped in their summer glory led me to a vast field of ripened wheat, and beyond, the spire of Chichester Cathedral pointing towards the heavens. Chichester would be the end of my day's walk, but first paths would take me to Fishbourne, through a copse of twisted dwarf oak and a patch of shade where I sat listening to the wind brushing through the leaves. It felt good to take off my rucksack, sticking now to my back, and feel the skies pressing down on me, swollen with rain like a bomb about to detonate.

One of only two medieval English cathedrals visible from the sea (the other is Portsmouth), and a landmark for seafarers, Chichester's spire prodded the clouds as if to rupture them. I felt no nearer the city as my path curved around the harbour. I was rotating inside a maze, never quite reaching its centre. For two clammy days I'd been snaking the edge of Chichester Harbour with its creeks and lagoons, walking parallel to the Roman road between Chichester and Havant. It was slightly demoralising to reach this road to find I'd only travelled ten miles as the crow flew, or as the Roman marched – a journey of twenty minutes by car. But I didn't envy people cocooned in those cars, missing the twisted oaks, the wading birds and the purple sea lavender.

Reeds twice my height bordered the final path into Fishbourne, and the air was clotted with salt. The village is best known as the site of Fishbourne Roman Palace, the largest domestic building discovered in Roman Britain and, in the opinion of the distinguished archaeologist Sir Barry Cunliffe, the largest Roman residence north of the Alps. With its mosaic floors, underfloor heating, corridors and courtyards, I'd planned to stop by, but it was closed so I pressed on to Apuldram.

Apuldram is another remote outpost on the peninsula – alone, rather than lonely – and my last stop before Chichester. The path led me straight to the tiny church of St Mary, which in normal times offers sanctuary to modern pilgrims who can spend the night here. Wind trembled through the plane and poplar trees encircling the church. I wandered around the graveyard, finding headstones half buried in the grass and silvered with lichen, tracing with my fingers the dates engraved into the stone. There was the grave of Mary Booker, who died in October 1771 aged eighty-six, and, just a few feet away, John Ormonde Gostling who died on 28 May 2020, aged ninety-six. People live long lives in these parts – except for those caught up in the fighting of the previous century's world wars, or lost at sea.

One area of the churchyard was dedicated to Commonwealth War Graves, where I found the headstone of Sergeant L. W. Bridger, a navigator with the Royal Air Force who died in 1942, aged just twenty-one. The churchyard was tranquil, just the whisper of sea winds in the trees, yet this fringe of southern England was not so long ago on the frontline of conflict, tragedy and heartbreak.

As I set off on the final leg to Chichester, I knew I was turning my back not only on Apuldram, but the sea. The next time I'd be close enough to see, smell and hear it simultaneously would be in Winchelsea 120 miles and two seasons away from this sublime spot. I may have turned away from the sea, but ahead lay the cathedral city of Chichester, and beyond, the great swell of the South Downs. The sea was behind me, but the chalk was yet to come.

Medieval pilgrims approaching Chichester first encountered the brick and flint city walls, designed to keep out coastal invaders and other unwelcome visitors. These still largely exist, built on the foundations of those laid by the Romans, fortified by sixty bastions and rebuilt following the Norman invasion. The Gough Map illustrates the city as two buildings, plus a spired church topped by a cross denoting a religious building. For author Nick Millea, the size and complexity of the illustration possibly denotes a town's importance. If so, then *cicestr* was not as significant as London, York or Canterbury, and a handful of other cities scattered throughout the land, but on a par with Southampton. More noteworthy than Havant though, which is represented by a single building.

From afar, Chichester looked remarkably like the perfect medieval city depicted on the Gough Map, though today's foot-sore pilgrims are met with a series of barricades in the form of busy roads, railway lines, and industrial estates. I pushed my way through on public rights of way, weaving around, behind and between the obstacles. Unlike the villages I'd passed through so far, where everything remained on an intimate, human scale, as a walker I didn't feel welcome here.

It wasn't until I'd reached the Cathedral Close that I sensed again the serenity of the past few days' journey.

VIII

Expectant clouds had hung heavy upon my arrival into Chichester. Overnight they'd given birth to rain, and the following morning dawned dank and dark. It felt as if I'd been following the cathedral's tall, slender spire for days, never getting any closer. Now, I was straining my neck as I peered up along its length towards the clouds. The spire topped a Norman building, a classic of its style with twin west-facing towers, round-arched windows and, uniquely, England's only surviving detached medieval cathedral bell tower. I went inside. A creamy light dripped from the clerestory windows, the air heavy with wood polish and silence.

Covid restrictions were still in place and I had the roped-off nave almost to myself. The few visitors were outnumbered by the cathedral guides who, genuinely pleased to see people after so many months, smiled a warm welcome. I asked one to stamp my Pilgrim Passport. A puzzled look, a few minutes' wait as he disappeared into the recesses of the cathedral, then my passport was returned to me. Inside was a simple sticker showing a pair of boot prints. It wasn't the medieval-style stamp I'd been anticipating, but it did the job.

On a nearby wall was a list of the bishops going back to 733, when they were the bishops of Selsey, former capital of the kingdom of Sussex and religious precursor to Chichester Cathedral. For the first four centuries names such as Eadbeorht, Withun, Æthelwulf and Æthelric dominate. Then, from 1070 onwards, come Norman French names such as William, Ralph, Simon, John, Richard. 1070 was four years after the Conquest, following which Æthelric II, the last Saxon Bishop of Selsey, was replaced by King William's chaplain, Stigand. Five years later the See transferred from Selsey to Chichester, eight miles away. Just a plaque with a list of names, but one revealing the wholesale Norman seizure of England. The revolution was far from peaceful, especially in the north of the country. Here, the genocide and scorched-earth policy inflicted upon the Anglo-Scandinavian population was known as the Harrying of the North, and is bitterly remembered in those parts 1,000 years later.

The Norman presence is still potent in Chichester Cathedral. Beyond the roped-off chancel I could see the massive, rounded piers in the nave and the transepts running the length of the cathedral. What a potent, if not outright intimidating, message this building style conveyed to the conquered populace. Norman buildings like Chichester Cathedral are known for their simplicity, their austerity, yet what we see today is deceptive. In the Middle Ages, the walls would have been brilliantly painted, garish to the modern eye used to bare masonry. If you look closely you can still see the original colouring in the tomb of Joan de Vere, who died in 1293 and her tomb apparently brought from Lewes Priory at the Dissolution. A few faint traces of red and blue, the medieval pigments that lasted longest. In the Middle Ages the costliest colour was ultramarine, a rich blue ground from lapis lazuli, a precious stone at that time only found in a remote valley in Afghanistan. The pigments were ground into egg tempura and pasted on the walls and ceilings of churches and cathedrals, manor houses and castles.

Monochrome masonry, the result of centuries of fading and rubbing, perhaps gives the impression that the Middle Ages were earnest, dour even, though medieval sensibility was more playful than today's visitors to Chichester Cathedral might imagine. Norman architecture, for all its gaudy colouration, was stern and forbidding. Its successor, Gothic, is graceful and spirited. In the cathedral you need only look at the carved figures on the roof bosses or corbels – a woman wearing a wimple, a Green Man, various birds and beasts – to appreciate the playfulness of the medieval sculptors. Often these gargoyles are cheeky, if not downright rude, such as the figure of Sheela-na-gig, a naked woman of probable pagan origin displaying her genitalia, commonly found in Norman churches across Northern Europe. Not in Chichester though, which is too genteel for such vulgarity.

Joan de Vere's tomb is thought to be the earliest example in England of one showing 'weepers', the miniature figures in mourning sculpted on the sides of the tomb chest. It's an impressive monument, but for non-art historians the most celebrated in the cathedral today is the fourteenth-century memorial to

Richard Fitzalan, Earl of Arundel, and his second wife, Eleanor. Carved from milky alabaster, and like Joan de Vere's removed from its original home at Lewes Priory sometime after 1537, it's renowned for its beauty and unusual iconography, showing the joined hands of the effigies of husband and wife. Above all, it's famed for a poem by the late Philip Larkin. Written in 1956, 'An Arundel Tomb' is a meditation on the nature of time and mortality, and ends with Larkin's oft-quoted line, 'What will survive of us is love.'

A tangle of residential streets escorted me out of Chichester that afternoon, taking me to St Peter's Church, Westhampnett. Accommodation in Chichester was expensive and largely booked now that we were released from lockdown, so I'd found an Airbnb near Boxgrove, around four miles further along the Old Way.

Looking more like a barn than a church, St Peter's tiled roof nearly met the ground. Narrow windows set in flint walls peeped out from beneath, like eyes under a hat. Large mature trees encircled the churchyard, as if shielding its buried dead. This was the first open parish church I'd met so far, and I stepped inside to evade the massing rainclouds. Founded shortly after the arrival of St Wilfrid's mission to the land of the South Saxons, the church repurposes Roman brick, tiles and even flue pipes – clues that it stands on a Roman road. This road was Stane (Stone) Street, which ran from *Noviomagus Reginorum* to *Londinium,* or Chichester to London. Medieval pilgrims used it when travelling to visit the shrine of St Richard in Chichester, a saint whose early sixteenth-century popularity once rivalled that of St Thomas Becket. Like the shrine of St Thomas in Canterbury, St Richard's shrine in Chichester was destroyed by Thomas Cromwell in 1538, the commissioners being paid £40 to carry out the work.

As a pilgrim church, St Peter's was one I most wanted to visit on my own little pilgrimage. Once inside, I made my way to the chancel, where medieval pilgrims had scored marks into a stone windowsill. They're hard to see today, and protected by Perspex, but I could make out various early Christian symbols: a shark-like fish, a triangle, several crosses. The chancel was cool, cave-like, its damp stonework clouded with mould. I inhaled, breathing in the medieval ambience of this place, and the palpable sense of walking in the footsteps of pilgrims who passed this way 1,000 years before.

Brought up an Anglican, I attended a Church of England primary school then suffered years of quasi-religious assemblies each morning at secondary school. Now I rarely attend formal services – just funerals and the occasional wedding – but my love of village churches, especially sitting alone in them, endures. The scent of damp stone, of candle wax and wood polish, the tangible sense of fathomless time, air laden with dust and silence. The connection with those who have lived before, the hand-smoothed wooden pews, engravings and paintings in stone and plaster, foot-worn steps. Perhaps, in some way, I would leave my mark, too.

Outside, the traffic of modern Stane Street trembled just a few hundred metres from the church door.

The clouds had burst while I'd been inside St Peter's, and heavy raindrops exploded onto the paved pathway of the church-yard. A notice beside the door invited me to sanitise my hands with the bottle provided, jolting me forwards five centuries from my medieval musings to twenty-first century tribulations. Covid-19 may not have been around in the Middle Ages, but outbreaks of disease, such as the bubonic plague (Black Death), which arrived in England in 1348, were frequent and devastating. Like coronavirus, the Black Death is thought to have originated in China, spread by travellers along the Silk Road and bringing social and economic turbulence in its wake. It was to give thanks for being spared illnesses like the plague that people undertook pilgrimages to the shrines of St Thomas in Canterbury or St Richard in Chichester, stopping at pilgrim churches like Westhampnett on the way.

Back on Stane Street, my hands sanitised and smelling of alcohol, I headed northeast towards London. Walking in a straight line along a Roman road, especially one as busy as this, is not as pleasing as following meandering medieval paths, but on this day of sudden showers I could stride out and cover the distance quickly. Medieval pilgrims would have done just the same, I told myself, altering their route to suit the circumstances and the weather. It's only human nature, and medieval folk were essentially the same as us.

Ahead lay the South Downs, swathed in mist. Those hills were for tomorrow. The afternoon was evaporating, and I was wet. Chris, the host of my Airbnb at Halnaker, on Boxgrove Common, was waiting to welcome me to his cosy flint cottage.

IX

From Halnaker (OE *healf+æcer*, plot of cultivated land) the following morning I took a diversion from the tarmac, and the

Old Way to Arundel, to continue up the original route of Stane Street. The modern road veers off to the right before rejoining the Roman road further on, but I was now on a track called Mill Lane. This was more tunnel than track, a darkening holloway, its banks twice as tall as me, where the temperature seemed to drop ten degrees. It's said that a holloway sinks by one metre every 300 years, so by that reckoning this one was nearly 1,000 years old, fitting perfectly with the Roman occupation of Britain from AD 43 to 410. The reason I diverged along Mill Lane, apart from its historic appeal as an ancient trackway, was the words *Pit (dis)* marked on my map. A disused gravel quarry, Eartham Pit is where, in 1994, archaeologists discovered the gnawed tibia (shin) bone and several teeth of what became known as Boxgrove Man.

Dating back some 500,000 years, these are the oldest human remains unearthed in Britain, and belonged to someone (now thought to be female rather than male) who crossed the land bridge that separated what is today southeast Britain and northern France.

Half a million years ago the white chalk of Sussex and Kent, its cliffs an emblem of 'fortress England', connected us with continental Europe. The first Britons walked to England, their footprints preserved on the beach at Happisburgh in Norfolk and only uncovered after the storm of May 2013. Those footprints, the oldest in Europe and briefly exposed to the world after perhaps 8,000 centuries buried in estuary mud, have now been washed back into the sea. The climate in Britain when *Homo antecessor* migrated here was similar to present-day Scandinavia, and the species survived by hunting mammoths, elk and horses. By the time *Homo heidelbergensis*, the tribe of Boxgrove Man (or Woman), settled in West Sussex the climate had warmed to Mediterranean temperatures, the people living off a diet of lion, rhino, bear, deer and horse, whose butchered bones were found in the quarry.

Fragments of bone and teeth can tell us a surprising amount about what this individual, man or woman, looked like, and how they may have lived. We know that they stood at around five feet eleven, weighed approximately fourteen stone and that they died at about forty years of age. The tibia's density shows that this was a strongly built individual, who ran a great deal – doubtless while hunting animals. Scratch marks on the teeth reveal how he or she ate, and worked flints found at the site show that the population who lived here were, say archaeologists, 'cognitively, socially, and culturally sophisticated'.

Eartham Pit is now fenced off for safety reasons and the quarry was obscured by late-July foliage, but peeking through the branches I glimpsed the deep chalk pit where prehistory was made. Surrounded by densely wooded slopes, the melancholy mewl of a buzzard overhead, I imagined this as virgin landscape, one that existed before the hills and valleys were cleared for agriculture. One that existed, in fact, when Boxgrove Woman walked here, perhaps on the same spot where this modern woman now stood.

I retraced my steps back down Mill Lane to Halnaker, and Stane Street. Soon, a meandering medieval path took me off the Roman road and once again I found myself among the black-berries and the birdsong. Like Mill Lane, the great age of this path was revealed in its depth. Either side were steep banks, from which ancient hedges had sprouted into full-grown trees, crocheted overhead and sheltering me from the rain far more effectively than my rainwear. This old, deep way escorted me to the ruins of the Benedictine priory of Boxgrove. Founded in the early twelfth century as a cell of the abbey at Lessay in Normandy, it originally housed just three monks.

By the Dissolution, Boxgrove Priory had grown to accommodate eight priests and a novice, plus their servants and retinue. The buildings included a guesthouse where visitors, including pilgrims on their way to London, Chichester or Canterbury, rested overnight. This was a step up in comfort from a hospice, as where you slept depended on your social standing. Royalty and aristocracy were invited to stay at the abbot's private lodgings, while folk on horseback such as Alice of Southwick were accommodated in the guesthouse. Those arriving on foot, the poorer pilgrims, the servants of affluent guests and other itinerant travellers, were shown dormitory-style rooms above the stables. Boxgrove was not a large or wealthy priory, so its guesthouse was simply furnished, with plaster walls (perhaps painted with religious scenes), divided into bays where guests would enjoy a modicum of privacy as they bedded down on straw mattresses. Assuming Alice stayed in the guesthouse, she was served a simple evening meal by the priory's servants before tallow candles were lit for the night.

After its suppression the priory church became the parish church of St Mary and St Blaise, while the rest of the monastic buildings were plundered or allowed to decay. The guesthouse, which incorporated the prior's lodging, was used as a barn after the Dissolution and by the eighteenth century had become ruinous.

From the church a mown path through meadows festooned with pink bindweed, heads drooping and jewelled with raindrops, led me to the shattered ruins of the old guesthouse. Apart from the church and one wall of the chapter house, the guesthouse is the only structure standing above ground. The north window gaped, having lost its tracery long ago. It looked like a mouth with the teeth knocked out – a painful memento of the vandalism and destruction wrought by Henry VIII on the ancient abbeys, monasteries and priories of medieval England. There was twenty-first century vandalism also, in the form of a Coca-Cola can discarded in the cloister.

Toothless and roofless, the lodging house offered little comfort that morning as I stood in the rain, encircled by the ruins and wildflowers of this beautiful, desecrated place.

The rain cleared, the air freshened, and the sun warmed the winds. I followed tracks away from Boxgrove Priory through fields of regimented vines. This was the Tinwood Estate, an award-winning vineyard whose sparkling wines are the fruit of a climate more French than English. The Romans were the first to bring vines to England, where they flourished. By 1086 the Domesday Book records forty-six places where vineyards were present, a number which had grown to 139 during the reign of Henry VIII. England's subsequent decline in wine production may have partly been a consequence of the Dissolution, as the monasteries owned many of the nation's vineyards, and it wasn't until the latter half of the twentieth century that wine was grown again on a commercial scale.

Further tracks led me across Boxgrove Common and into woodland, the way sandy and indented with horses' hooves. I was only a few hundred metres from a settlement, yet saw nothing except woods and fields of sheep. I had the landscape to myself, the trees offering their shade and company as I climbed up through Eartham Thicket. Up, up onto the chalk hills of the South Downs.

On Long Down, Sussex unfolded before me, the faint glint of sea beyond. Long Down may only rise 100 metres above sea level, but on the intimate scale that is the southern English landscape it felt like the crest of a mountain. Parched barley waved as I passed, its quivering ears reminding me again that Lammas

Day, and harvest, was near. At Lammas, loaves were baked from the first-gathered grain, and brought to the churches to be consecrated. Feasting, celebrations and matchmaking followed in a bucolic ritual befitting a rooted, rural population. With increasingly erratic weather patterns playing havoc with harvest time, and with our ever more secular, urban lives, Lammas is barely observed today.

A few stray poppies, outcasts from glyphosate-ripened fields, fringed the path down to the village of Eartham. Huddled in its valley, it's a rapture of rose-wreathed cottages, apple orchards, fertile farmland, flint-built church and old country pub. I could quite see why Eartham's inhabitants, modern Boxgrove Man and Woman, would want to settle here.

Inside the flint-built church, beyond the nave of stumpy, rounded columns, I found two Corinthian capitals carved with acanthus leaves. A Mediterranean shrub not commonly seen in twelfth-century Sussex, the acanthus is characteristic of classically inspired Romanesque architecture. So far, so Norman. Between the acanthus fronds peeped the face of a bearded man and the head of a hare, thought to represent Ostara or Eostre, the Saxon goddess of spring. Impervious to its classical pretensions, the church of St Margaret embraced a pagan and intensely rustic heritage that reached beyond the grasp of medieval Christianity.

It was too early to stop at the George pub so I strode on, up tracks of mud and flint, towards Slindon. I was walking through three seasons that July morning. Relics of spring clung on in the withering sprigs of cow parsley, and mingled with the purple vetch, pink geranium and magenta thistle of high summer. Embryo blackberries, a late-summer fruit, were a forewarning that autumn wasn't far off.

Slindon is a picturesque – there's no other word for it – estate village of flint and ashlar, now in the care of the National Trust. That it was once an important settlement, with a history reaching back some 100,000 years, is clear from the myriad paths, tracks and roads that converge here. Archaeologists have uncovered evidence of Palaeolithic occupation, a time when the sea lapped against the hillside. The Saxons named it Sloping Hill (*slinu-dun*), and the village was passed to the archbishops of Canterbury and then to Henry VIII, who created a deer park. The deer have largely gone now, and most of the stately beeches blew down in the Great Storm of October 1987, but today's South Saxons still enjoy the woods, especially in April, when a mist of 10,000 bluebells hovers beneath the trees.

A sunken track, earthy and sweet-smelling after the rain, passed through the near wilderness of Rewell Wood, where I walked on alone, my pace quickening as so often when in woodland. Beneath the mulch of long-fallen leaves lay the ribcage of downland chalk, protruding through its skin of foot-worn earth. Rewell Wood is now largely a commercial conifer plantation, though on my OS map were marked earthworks, enclosures and tumuli, affirming that this was once an open landscape, farmed by our prehistoric ancestors. The story of mankind, etched in chalk.

I strode on. Rewell Wood was behind me and the track now ran parallel to the A27, where, on the other side of a hedgerow of ripening blackberries, unseen traffic had groaned to a halt. Exhaust fumes wafted over the hedgerow, impatient horns honked and an ambulance whined, drowning out the skylarks. Soon the track veered away from the road, taking me down through the prettily named Waterwoods to a sign announcing the threshold of the historic market town of Arundel, ancestral home of Larkin's Earl of Arundel and wife, Eleanor. On the Gough map, *arundell* on the banks of the River Arun is represented by two castles, walls and one gate, boasting its former importance as a fortified medieval port.

Hot, sweaty and footsore, I let the Old Way lead me deep into Arundel's heart.

I had now completed three stages of the Gough Map's itinerary, and had ended my Lughnasa walk along the Old Way. Throughout spring in Yorkshire, after my Ostara walk had been curtailed and when lockdown felt unending, I questioned whether I'd ever make it to Arundel, let alone Canterbury. Now I was here, with some seventy miles under my belt. Weariness gave way to elation, and relief when I saw Chris, who had come to Arundel to drive me back to his cosy flint cottage in Halnaker.

The Book of Margery Kempe

Margery Kempe, c.1440

The earliest autobiographical work in English, the book was dictated by the illiterate mystic Margery Kempe (c.1373–c.1440) in the 1430s. The manuscript was lost until its rediscovery in the 1930s, and is now kept in the British Library. In this extract, Margery is on her way to Aachen, then an important site of medieval pilgrimage.

The next day, she paid for her lodging, enquiring of her hosts if they knew of any party travelling towards Aachen. They said 'no'. Taking her leave, she went to the church to find and prove if her feeling were true or not. When she came there, she saw a company of poor folk. She went up to one of them, asking where they were intending to go. He said, 'To Aachen'. She asked him to allow her to travel in their company.

'Why lady,' he said. 'Don't you have any man [servant] to travel with you?'

'No,' she said. 'My man has left me.'

So she was received into this company of poor people, and when they came to any town, she bought her food and her companions went about begging. When they were outside the towns, her companions took off their clothes, and, sitting about naked, picked themselves [for lice]. Need compelled her to wait for them and prolong her journey, and be put to much more expense than she would otherwise have been.

This creature [Margery Kempe] was afraid to take off her clothes as her fellows did, and therefore, through mixing with them she caught some of their vermin and was dreadfully bitten and stung both day and night, until God sent her other companions. She remained in their company with great anguish and discomfort, and much delay, until the time that they reached Aachen.

SAMHAIN

'A holiday, falling on the night of 31 October to 1 November, celebrated by the ancient Celts as the beginning of winter and the new year, and a time during which the spirits of the dead could return to the earth'

ARUNDEL TO LEWES

X

My memory of late summer was of baked earth and desiccated air, rucksack sticking to my back as I walked off the Downs and into medieval Arundel. Now, three months on, I was returning under gunmetal skies, newly fallen leaves spiralling on the ground in tropical gusts. A season had passed, and autumn had settled over the landscape as I sat on the bed in my hotel beside the A27 on the edge of Arundel.

It was late October, and approaching the Celtic festival of Samhain, or, in the Christian calendar, Halloween. The midpoint between the autumn equinox and the winter solstice, Samhain was a time to celebrate the harvest, welcome the darkness, commune with the dead. Druids were summoned, ancestors honoured, fires lit, cattle sacrificed. Two thousand years on, children dressed as spooks knock on doors demanding a trick or treat, candles are lit inside grinning pumpkins and effigies are burnt on bonfires as spell-bound crowds watch on. The Romans may have outlawed Druidry two millennia ago, and Christians appropriated their festivals a thousand years later, yet the pagan spirit clings on.

I had been thinking about time, and the games it plays with your mind, as I arrived at Arundel station. It felt like forever since I'd walked into the town on that hot July afternoon three months earlier, but it also felt like no time at all. The year had shifted, and so had I. Returning to domestic life after my summer walk, to my family and my work, I'd lost the protective carapace nurtured during that week in Lughnasa.

Now I was alone again, and about to set off on a week of walking. A solitary walk might be the ultimate in freedom, but a woman walking alone is still seen as militant, still attracts attention and comment. You learn to forge a layer of mental armour around yourself, to ward off hazards – physical or psychological, real or perceived – you may meet along your path. As I started out on the next leg of my pilgrimage, that armour had peeled away. I was a mollusc that had lost its shell, and I needed to regrow it quickly, lose the vulnerability and loneliness I now felt eating a takeaway in my room at the Premier Inn, next to a convent at Crossbush on the outskirts of Arundel.

I was given a room overlooking the convent housing the Poor Clares, a community of nuns who normally offer hospitality to passing pilgrims, but who were sheltering from Covid. I could just see the convent now behind its high brick wall, surrounded by a protective ring of trees. When I phoned to book the hotel, asking to be at the back and away from the main road, the receptionist had cautioned me about my choice of room.

'Are you sure you want to be at the back? Some guests have complained about the noise from the convent bells in the morning,' she'd asked.

'I'd rather be woken in the morning by bells from the convent than by HGVs on the road,' I reassured her.

And ring the bells did, calling the nuns to prayer throughout the day and evening, and in the early morning just as the receptionist had warned. Not as early as the dawn *adhan*, the first of five daily calls to prayer which, like the convent bells in the Christian tradition, punctuate the lives of the faithful throughout the Muslim world. In my travels in Arab countries I loved being woken in Damascus, Muscat or Amman by the *adhan*. First came the chant from one solitary mosque, amplified across the roof-tops, then others would join in. Layer upon layer of symphonic sound before the calls faded away, and silence settled over the city once again. Like the *adhan*, the convent bells of the Poor Clares hinted that beyond a world ruled by timetabled work and leisure, TV programmes and TV meals, there existed a parallel universe where lives were measured by a different, more ancient, clock. I was unable to stay with the Poor Clares, yet felt connected to them by the bells tolling their religious observances. The same bells that once tolled from countless convents, abbeys and priories of medieval England before Henry VIII obliterated them all.

My takeaway eaten, I laid the OS map out on the bed. Like almost everyone else these days I use my phone for navigation, but still prefer to look at a paper map for walking and to see my whole journey unspooling before me. Seven centuries previously, the red line drawn on the Gough Map ended stage four of the itinerary at Bramber. As Bramber was only twenty-two miles from Arundel I'd opted to make the most of being on the Downs and finish this stage in Lewes, a major medieval settlement around fifty miles along the Old Way. It didn't sound much, but it was now over a month past the autumn equinox and the nights were drawing in. The clocks would go back later that week, further shortening my days.

From Arundel the Old Way follows the South Downs Way, itself tracing an ancient ridgeway used for perhaps eight millennia. With no new roads built in England from the end of the Roman Empire around the year 400 until the toll roads of the eighteenth century, medieval travellers, including pilgrims, walked or rode the safest and driest routes. Tried and tested routes that had been used by millions of fellow travellers before them, like the ridge path over the South Downs. And now I'd be walking that same path, striding over open chalk hills etched by aeons of human life, descending each day or evening to Sussex villages lying beneath the escarpment: Storrington, Steyning, Bramber, Saddlescombe, Pyecombe, Offham. At the end of the week I would drop down into Lewes, the historic county town of East Sussex that spans the River Ouse before it bleeds into the sea.

Woken by those convent bells, I set out on a morning more summer than autumn, the sun watery after the night's rain, the air mild, the wind soft. Sodden leaves sticking to the pavement were the only sign of the new season as I walked towards Arundel's historic centre, its great castle rising above the misted valley like a fantasy. Coming from the north of England, where autumn was well underway, here it was as if it had barely begun. Some trees still wore their summer greens, others had begun their transformation to autumn golds. Arundel, buzzing with holiday visitors when I was there in the summer, was now a workaday town with residents going about their business.

I crossed the River Arun, passing the remains of a Dominican friary founded in the second quarter of the thirteenth century. Unlike the Cistercians, who preferred to secrete themselves in remote valleys where they farmed large estates and amassed vast wealth, the Dominicans, or Black Friars, chose to live and preach within the community, begging for alms. For Alice of Southwick, the diversity of monastic orders in England – Cistercians, Cluniacs, Benedictines, Carthusians, Dominicans and many others – had formed the warp and weft of everyday life since the beginning of known time. That they would all be extinguished in one fell swoop by a headstrong and spiteful monarch for his personal gain 300 years later was inconceivable.

On I climbed up the steep High Street, out of condition and

out of breath, towards the castle and the parish church of St Nich-olas. Timber-framed and brick facades crested with tiled roofs hemmed the street, its jumble of epochs and architectural styles blending into one satisfying whole. No one building looked out of place, as if by design rather than pure luck. Dominating the tangle of medieval streets, at the top of the hill, stood Arundel Castle and its adjacent church of St Nicholas.

Busy with visitors in summer, St Nicholas was now empty except for me and a cleaner in a surgical mask, spraying and wiping down the pews. Keeping my social distance I walked up the nave. Dividing it from the chancel is a glazed iron grille, and behind the grille is the Fitzalan Chapel, the private mausoleum of the Catholic Norfolk family of Arundel Castle. As the nave is used for worship by the Anglican townsfolk, St Nicholas is a rare surviving example in England of the medieval practice of two ecclesiastical foundations existing under one roof.

It's been this way since the Reformation. Quarrels between the Norfolks and the parishioners over who owned which part of the building came to a head in 1879 when the vicar took to the law, claiming the chapel for the town. He lost, and the chapel remained shut off to the parishioners for nearly a century. In 1977, for the first time in over 500 years, the grille was opened. Since then it has been unlocked a further seven times, but only once this millennium, in November 2018 to commemorate the centenary of Armistice day. The 1534 Act of Supremacy, when Henry VIII formally broke with Rome, shook the foundations of the country like an earthquake. Five hundred years on and its tremors still reverberate as we again turn our backs on Europe, repeating those centuries-old debates over identity and sovereignty.

Leaving the divided building I walked through the church-yard, where crocuses, a rich deep pink, nudged up through wet turf. Robins still sung from branches as if spring rather than winter were approaching. Churchyards like this are sanctuaries for nature and for humans also in a chaotic world, havens where hush descends like the softest of autumn rains. Holly trees, ripe with crimson fruit, foreshadowed winter. For Christians, holly is a symbol of Christmas, its berries representing the blood of Christ, its sharp leaves the crown of thorns. Like many other Christian traditions, reverence for holly is borrowed from earlier pagan beliefs, when the tree was a symbol of fertility and eternal life.

I cut up through the grounds of Arundel Castle, where beech leaves like beaten gold fluttered on branches. The trees looked singed – still rich dark green in the middle, their tips burnt brown. Autumn is, of course, John Keats's 'season of mists and mellow fruitfulness', and although it can be a melancholy time of year, with its recollections of the new school term, it's a season I love – sun low in the sky, rich light and deep colours, the land still warmed by westerly winds.

At the top of the hill, austere and alone, stood a memorial to the Siege of Sevastopol (1854–5), one of the most arduous of the Crimean War. This year-long blockade produced Tennyson's poem 'The Charge of the Light Brigade', and made a household name of Florence Nightingale, who tended the wounded in battles such as Balaclava. I was about to walk away from the monument when I spotted a bunch of flowers laid on its plinth, droopy and rain-sodden after last night's storm. A small piece of soggy note-paper had been slipped into the bouquet, on which were scribbled these words:

For ALEC

Miss you mate

Love Tom

I did not need to know who Alec was, only that this blustery hilltop with its memorial to a forgotten war held meaning for Tom. A fitting place to leave a short yet eloquent tribute to a lost companion, the South Downs swelling beyond.

Now, at last, were the chalk downs as I'd imagined them. Or remembered them from my Chilterns childhood, rising and spilling, steep valleys snaked with white paths, copses of beech clinging to the slopes, sheep grazing on the hills. Open hills, very different from the extensive woodlands I'd passed through in the landscape before reaching Arundel in the summer. Turf sprang underfoot, and the air was sweetened with sheep droppings. For me, sheep country is the best country. I'd seen few sheep on my walk so far, and I missed them. At home in the Yorkshire Dales, sheep are the visual and aural backdrop to my life, their calm presence a constant comfort. And spring would not be spring without lambs – new life so apparent, leaping around the fields surrounding my home.

For centuries, sheep were the lifeblood of the South Downs too. In the Bronze Age the original forest was cleared for agri-culture, with crops grown in the valleys and sheep grazing the hilltops. Unlike today's fat, fluffy sheep bred for meat, Bronze Age sheep were smaller and hardier, akin to the wild, gazelle-like beasts still roaming the Hebridean island of Soay – the Old Norse for 'sheep island'.

By day, sheep grazed the Downs, and at night they were 'folded' into the lower fields, their dung a natural fertiliser on chalky, infertile soil. For thousands of years this system continued, granting a livelihood for generations of Sussex farmers, with teams of oxen ploughing the available arable land. The nineteenth century brought change. Horses replaced oxen for ploughing, and with three horses the equivalent of eight oxen, further sheep pasture was ploughed up. In the early twentieth century it was the turn of horses to be supplanted, this time by tractors, though oxen clung on longer in Sussex with the last team ploughing on the Downs between the two world wars. The final nail in the coffin for widespread sheep farming on the South Downs came after the Second World War, when artificial fertilisers were introduced, allowing more of the thin, chalky soil of the hilltops to be ploughed for crops.

For some environmentalists sheep are a menace, 'woolly maggots' accused of destroying the natural environment in upland areas of Britain through overgrazing. Yet traditional sheep-grazed downland is England's most diverse habitat, with up to forty-five flowering plants growing in one square metre – the equivalent density and diversity of a tropical rainforest. When the sheep disappeared from the South Downs so did the flower-rich grassland and the insects it supported, like the exquisite pastel-winged chalkhill blue butterfly, whose home is the dwindling chalk and limestone grasslands of southern England, and the wart-biter bush-cricket. Now threatened with local extinction, in the British Isles this cricket is only found on the fringes of southern England, although it has also declined in other regions of Northern Europe. Half of the world's surviving chalk grassland is in Britain, but with 80 per cent lost under the plough it's one of our most threatened habitats. Much of the remaining grassland, around 41,000 hectares, now clings to the hillsides, which are too steep for tractors – though not for sheep.

I walked on, and up, to the top of the hill, where I rested under a huge and ancient holm oak, its roots writhing deep into the earth. Introduced into Britain in the late 1500s, the holm oak is a tree of many names, and many guises. In Latin it's *Quercus ilex*, a native of the eastern Mediterranean and in classical mythology a symbol of fertility. In modern English vernacular it's ever-green oak. In history (and in some quarters still) it's known as a holly oak, its dense canopy of glossy leaves offering year-round shelter for birds. I sat beneath its branches, and looked down past Arundel to a silver glint of sea. I was high on the chalk, yet the sea was only a few miles away, my ever-present consort. The view was perfect, timeless, soured only by a bag of dog poo which someone had carefully placed beside the tree's twisted trunk.

The path began its descent through pasture where bloomed dandelion-like flowers, a disconcerting yellow. Yellow is the colour of spring, of buttercups, of daffodils and gorse. Summer is the season of rich deep pinks and purples, and autumn is the red of hawthorn berries, rosehips, holly and rowan berries. Yet here the down was spritzed with springtime yellow. I looked the flower up on my phone. Autumn hawkbit (*Leontodon autumnalis*), a relative of the dandelion and a member of the sunflower family. Described by the Lawnhealth website as 'a perennial weed that forms as a basal rosette . . . often referred to as fall dandelion' it can apparently be 'controlled with a selective herbicide'. It may officially be classed as a weed, but the autumn hawkbit brought to mind some of my favourite lines of poetry:

> *To me the meanest flower that blows can give*
> *Thoughts that do often lie too deep for tears.*

(William Wordsworth, 'Ode on Intimations of Immortality', 1807)

Dropping down steeply through woodland I found myself back at the River Arun, where the nettles were still in fine fettle, surprising me with the ferocity of their late October sting. Nettles aside, it was good to be down by the river once again as it flowed softly south. Wildlife – mostly squirrels and pheasants – scuttled across the path, as if trying to cross a busy motorway. The woodland air was syrupy, the river a deep muddy brown after the previous night's rain. Reeds shook and murmured as I passed, the atmosphere that sultry morning more River Nile than River Arun.

Just a mile or so from these banks people were going about their working day, in shops and offices, schools and hospitals. It was hard to get my head around. When walking through nature you lose all sense of time, of weekdays and weekends. Nature is not constrained by human timetables, and when you move unhurriedly through, and deeply into, the landscape, you also are released from timetables. You are autonomous, unfettered. You are free. And freedom, especially for a woman, is a threat. Why else did medieval society, and some cultures today, forbid women from going out alone, unchaperoned? Is it for their own protection, as is claimed, or because it demonstrates that women do not need men as much as they'd like to think? As late as nineteenth-century Europe, women such as the Swiss explorer Isabelle Eberhardt adopted a male identity and wore men's clothes so that they could travel freely, unencumbered by societal expectations.

Unchaperoned, I followed a track past South Stoke's grand farmhouse and modest farmworkers' cottages, and through an archway of holly, to the holy church of St Leonard. Although the church dates from the eleventh century you'd hardly know it from its present appearance, the upshot of a harsh Victorian restoration. Ian Nairn, in Pevsner's *The Buildings of England*, describes the interior as 'just bare and swept clean'. Like a bad facelift, the church looked like it had lost its personality. Only the Norman doorway and thirteenth-century porch remained unscoured, greened with damp and time. Beside the peeling stonework of the old porch someone had placed baskets of autumn cyclamen, dramatic eruptions of life and colour. This church was still cherished, even after its Victorian hatchet job.

From South Stoke the track continued to a footbridge over the Arun, fast-flowing and heavy with rain. I squelched and slithered my way beside the muddy riverbank and over fields where cattle rested, and through a copse matted with leaves. This path through the woodland was atop an embankment raised above the floodplain, creating a causeway between the two villages of South and North Stoke and keeping the traveller's feet largely dry. The name 'stoke' is commonplace throughout Anglo-Saxon England, deriving from the Old English word *stoc*, or outlying settlement. Many such 'stokes' have grown and flourished in the intervening millennium to become villages, or even large industrial cities. South Stoke and North Stoke, in their crook between the River Arun and the Downs, remain rural hamlets.

North Stoke was as delightful as South Stoke. The same substantial farmhouse and flint-and-brick estate workers' cottages, same little Norman church, an enormous yew in the churchyard at least as old as the building. Cruciform in plan, its timber bell turret topped by a weathervane, St Mary's missed South Stoke's overenthusiastic Gothic Revival renovation, instead undergoing a gentle repair in 1910, when attitudes towards restoration were more sympathetic. Under the care of the Churches Conservation Trust since 1992, St Mary's in North Stoke is now in safe hands.

I pushed open the doors. The interior was how St Leonard's had once been, and should have remained. Old plaster walls, peeling and patinaed, a glorious buttercream matching the limestone dressings. A Norman font, mossed with age. Fragments of medieval stained glass. A carving of a human hand supporting a corbel stone. Remnants of wall paintings lingering above the chancel arch, where I made out an owl, flowers, foliage and vines. The Victorians loved to scrape away plaster, keen to reveal rubble walls that were never meant to be revealed. Unknowingly, they also scraped away swathes of medieval wall paintings, hidden under the limewash of sixteenth-century Protestant reformers who viewed such images as idolatrous. This fanatical limewashing saved numerous paintings from the Puritans a century later, leaving those that escaped the Victorian builders to be revived by twentieth-century restoration. A country church built for country folk. The vines, the foliage, the owl and, most charming of all, the head of a beaming sheep carved on a corbel in the south transept. This was sheep country, and always has been.

In the tilted sunlight, glowing the same ochre as the autumn leaves and layered in centuries of dust and prayer, the church felt peaceful and holy and timeless.

Another sodden hedge-lined causeway led me over a floodplain grazed with sheep back to the banks of the Arun, from where I wended my way to Houghton. Seeing southern buildings after the millstone grit of North Yorkshire was a shock. Half-timbered cottages infilled with cob and flint, their thatched roofs pierced by massive brick stacks, with names like Spindleberry, Bumble Cottage and Rhubarb Cottage, redolent of an English pastoral dream. The George and Dragon pub wasn't open so I pressed on, the Arun Valley spreading out before me. At Amberley station I stopped at a riverside café with a deck overlooking the water, peaceful and summer-like this October afternoon. A waitress came over to take my order.

'Just you?' she enquired, notepad and pencil in hand. Yes, still just me.

XI

I left Amberley station the next morning via High Titten, a narrow lane of bronzed hedgerows, following the chalk path up onto grass downland, where summer wildflowers lingered in this most southerly fringe of southern England. Flowers like the mauve Michaelmas daisy, a member of the Aster family, named for their late flowering, often blooming well into November. A much loved and familiar flower in the landscape, Michaelmas daisies are a North American import which gained popularity in the gardens of Victorian England, soon spreading over their cultivated bounds into the countryside. Common toadflax, also known as butter-and-eggs, is another immigrant, this time from Southern Europe, and rich pink knapweed, loved by pollinating insects, flourishing on meadows and grasslands.

Even more pinks. Rosebay willowherb, leaves now reddened and withering and known in its North American homeland as fireweed, is often seen on waste ground: railway embankments, verges and, after the War, bombsites, where it was renamed bomb-weed. An occasional poppy, its blood-red petals heralding the Remembrance commemorations that would take place in a couple of weeks. Once sparkling like rubies over the ripened cornfields of England, the poppy has followed farming from its origins in the Fertile Crescent across the world. Like rosebay willowherb, poppies love disturbed soil, springing up in the battlefields of the Somme after the First World War as a symbol of renewed life. Officially classed as weeds, they are no longer tolerated in the herbicide-drenched cornfields of England, but cling on in the margins along with their cereal-loving companion, the sapphire-blue cornflower.

Through gaps in the hedgerow I spied Amberley Castle. This massive medieval construction set majestically against its back-drop of the lush Arun Valley is now a luxury hotel, and for the medievalist best appreciated from afar. High overhead a buzzard skimmed the warm October air. I was walking on my own that morning, but I was not alone. My map revealed a landscape pock-marked with Bronze Age burial mounds, dykes, field systems and other prehistoric earthworks. Humans made their mark on this chalkscape some 5,000 years ago, just as I was now marking the chalk with my boots as I climbed. They're now entombed in turf, but these circular burial mounds would have dazzled onlookers when first raised, white beacons visible from the valley far below.

High on the South Downs I trod, following a skylark as it swooped and dived ahead, like a rainbow just out of reach. A few hawthorns still clung on to this exposed hilltop. Naked and lichened, speckled with red berries, they bent sideways in the stiffening wind. Hot on the heels of Alex, the first of the year's autumnal storms, Barbara was closing in. I quickened my pace, wanting to reach Storrington before Barbara caught up with me as on the hills there was no shelter at all.

I passed virtually no one all day. Just a few grey-haired couples, the odd solitary hiker and a flock of sheep, who paused their grazing to look at me with faint surprise as I passed. The chalky track unravelled before me as I strode on. My body revelled in the rhythm, my thoughts untethered flew away with the skylarks. A bellow, very like a cow mooing, came from the path behind me, and I jumped aside. A bearded man sped past on a mountain bike.

'Sorry! My bell doesn't work!' he called back.

'I thought you were a cow!' I shouted above the wind.

'Charming!' he laughed, and cycled on. In my ordinary more frazzled life, I might have resented the near miss. High on the Downs, with just the sheep for company, I was as untroubled as the wind.

So free and so high that the red kites gyrated below me, and below the kites unfurled the Weald. Bridging the chalk escarpments of the North and South Downs, the Weald (from the Old English *wald*, or forest) was once thickly wooded. Now it's a landscape of undulating hills stippled with rocky outcrops, scattered with farms, hamlets and villages. To the south a silver strip of sea, and my journey's beginning. To the east, beyond sight, lay Canterbury, and its end.

The wind picked up and the skies darkened. So I picked up my pace and marched on along the ridge, following a cross-dyke as it ran over the top of the hill. Such linear earthworks of Bronze Age construction are thought to be territorial boundary markers, although they may also have been used as drove roads or trackways. The landscape I now paced was a trellis of prehistoric activity, hidden beneath a thin skin of green, sheep-cropped turf. When the turf was ploughed for arable land, the archaeology disappeared, along with the sheep, the flowers and the butterflies.

Just when I thought the heavens were about to open, the skies cleared, the clouds split apart, and the sun slid out again. I could see the South Downs rolling out ahead, their tops drenched in a watery light. Hovering just a few feet away was a kestrel – head quite still, wings navigating the thermals, eyes pinpointed on the verge below. She was completely oblivious of me. I stood and watched, admiring her milky speckled breast, then continued on my way, expecting her to fly off as I approached. Instead, she swivelled her head to glance at me then returned to the serious business of hunting. Our eyes had met, and for one brief, enchanted moment two spheres – human and avian, civilised and wild – coalesced.

Storrington was my destination that day and I passed first one then two paths that would have taken me down to the village. Still buzzing from my avian encounter I wanted to stay up on the Downs as long as possible, up with the sheep, the skylarks and the kestrels.

Chantry Lane was my final chance to descend to Storrington before passing it altogether, so I turned downhill towards the village far below. Cut deep into the chalk of Chantry Hill the lane dropped steeply, and gravity pulled me downward. The wind had dropped and, after hours on the bare, wind-blown ridge, my way was now thick with trees: sycamore, ash, beech, hazel, all in mutating shades of gold. The final path into Storrington crossed meadows, and passed under majestic oaks and fields where ponies grazed and galloped, kicking out their hoofs. It threaded its way through housing estates, past village allotments, and ended in the centre of the village. An old way that existed long before the strata of modern life settled over it like drifted sand. Like the tumuli on the hill above, long buried, but never forgotten.

The Gough Map doesn't depict the country's hills, even ones as notable as the South Downs, but emphasises its rivers. Rivers were the principal means of navigation in medieval Britain, and the rivers on the map are thought by historians to be of greater significance than its roads. As Nick Millea points out in his book *The Gough Map*, mountains tended to impede navigation, while rivers facilitated it. Medieval travellers would have avoided crossing mountains where possible, instead choosing paths through the valleys. The exception would be where the valleys were less safe, or less passable, than the hills or mountains, which might depend on the season when you were travelling. In summer weather, the low routes would usually be the best, while in winter the higher routes, especially on chalk landscapes, would be drier. This is why another of England's ancient trackways, the Icknield Way, has both a lower and a parallel upper route.

In the thirteenth century, when the Gough Map was first drawn up, roads, as we imagine them today, did not exist. They were routes rather than roads, and the red route from Arundel to Bramber leaps straight over the South Downs, missing out villages like Storrington, where that early evening the air was warm and soft. I had left Storm Barbara still scowling over the Downs, and was happy to be back in summer once again.

Hospitality for tourists was limited that autumn, with many Covid measures still in place, so I took a bus back to Arundel and the Premier Inn, which I shared with the BT workers, gas engineers and road maintenance staff whose jobs took them away from home during the working week. As Chaucer's colourful characters showed, medieval pilgrimage was a leveller, one of the rare occasions when the different professions and social strata mixed. My Premier Inn was not unlike London's Tabard Inn on the south bank of the Thames, where pilgrims to Canterbury began their journey.

I enjoyed being among others staying here for work rather than leisure as it lent my pilgrimage, my walk with a purpose, a legitimacy which, as a 'tourist', it may have lacked. Chaucer's fictional characters, and Margery Kempe's real-life companions aside, pilgrimage was supposed to be a test of endurance and faith, not just a holiday. It's perhaps no coincidence that the word 'holiday' derives from 'holy day', as holy days were an excuse for making merry as much for medieval Christian folk as for the pagans before them.

XII

The Gough Map does not relate where pilgrims rested on their way to Lewes, though they may have been luckier than me, and found accommodation in Storrington. After passing on the Premier Inn's all-you-can-eat breakfast, I returned to Storrington the following morning, where I found a village with a split personality. On the one hand it's a bit of a local celebrity, a community humming with shops and restaurants, cafés and tea rooms, estate agents, galleries and all the buzz of a prosperous town. An urban village of 7,000 souls, punching above its rural weight.

If you cross the A283 from Winchester to Shoreham slicing through the village and hugging the South Downs, you encounter Storrington's more sedate twin. The moan of traffic fades and in its place there is hush. This Storrington wears its antiquity with pride, paying little attention to its social-climbing counterpart over the road. Or that's how it appeared to me that morning, as I walked along Church Street towards the South Downs.

In Church Street I found the soul of the medieval village, the Storrington that Alice would have known. Opposite St Mary's Church is St Joseph's Abbey, a Tudor-style mansion that has, over the centuries, housed a rectory, a Dominican convent and a boarding school. Past the church, along School Lane, is Storrington Priory, a former Premonstratensian house secluded behind its high brick walls, hills rising beyond. The priory is now inhabited by the Chemin Neuf Community, an ecumenical order hosting retreats, missions and educational programmes, a contemporary blend of sacred and secular. Over five centuries have passed since the pinnacle of medieval religious fervour in this country, yet its essence still underpins places such as old Storrington, sheltered beneath the swell of the South Downs.

I left Storrington to the echo of church bells, and headed once again for the chalk hills. Church Street had become Greyfriars Lane, Storm Barbara had done her worst, and all was clear blue innocence as I walked up onto the Downs. The burn in my leg muscles as I climbed felt good, as did leaving behind the twenty-first century with its politics, its pandemics and its frenetic populace. Greyfriars Lane turned into a bridleway – a stony track as old as the hills I was now climbing, becoming increasingly sunken and hollowed as it steepened. For thousands of years travellers like myself used the ridgeways at the top of the hills to cover longer distances. And, like me the previous evening, they needed to come down into the valleys to find places to stay. In settlements such as Storrington, villagers from prehistory onwards have used these same paths to climb into the hills, leading their sheep and cattle up to pasture on the verdant down.

The previous night's rainstorm had turned the chalk paths to sludge but soon I was above the treeline and the sludge, the South Downs unravelling as I made my way east. The warm Samhain sun pounded my scalp, my boots trampled the skeletons of coccoliths – minute marine algae that floated in these once-tropical seas in their trillions. Over a period of eighty million years the coccoliths sank to the ocean floor, becoming sediment and compacting into the rock of the late Cretaceous Period, *creta* being the Latin for chalk. Upper Cretaceous rock, which is 95 per cent calcium carbonate, is the softest and purest of the limestones. Like its limestone cousins – marble included – it is the only rock that can be scored with a butter knife, as biddable as if still living. Unlike every other ancient rock, chalk was once alive, and walking across chalk is walking over time at its deepest.

At last I reached the ridge, where the grass still smelled summer sweet and skylarks greeted me to their hilltop habitat. My destination that morning was Chanctonbury Ring, one of the many Iron Age hillforts strung along the South Downs like pearls on a necklace. Chanctonbury is not the most impressive of these hillforts. That honour belongs to Cissbury Ring, the largest hillfort in Sussex, and the second largest in England after Maiden Castle (from the Celtic for 'great hill') in Dorset. Though it is the most captivating, swathed in myth and legend.

Chanctonbury and Cissbury are only two of the thousands of similar earthworks dispersed throughout Britain, many of which were constructed between 600 BC and 400 BC. The earliest were those archaeologists call 'univallate' – surrounded by only one defensive bank and ditch. Later, more complex 'multivallate' forts were built, often developing from their simpler predecessors. Their purpose, as well as defensive, was perhaps as gathering places for the farmers who lived and worked in the surrounding countryside. Excavations of timber round houses, shrines, temples and granaries in Danebury, Hampshire, are proof that some were occupied for some of their existence. By 100 BC most hillforts were abandoned, or had shrunk in size and importance leaving only ghostly indentations on the landscape, like fingerprints.

Ahead I saw Chanctonbury Ring, or so I imagined, a cluster of trees crowning a distant hilltop. Other hilltops lay between me and Chanctonbury, and other paths and tracks splintered off the ridgeway, coiling across the Downs to their furthest horizons. I stuck to my guns, and to the ridge path over chalk grassland still studded with summer wildflowers – dandelions, daisies, red clover. Some fields were already planted with winter wheat, its acid-green shoots poking between nodules of flint lodged in tawny earth. I had thought my pace would quicken on top of the Downs, with no obstacles, no gates, no stiles to impede my progress. In fact, the opposite happened. I slowed right down, delighting in every flower, every bird, every moment. I didn't want the chalk to end.

As a travel journalist, I'd spent years flitting around the world on writing commissions. At first I'd loved it, revelling in the excitement of new places, new sights, new sounds, new smells. I'd especially liked travelling in what is Eurocentrically called the Middle East, finding the landscape, politics and people fascinating.

On one such travel-writing foray I found myself in the Sinai Desert, on a solitary retreat and fast. For three days and nights I consumed nothing but water, a little salt, and a few squares of melted chocolate I'd hidden in my rucksack. There was nothing to do except sleep, sit and collect armfuls of acacia branches for my fire, along with a down sleeping bag my only protection against the cold desert nights.

I thought I'd be bored, but the three days and nights passed quickly. As each day dawned I awoke with the sun as it rose over the mountains, and dozed off when darkness fell, wrapped in camel-scented blankets, watching shooting stars fizz across the sky into nothingness. I traced intricate patterns in the sand with my fingers, and created swirling designs from small pebbles scattered around my camp. Clock time evaporated, leaving only the infinity of night following day.

In those three days and nights I came to know my little patch of desert intimately – the tracks and footprints of mammals and lizards, the spiky acacia trees, the rocks. The words of William Blake never rang so true as here in this boundless desertscape:

> *To see a World in a Grain of Sand*
> *And a Heaven in a Wild Flower*
> *Hold Infinity in the palm of your hand*
> *And Eternity in an hour*

(William Blake, 'Auguries of Innocence', 1803)

A world in a grain of Sinai sand, eternity in a desert hour. Why did I need to fly vast distances to discover the world, when if I looked closely enough I could find the world all around me? Rather than travelling horizontally across the surface of the globe, I could travel vertically, delving deep into the landscape, journeying through time rather than space. I could travel slowly and more meaningfully, walk instead of fly, discover my own country at my own pace.

I could walk across the chalk hills of England, all the way to Canterbury.

Canterbury still seemed a long way off that late-October day, but I didn't care. I was happy to be flying high above the civilised world. Below I could see cars glinting along the A283, but I couldn't hear them. All I heard were the skylarks and the wind. I met virtually no one, only a pair of young men yomping with backpacks, and a flock of Herdwick sheep. They looked out of place here on these soft, chalky downs of southern England, far from their usual Cumbrian habitat of granite and slate.

Their unexpected presence here is no fluke. Unlike modern Southdown sheep, their well-bred southern cousins who for centuries have roamed the downs of England, Herdwicks will happily graze on local tor-grass (*Brachypodium pinnatum*). This tough, densely clumped plant grows freely and invasively on chalk grassland, swamping the indigenous downland flora and decreasing plant diversity. To counter its spread, heritage breeds such as Herdwicks, Shetlands and Hebrideans have been introduced as part of the South Downs conservation grazing programme.

Restricted to an area with poor feeding choices, these breeds will graze on less-desirable plants, allowing traditional chalk-loving plants and flowers to repopulate the grassland. Herdwicks and their fellow breeds are similar to the animals roaming the South Downs before the eighteenth century, when Sussex stockbreeder John Ellman (1753–1832) 'improved' the breed for meat, so creating a stockier animal. Although descendants of the sheep grazed here since Neolithic times for their wool, modern Southdowns' preference for high-nutrient grass has proved detrimental to the biodiversity of the South Downs – paradoxically so, as these are the hills they're named after.

The fathomless peace of the hills was interrupted by the A24, which cuts across the South Downs at Washington. I was soon up on the hills again, nearing Chanctonbury Ring. Etymologists tell us that the name Chanctonbury comes from the Old English *burh* (stronghold) near the *tun* (farmstead) belonging to *Cenga*. Archaeologists relate that this is an Iron Age hillfort, prominent on the north ridge of the South Downs and in use in various periods throughout history. They explain that it dates from the sixth and fifth centuries BC, measures around 168 by 122 metres, and has two entrances – one in the east and another in the south-west. Foundations within the ring indicate that it then became a Romano-British temple. Historians add that after many centuries of abandonment it became the pet project of landowner Charles Goring, who, in the mid-eighteenth century, planted the distinctive ring of beech trees that have established Chanctonbury as a prominent Sussex landmark.

Ask a folklorist, and you hear a different story. You learn that local people believe the ring was created by the Devil, and that if you walk around it anticlockwise seven times, he will appear and offer you a bowl of milk (or soup) in exchange for your soul. The

Devil seems to have been remarkably busy in pagan England. Innumerable sites like Chanctonbury were deemed by advocates of the new religion to be the Devil's work, and many bear his name. One thousand years after the official adoption of Christianity, Chanctonbury still holds fascination for pagans, and for occultists such as the late Aleister Crowley, who lived in Steyning – my own destination that night.

Eyewitnesses have reported fairies dancing around Chanctonbury Ring on Midsummer's Eve, while others have documented UFOs hovering overhead. On this mild autumn afternoon, though, all was tranquil. Following in the footsteps of the tens of thousands before me I walked – clockwise – around the ring. My feet propelled me around the ramparts as if they had no choice, and in each direction the landscape flowed into the horizon. Beyond the Weald lay the North Downs, a far ribbon of blue. Towards the east, the rounded chalk hills of the South Downs escarpment rippled away. To the south shone a glimmer of sea, its shape-shifting presence the chaperone of my downland walk. Sometimes visible, sometimes just out of reach, but always reassuringly present – though a presence more felt than seen.

I walked into the centre of the ring, now also planted with trees. Charles Goring's original beeches have long gone, after reaching the end of their natural lifespan, and new trees were replanted in 1977. Just ten years later the great storm of October 1987 felled most of the beeches, their shallow roots leaving them vulnerable to high winds. Their replacements are now reaching maturity, though the ash trees that have also sprouted within the ring looked sad and spindly, dropping their feathery leaves onto the ground before their time.

This was a shock, but not a surprise. Ash dieback, imported into England in 2012, has advanced into Sussex and millions of trees will need to be felled to prevent further spread of the disease. *Hymenoscyphus fraxineus* originated in Asia, and although it doesn't cause much damage in its native habitat, its introduction into Europe has been catastrophic. The European ash has no natural defence against the fungus, which is expected to kill 80 per cent of British ash trees –around 60 million of them, or one per head of the population. Along with the trees will go the many species that rely on the ash as a habitat. Birds such as tawny owls, woodpeckers and nuthatches, which nest in holes and crevices in its trunk and branches, and bullfinches that feed on its seeds. Spring flowers – bluebells, speedwells, celandine – that flourish under its open canopy, and the insects that feed from them, will also disappear. An unhappy consequence of global markets and climate change.

I continued through the hillfort to its furthest side. A Mars Bar wrapper lay buried in the ground, half swallowed by the earth. Another contribution to the Anthropocene, the geological epoch invented by scientists to explain the impact of human activity on the earth's crust, climate and ecosystems. The wrapper was just the latest fragment of two millennia of history under my feet, but I couldn't bear to leave it for future archaeologists so I plucked it out of the ground and stuffed it into my pocket.

Chanctonbury Ring was the high point, both literally and metaphorically, of my day's walk. I didn't want to reach Steyning too soon, so I continued along the wide chalky track. Then, as the sun began to dip, so did I, dropping quickly off the hilltop along a path hemmed with last summer's blackberries, rosehips and hawthorns, their berries hanging like grapes. The slow-sliding sun threw shadows across the valley, lengthening the sheep as they grazed on the hillsides. Delaying my descent still further, I sat on a bench dedicated to Mary Virgo – 'a great lover of the

Sussex countryside' – and looked out over the steeply wooded escarpment. Next to me on the bench was a poetry box, inviting visitors to take a pen and paper, and leave some words. But the light was thinning, I still had to get off the hill and poetry is not my strong point.

I looked up. The tree I was sitting under was an ash – still sturdy, still strong, not yet dying. Getting up from the bench I caressed its trunk, wishing it good luck, and continued on my way down the hill to Steyning.

If Storrington is a village aspiring to townhood, its near neighbour Steyning seems determined to cling on to its provincial past. Pronounced 'Stenning' by Sussex folk, the name possibly derives from the Old English *stæning*, or 'stony places' – perhaps after the flint nodules that strew the Downs and from which the village is largely built. Flint nudges half-timbering and mellow brick, a pleasing assortment of facades on Steyning's High Street of health food stores, tearooms, antique shops and estate agents. There was even a shop displaying just baths and taps, its wares glowing from the window into the evaporating light.

It was dusk now, and getting cold. Tempted as I was by the promise of a hot chocolate in one of those cosy tearooms, I didn't stop. Instead, I headed out of the village centre towards the parish church of St Andrew, hoping to visit before it shut for the day.

Architectural historians generally agree St Andrew's is the best example of a Norman church in the county, and among the finest in the country. They extol its 'virile and inventive' twelfth-century styling, its magnificent nave, exemplary roll-mouldings, richly carved label stops and delicate rosettes. And who am I to argue? For me, though, a historic building is as much about its atmosphere as its architecture. And St Andrew's had atmosphere in spades – layer upon flaking layer of it, each layer unveiling a history reaching back over a thousand years.

The earliest chapter in this history is its pre-Norman dedication to the Saxon shepherd, St Cuthman. The same Cuthman I'd encountered in the summer, by the sea at Chidham. The same Cuthman who, after the death of his father, wheeled his invalid mother across the Downs to Steyning, where the rope pulling the cart snapped. Legend relates this incident in colourful and extensive detail, but the abridged version is that, taking the snapped rope as a sign from God, Cuthman settled in Steyning, founding a church to tend to his new flock. In 1884 the *Light from the Lowly, Or, Lives of Persons Who Sanctified Themselves in Humble Positions* described how Cuthman:

> assisted by the generosity of some farmers of the neighbour-
> hood, built a hut to shelter his mother, and with the abundant
> alms he received laid the foundation of a small church.
> Crowds from the surrounding country flocked to the place,
> not only to see the new building, but to hear the holy words
> of the servant of God.

After Cuthman's death sometime in the eighth century, pilgrims continued to converge on Steyning. Nineteen years before the Conquest, his monastery was granted to the abbey of Fécamp in Normandy, rebuilt and rededicated to St Andrew. The local saint was never forgotten, even 500 years after Henry VIII decreed saint veneration illegal, and in 2007 the church was renamed St Andrew and St Cuthman. Pilgrimage, likewise outlawed by Henry, also lives on in ancestral memory. Only an hour earlier, on my way into Steyning, I'd passed a nameplate for three houses affixed to an old flint wall. One of these houses was Pilgrim Cottage. Surely Alice of Southwick, on her way to Canterbury in the thirteenth century, also stopped at Steyning to pay her respects to St Cuthman.

Maple leaves gilded the stone-flagged path of the churchyard, and an organ's piped notes wafted from inside as I approached the church that darkening autumn afternoon. Not wishing to disturb the organist I strolled around to the back of the building, where I spent a few minutes reading the gravestones and listening to the birds settling down in the hedgerows and treetops.

I was about to walk on when my eye caught a flash of bright green canvas. In a nook between the tower and the north wall of the church someone had set up camp. Not just a tent but a whole encampment, and one that had evidently been there for a while. Pots and pans, a firepit, a battered kettle, plastic bottles of water, storage boxes of tinned food, folded piles of clothes, a basket of wood, a canvas director's chair, brushes, brooms and a washing line held up with crutches surrounded the tent. There was even a mosaic hanging on the wall and, beside the tent flap, a water-logged biography of Tom Jones. It brought to mind a hermit's cave, or the cell of a medieval anchorite. And it didn't seem out of place. Many churches in the Middle Ages had an anchorite, or anchoress – men or women who locked themselves in a cell inside or adjoining the main building, never to leave. One window looked into the chancel, where the incumbent received sacrament. Another small window opened onto the churchyard, through which parishioners, for whom their local anchorite was an oracle, would seek advice.

But this was not the Middle Ages, and the camp beside the church was unlikely to belong to an anchorite.

'Hello, anybody home?' I called out to the tent. No reply. I walked back to the south side of the church and stood in the porch, listening. The organ music had stopped, so I went inside. A well-groomed woman of middling age was busy sanitising and polishing the pews. Her hair was short and neat, and she wore ankle boots, jeans and a leather jacket. We exchanged the custom-ary pleasantries. Her husband had been practising on the organ, she said. Now he'd finished, and it was time to close the building for the afternoon, so we processed outside. As she was locking the door, I asked about the camp at the back of the church.

'Oh, that's Michael,' the woman replied. 'Horsham Council gave him a tent, and the churchwarden allows him to live in the churchyard. He's been there a long time.'

'I'd love to talk to him,' I said. 'I'm doing this pilgrimage you see, and it would be good to meet someone who isn't . . . living in a house.' It was hard to express to this chic, cordial woman exactly what I meant. Most of the people I'd met so far were, I guessed, like her, or me: well-spoken, middle-class, living in comfortable houses. Outside by choice rather than necessity, for recreation rather than by obligation. Hikers, dog walkers, runners, mountain bikers, horse riders – and the occasional pilgrim. 'Maybe he'll be there when I come back in the morning?' I ventured.

'Maybe. I don't know. He's sometimes a little . . . worse for wear,' she said, choosing her words. 'Perhaps you can talk to the church warden. She takes care of him, in a way.'

The churchyard camp wasn't without precedent. Book II of the *Codex Calixtinus*, the twenty-two miracles associated with St James of Compostela, tells the story of a Greek pilgrim called Stephen. On arriving at Compostela Cathedral he approached the guards and 'cast himself at their feet and begged them to grant him an out-of-the-way place in the church where he might be permitted to devote himself to continuous prayer'. The cathedral guards:

> prepared a sort of dwelling for him . . . out of rushes in the manner of a cell and located inside the basilica of the blessed apostle, and from its right front he could look at the altar. In this place Stephen spent his celibate and most blessed life in fasts, vigils, and prayers both day and night.

(*The Miracles of Saint James*, ed. Coffey, Davidson and Dunn)

The organist and his wife said their goodbyes, and strolled off down the flagstone path with its carpet of maple leaves and well-tended borders. The parishioners clearly took much pride in this exemplar of Norman architectural splendour that also happened to be their local church. But they were also taking care of one of their own, someone who had fallen on hard times and was not fortunate enough to live in one of the fine flint houses of Steyning, this prettiest of Sussex villages.

XIII

After a night of rain Steyning was washed clean, looking even more salubrious than it had done when I arrived the previous evening. I now had two days' walking under my belt, and was getting into my stride again, both physically and mentally. The mild ache in my calves, unused to the steep escarpment of the Downs, was subsiding, and I couldn't wait to be up on the hills again with the skylarks and kestrels. Before leaving Steyning I hoped to meet the occupant of the tent at St Andrew's, so retraced my steps to the church. The camp was just as I'd seen it the previous evening.

'Hello . . . Michael?' I called. I thought I heard rustling from within the tent, but there was no reply. I would like to have known more about him; how he came to be living beside a church, and whether he found safety and solace there. It was not to be, so I left St Andrew and St Cuthman for a final time and went on my way. Back through the well-heeled village centre with its health food stores, tearooms, antique shops, estate agents and the shop that sold nothing but baths and taps.

I turned down Maudlin Lane, feeling anything but maudlin as I strode out of the village and into the country once again. However charming a place is – and Steyning was charm personified – I longed to be away from civilisation, walking free over the hills. Rainstorms had been forecast for that morning. Perhaps it was good luck, or divine providence bestowed upon pilgrims, but so far I'd managed to evade Storm Barbara. Inside my backpack was a raincoat, packed as insurance. It put me in mind of a proverb I'd once heard on my travels in Syria, a *hadith* (or saying) of the Prophet Mohammed. It tells the story of a Bedouin who was about to leave his camel without tying it down.

'Why aren't you tying down your camel?' Mohammed asked the Bedouin.

'I put my trust in Allah,' the Bedouin answered.

'Tie your camel first, and then put your trust in Allah,' advised the Prophet. An elegant rendering of the old proverb: God helps those who help themselves.

Ahead soared the Downs, soaked in sunshine. They looked so inviting, but the Old Way first detours via the hamlet of Botolphs, burrowed beneath the hills and an unmissable landmark for pilgrims. I would visit Botolphs, but would miss Bramber (*brimbr* on the Gough Map) and its medieval pilgrim inn, which I badly wanted to visit but which had been closed for the past few months.

Promising myself I'd return to Bramber in better times, I headed south to the church of St Botolph's, after which the settlement took its name. The church now sits within its flint walls, encircled by open country where piebald sheep nibble at the turf. Dating from around 950, St Botolph's was built near one of the first industrial trade routes in Britain, a Roman road along which tin was carried from the Cornish mines to the East Sussex seaport of Pevensey. Two thousand years on, and industry still stamps its mark in this nook of rural West Sussex, with the railway line and modern cement works visible just a few hundred metres away.

Like St Mary's in North Stoke, the exterior of St Botolph's is simple and unpretentious. Since 2013 it has been maintained by the Churches Conservation Trust and, so says the website, 'still welcomes wayfarers'. Considering myself a bona fide wayfarer I pushed open a nail-studded door, the date 1630 incised into the oak. Inside, it resonated peace. A blocked arcade on the north side revealed a formerly sizeable church that ministered to a larger population than the scattering of farms and houses of today's shrunken hamlet.

It was hard to imagine in this serene spot, but 700 years ago Botolphs was a busy port on the tidal River Adur. Then the sea receded and the river silted up, leaving the settlement much reduced and the church marooned in its meadow under the hills. This pattern of once-thriving ports now stranded inland, or entire towns submerged never to be seen again, was one I was to encounter repeatedly as I neared the coasts of Kent and Sussex. It may seem immutable, but this has always been a landscape of loss and transformation. In an age when we seek to control nature, to shackle it, this fringe of southern England can't be constrained. Perhaps that's why I, always railing against stasis, ever refusing to be pinned down, felt at home here. Home is not just a house, after all. It is a place that aligns with your nature at its most elemental.

A late-Saxon arch led me through to the chancel, where the walls heaved with age. Above the chancel arch, medieval wall paintings once educated illiterate parishioners and pilgrims. Peeling, fading, but after many hundreds of years enduring. I walked back into the nave. A notice on the wall read that St Botolph was a Saxon hermit, patron saint of travellers and fishermen and sometimes called the Boat Easer. The right saint to see me off on my day's walk, then.

Like all buildings under the care of the Churches Conservation Trust, 'St Bots' as it's affectionately known is no longer used for regular worship. This doesn't mean the church is unused, and local people still congregate to celebrate the highlights of the agricultural calendar. Early January is Plough Sunday, the traditional beginning of the farming year, followed by Clipping Sunday in April. Clipping, or *clypping*, is the Anglo-Saxon custom whereby parishioners celebrate their love for the church fabric, holding hands in a circle around the building or using rope if there aren't enough people. Rogation Sunday, with prayers for crops, is in

May, followed by a sheep-shearing ceremony in July and ending with Lammas in early August. This church was over a thousand years old, cut adrift by the river and the tides, and virtually abandoned by previous villagers. For the current population of Botolphs, though, it is a living, breathing entity and the heart of their community.

I would love to have spent longer in this peaceful spot at the foot of the Downs, but the hills beckoned, and rainclouds threatened. After crossing the River Adur, now flowing a good 500 metres from its medieval course, and darting across the A283, I climbed up the chalk track to Beeding Hill. Here, as at other sites along the South Downs Way, I found a water point – one of the troughs or taps where modern pilgrims can refill their bottles. There is little water on top of the chalk hills, and water is as vital to twenty-first century travellers as it was to medieval wayfarers. For our ancestors, the wells and springs from which water gushed were believed magical and then, when Christianity arrived, holy. You can still find ancient wells near medieval churches, such as at Binsey in Oxford. Grafted onto earlier, pagan, sites a new religion assimilated the old. Here beneath the Downs, the even newer religion of canine worship was also honoured, and beside the trough someone had placed a tub of water for thirsty wayfaring dogs.

I climbed, and the wind strengthened. Once again my legs complained, and once again the skylarks saluted me as I reached the top, rewarding me with their unseasonable song. The entirety of southeast England expanded before me, by turns drenched in sunshine and shrouded in shadow, clouds throwing the Weald into light and shade. To my right the sun bounced off a luminous sea.

There was nobody else on the ridge path that morning. Pausing for a moment, I gazed down at the settlements scattered along the coast. This is a densely populated part of the country, yet how easy it was to feel deliciously alone. I turned round for a last look at Chanctonbury Ring. In prehistory, fires were lit on hillforts in times of celebration, just as beacons are lit on today's significant occasions: the Millennium, the Jubilee, the Queen's ninetieth birthday.

Below me, and marked on my map in gothic script to indicate antiquity, cultivation terraces cascaded down the hillside. Probably of Bronze Age origin, these terraces, or strip lynchets, were ploughed by early farmers and may still have been in use in the Middle Ages. Many centuries later they are clothed in grass. Five thousand years of history hidden just beneath the turf of chalk hills, skimmed by enormous shifting skies.

I was now just two days' walk from Lewes, floating above the villages of Upper Beeding, Edburton and Fulking threading along the valley at the foot of the Downs. These were Saxon communities, established when people abandoned the settlements on top of the hills and settled in the fertile sands and clays of the Weald, the river valleys and the coastal plain. Medieval pilgrims, like their fellow travellers, would have used this well-drained ridge route in bad weather, avoiding the damp valley bottom. A noticeboard alongside the path reported that this was a pilgrim route between Winchester and Canterbury, though not the Old Road over the North Downs rediscovered by the writer Hilaire Belloc, now called the Pilgrims' Way. This more ancient one, spanning the South Downs, may have converged with the Old Way from Southampton.

Wherever they originated, pilgrims on their way to or back from Canterbury needed to descend to the villages for water, food and rest. That Upper Beeding was an important stopover on this route is suggested by the many references to 'travellers' in the parish registers, some of whom – perhaps even Alice herself – stayed in the Benedictine priory of Sele before it was decommissioned by Henry VIII.

I was tempted to take one of the many paths off the ridge down to one of these villages, but I had enough food and water for the day and didn't need to rest. So rather than tread the sodden paths of the valley bottom I stayed high, contouring smooth primordial hills, prehistoric chalk under my feet. The clouds were darkening and thickening, animating the landscape, yet here I was striding free over the Downs in a drifting pool of sunshine.

In one of those pools of sunshine was Devil's Dyke. Or, more accurately, the Iron Age hillfort above the mile-long ice-carved valley of the same name. According to legend, Devil's Dyke was dug by Satan himself to drown the pious Wealden folk, although any meltwater that remained after the Ice Age has long gone, leaving in its wake the steepest, longest, deepest dry valley in England. For the painter John Constable, the prospect from the hillfort was 'the Grandest in the world'. I couldn't vouch for this, but it was certainly the grandest in southeast England, with West and East Sussex laid out like a banquet. Whether Alice and her fellow pilgrims would have wanted to consort with the devil, even for the view from the top of the dyke, is doubtful. Landscapes as objects of beauty were an invention of Romanticism, and a concept completely unfamiliar to medieval pilgrims. Safety and sanctity rather than picturesque views were their priorities.

Devil's Dyke is the only Iron Age hillfort I know that has a pub on top. For motorists, the advantages are obvious – you can drive up the 200-metre hill for a drink and a bite to eat, then have a wander around without getting seriously out of breath. I could see them as I approached the pub. With their dogs and metropolitan outdoor uniform of Puffa jackets and ankle boots, they stood out from the Vibram-soled, Gore-tex-clad and somewhat dogged countenance of the serious hill walkers I'd met on my downland walk that week.

Still, it was good to see people enjoying the countryside, asserting their civil rights. The right to roam in England and Wales over 'open country' (mountain, moor, heath or down, as the terminology quaintly has it) was only granted with the Countryside and Rights of Way Act of 2000. This act covers just 8 per cent of the land (much more is open access in Scotland), and younger people, those from ethnic minorities or with disabilities are still under-represented among countryside users. The Countryside Act also set 1 January 2026 for applications to include historically and currently used routes as rights of way on a definitive map, though after action from organisations such as the Ramblers, with their *Don't Lose Your Way* campaign, this date has now been postponed. Just like the Kinder Mass Trespass ninety years ago, the public are still fighting for their rights of way.

How odd it felt to be so high, and so far away from any of the valley settlements, yet to find myself among so many people. In Arab countries, a distinction is made between the traditionally nomadic Bedouin, who roam the land in search of grazing for their camels, goats and sheep, and the *fellaheen*, or farmers who settled in one place, put down roots and built villages. Settled peoples versus nomads, and, like our often fractious relationship with traveller communities, riven by a deep mutual suspicion.

Arriving at Devil's Dyke that morning, after three days virtually alone on the Downs, I felt some of the same misanthropic suspicion towards these folk strolling around the hilltop without having walked there. Not that I thought I was any better for arriving on foot, I just felt different. After a few days my protective carapace had regrown, and I had forgotten how to be with people. So although it was a cold day, and my legs ached from battling the hills and the winds, I didn't enter the pub, warm and inviting as it looked. I didn't want to break the spell of being out on my own in the hills with only the sheep and the birds and a few solitary, monosyllabic walkers for company, so I sat down on a bench, re-tied my bootlaces, and walked on.

It was good to be alone again, descending the gusty ridge path towards Saddlescombe. This hill was Summer Down, and I was within the tree belt once again. Not bent and stunted hawthorns, the only trees brave enough to bear the brunt of the winds on top of the Downs, but proper broadleaf trees like ash and birch, beech and oak. In my hurry to get off the hill I overtook a couple, a man and woman in their seventies, both grasping walking poles in each hand.

'That's the way to do it,' I said as I passed. 'Slow and steady.'

'Can't do it any faster,' the woman replied. There was clearly a lifetime of hill walking under their combined belts, and advancing age and steep slopes weren't going to stop them now.

At Saddlescombe, a historic farmstead now owned by the National Trust, I ordered hot chocolate with marshmallows and cream from a pop-up café housed in a vintage caravan, warming my hands on the mug. Summer Down was behind me, and it was chilly autumn in the valley. I had one more hill in me that day, so under marshalling clouds I set off again, following a holloway trampled deep by innumerable feet, up to Cow Down. Tree roots bulged from the banks, grasping the chalky sub-soil with arthritic fingers.

On Cow Down, where cattle aptly grazed, I walked alongside a row of twisted hawthorn trees that had once been knitted into a hedgerow, but were now isolated and winter-bare, a few berries, or haws, shrivelling on their branches, trunks silvered with lichen. Just six months ago, these trees lathered with the cream-white or pale-pink May blossom that gives the tree its alternative name. Mature hawthorns are havens for insects, supporting over 300 species, while winter visitors from the north, such as fieldfares and redwings, feed off its haws. In folk mythology, the hawthorn is the tree of fertility, the forebear of the Maypole around which people danced at the pagan festival of Beltane, or the Christian one of May Day. If you look closely inside country churches you'll often glimpse a very pantheistic Green Man carved into a stone capital or hidden under a wooden misericord, peeping through a sprig of hawthorn leaves.

Turning to look back at the ripple of hills, and the ridge path I'd trod since Arundel, I saw Chanctonbury Ring in the misty distance. For the eighteenth-century naturalist Gilbert White, South Downs scenery was the finest in England. 'I still investigate that chain of majestic mountains with fresh admiration year by year,' he wrote in *The Natural History of Selborne*, 'and think I see new beauties every time I traverse it.' It had only been three days since I'd left Arundel, but high on these chalk hills, both ancient and ageless, time expanded and days became meaningless, stretching into eternity.

The old, chalky track led me off Cow Down into Pyecombe, a less lovely place than Saddlescombe on the other side of the hill.

Its name, from the Old English *pie* + *cumb*, or the 'insect-infested valley', did not recommend it so I crossed the A23 London to Brighton road to find my path again. After so long on the empty hills, seeing the debris strewn along the roadside was painful. There was the usual scattering of Costa Coffee cups and Red Bull cans, and among them a sombre newcomer – a blue surgical face mask lying crumpled and sodden on the verge.

It was not with a light heart that I began the climb out of Pyecombe. I so longed to be up on the unsullied hills again, away from the symptoms of twenty-first century life, that I almost didn't spot the little church set back from the lane. And with a good few further miles to walk that day, having spotted it I almost didn't stop but for a board which read:

The Church of the Transfiguration
Pyecombe
The Shepherds' Church
For around 850 years we have offered rest
hospitality and refreshment to pilgrims and visitors

I was a pilgrim, a tired and downhearted one at that. And, with a climb to the highest point in East Sussex ahead, I was definitely in need of rest. The village of Pyecombe stands on an old drovers' road, and for centuries shepherds drove their flocks along it up onto the Downs, gathering here before taking their sheep to market in the local towns and villages. Even before the church was founded in around 1170 – the year Thomas Becket was murdered – a prehistoric track passed by the village, starting at Wolstonbury Hill to the west and possibly continuing to Stonehenge. The Roman road from London to the south coast also crossed here, confirming Pyecombe's location as a major crossroads for two millennia. After Thomas Becket was canonised in 1173, Pyecombe became a waypoint on the southern pilgrimage route between the shrines of St Swithun in Winchester and St Thomas in Canterbury, and a century later between St Richard's shrine at Chichester and London. Edward I, who lived from 1239 to 1307, is said to have made this pilgrimage at least once.

Flint-walled and tile-roofed, the exterior of the church was as charming as St Botolph's. The interior, whitewashed and almost bare, was not. Its Norman heritage was barely visible except to sharp-eyed church historians, and I was about to continue on my way when I saw a room off the nave, opposite the door. 'The kitchen is open, please come in and use the facilities. Help yourself to tea and coffee,' a notice read. It was, and I did. I also used the pristine new toilet, paired with one in a Cambodian village as part of a toilet-twinning scheme ('flushing away poverty, one toilet at a time'). Hospitality for pilgrims and travellers was as genuine today as it had been to Alice of Southwick passing by more than seven centuries earlier, albeit with a modern twist. This was one of the most significant pilgrim churches on my entire journey, and I'd nearly walked right past it.

The Shepherds' Church had one further revelation for me, one I'd not spotted on arriving half an hour ago: the wooden church gate swinging on a central pivot like a turnstile. This was a Tapsel gate, named after the family who invented it in the eighteenth century and unique to Sussex. For the coffin bearers of the South Downs it was wide enough to allow easy access to the churchyard, yet narrow enough to prevent animals from entering. Only seven Tapsel gates remain, this one being a twentieth-century replacement. A Pyecombe hook, the local shepherds' crook, formed the latch. Until a few decades ago Pyecombe hooks were made in the forge opposite the church, their elegant shape and perfect balance earning them fame not only among shepherds throughout the land but bishops all over the world, who use them as croziers. The last Pyecombe hook was made by blacksmith Sean Black in 1946 – perhaps the one that is now locked safely inside the church and displayed on special occasions.

My mood had lifted by the time I left the Shepherds' Church, and I was ready for the climb up to Ditchling Beacon. The track passed by Pyecombe Golf Club, a mowed, clipped, strimmed and weed-free swathe of grass, a preposterous green against the ochres and buffs of its autumnal downland backdrop. But nature was making a comeback, rebelling against the neatness of the golf course with a few renegade wildflowers left over from the summer strung along its edge. How did the golfers keep their shoes so pristine and white when my boots were caked with clay and chalk? It was bizarre, sharing these billowing downs on this blustery day with men dragging carts over manicured grass. Two parallel worlds which nearly touched, but never quite converged.

The gorse was in bloom as I crossed into East Sussex and approached Ditchling Beacon, a portent of spring rather than winter. It had been a long day, and the summit seemed out of reach, always on the horizon. And then I was there. A trig point decked with flame-orange strawflowers confirmed this was truly the top, 248 metres above sea level. Like so many of the hills I'd climbed, Ditchling Beacon is an Iron Age hillfort, and even on a bright autumn afternoon, and even with the walkers who had driven up to the car park, it was an intensely atmospheric place. My friend Rebecca, who I'd met when we both worked as hiking guides many years ago, had also driven up to the car park as she'd offered me a bed for the night at her home on the edge of the Downs.

Waiting for Rebecca to arrive I savoured the panorama, and the moment. I was at the highest point of the Old Way, and halfway through my pilgrimage. From the pinnacle of Ditchling Beacon, it would be downhill all the way to Canterbury. Geographically speaking, at least.

XIV

The wind had whipped into a frenzy and dirty black clouds were flinging down showers of rain when Rebecca drove me back to the top of Ditchling Beacon the following morning. The plan was to drop her car off at home, then meet me on my way down into Lewes. For many years Rebecca worked as a lecturer in country-side management at nearby Plumpton College, and she'd offered to accompany me on the final leg of my Samhain walk so she could share her knowledge of the Downs.

As she stopped to let me out of the car, Rebecca pointed to a derelict dew pond near the car park where sheep would once have sipped. Being chalk there is no natural water source on top of the Downs, so farmers created concrete saucer-shaped ponds to collect the overnight dew and rain. As I gathered my rucksack and maps from the back seat of her car Rebecca explained that the chalk downland we see today is a 'Plagioclimax community', or a man-made landscape.

'Without the sheep you wouldn't have the Downs,' were her parting words as I climbed out of the car. It was humans who cleared these once-wooded hills five millennia ago for agriculture and grazing, creating the cropped grass so characteristic of today's downland landscape. Much, it seemed, about these apparently natural hills was not natural at all.

We agreed on our rendezvous, and Rebecca drove away leaving me to navigate the other visitors who'd driven up to the beacon that Sunday: dog walkers, hikers, mountain bikers and neon-clad runners who sploshed in the puddles as they zipped past. I was sharing the landscape I'd lost my heart to with others, and I felt like a jealous lover. In the valley below was Ditchling, where for sixty years the singer and 'Forces Sweetheart' Vera Lynn lived until her death in 2020, at the age of 103. Vera's White Cliffs of Dover were seventy-five miles from Ditchling, but the white hills of the South Downs swelled behind her Tudor manor house, opposite the churchyard of St Margaret's, where her ashes are buried.

The wind had turned bitter and for the first time that week I felt underdressed. The clocks had gone back the previous night, and British Summer Time had ended. A long winter lay ahead before I'd feel the sun's warmth on my back once again. The OS map, nearly ripped from my hands by the wind, showed a terrain bristling with archaeology – tumuli, dykes, enclosures, settlements. And, on Plumpton Plain, some of the oldest field systems in the country, probably dating from the Bronze Age. Rebecca had told me about these the previous evening as we drove past the college where she used to work, on the way to her home on the edge of Lewes.

'One of my students found half a bronze axe-head at Plumpton, which may have been thrown into the pond,' she'd said. 'As a water source, it will have been viewed as a sacred place.' The pond was quite close to the present church, so this fitted with the theory that Christian sites appropriated pagan ones to smooth the transition between religious belief systems.

I'd been walking for twenty minutes or so, and most of the runners, mountain bikers and dog walkers had thinned out. The cold wind tearing at my hair, the rain splattering against my face – it felt so good to be striding out on top of the Downs again, the Weald stretching below. Scattered around me on the ridge were a multitude of tumuli, or burial mounds, now half hidden beneath their skins of turf. When they were first made, these circular earth and stone barrows were covered in shimmering white chalk, and visible for miles around. Although primarily burial mounds for the upper echelons of Bronze Age society, it is thought that they also had a ceremonial or ritual purpose, and it was not hard to imagine the effect of these high, gleaming mounds on the ordinary folk living in the darkly wooded valleys below.

The clouds detonated, the temperature plummeted, my fingers froze and my trousers stuck to the back of my legs. Regardless of the turn in the weather and the change of the clocks, skylarks sang resolutely on. After a tussle between the seasons so characteristic of Samhain, autumn now had the upper hand. The Weald had disappeared under a veil of mist, so I kept my head down and marched on.

The inclement weather didn't dissuade Rebecca from joining me for my final plunge off the Downs, and we met as planned on Mount Harry – at only 195 metres less impressive than its lofty name suggests. Rebecca, striding tall and confident through the mizzle, looked just as she did when I first met her thirty years ago in the high, ragged mountains of Andalucía. Her hair was greyer now, but so was mine. Since leaving the walking holiday company

'We are not finished with this fellow yet'

Henry may have assumed that having his friend as head of the Church in England would resolve the longstanding power struggle between Church and Crown.

Instead, Becket appears to have undergone a spiritual transformation, turning his back on his previous life of luxury. He resigned from his role at court and became a champion of the privilege of the clergy to be tried in ecclesiastical courts, whatever crime they may have committed.

It was a struggle between two authorities, headed by two men who'd once been close friends. Thomas, the stubborn one. Henry, the short-tempered one.

An attempted resolution ('the Constitutions of Clarendon') was rejected by Becket. Henry retaliated by charging him with embezzlement and summoning him to a trial.

Becket, fearing for his life, fled the country, not to return for six years. 'We are not finished with this fellow yet,' Henry is reported to have said, ominously.

we'd both worked for, she lived in southern Spain and then in East Sussex with her family. With me settling in Oxford, and then in North Yorkshire, we'd not seen much of each other in recent years, and had spent the previous evening catching up with our news over a bottle of Rioja.

It was from Mount Harry that, in May 1264, the rebel baron Simon de Montfort surveyed the town of Lewes, where King Henry III, grandson of Thomas Becket's nemesis, was holed up at the priory of St Pancras. De Montfort's army's height advantage meant Henry's troops had to fight the ensuing battle uphill, leading to the defeat of the king and the establishment of England's first representative parliament. A contemporary chronicle records a vision of St Thomas and St George, two saints associated with England, floating above the Downs:

> There were some in the army at Lewes who saw, clearly, an unknown knight, clad in armour and holding before him an unknown banner, and an archbishop clothed in pontifical garb blessing the baronial army; and they vanished, suddenly, when the battle was done. They were reckoned to be St Thomas the Martyr and St George.

Thomas had, since Henry II's repentance, been reclaimed by the monarchs of England, but it was de Montfort's rebels who won the day. Chronicles tell how Henry III was 'much beaten with swords and maces', and his brother Richard of Cornwall was taken hostage. When the battle spilled into Lewes itself the troops defending the castle fired arrows onto the thatched roofs of the houses in an attempt to hold back de Montfort's men. 'The town on fire, and its streets filled with objects of indiscriminate slaughter,' wrote a contemporary of the devastation. The parliament only lasted a year before Simon de Montfort was killed by royalist forces at the Battle of Evesham, but his legacy in the constitutional story of England endures.

All this mayhem seemed a far cry from the tranquillity of the South Downs that Sunday morning, although battles are being fought on other, more insidious fronts. Across the valley from where we were now walking Rebecca pointed out a wood called Ashcombe, from the Old English meaning 'the valley where the ash trees grow'. With the rapid advance of dieback, ash trees such as those at Ashcombe will soon be gone and largely replaced by sycamore. Like ash, sycamore is a broadleaved woodland tree but as a non-native species will bring long-lasting implications for the countryside. This I learned from Rebecca, as we marched over the hills, me trying to match her long-legged pace.

'The advantage of sycamores is that they spread quickly, and they're hardy,' she said as I paused to take a breath. Rebecca was not out of breath. 'Their disadvantage is that climate change could increase their growing season, which might shade out our traditional woodland plants. But if the south of England becomes warmer and drier, we could see a decline of not only sycamore, but also bluebells and other iconic species.'

'Oh no, that would be awful!' I panted.

'We'll just have to see what happens,' said Rebecca, a note of consolation in her voice.

Bluebells, my favourite spring flower, thrive in the mottled light of trees just coming into leaf – trees like the dying ashes all around us. Almost half the world's bluebells are found in the UK, but our native variety, *Hyacinthoides non-scripta*, a delicate, drooping purple-blue flower, is being crowded out by the 'Spanish' bluebell (*Hyacinthoides hispanica*), forming the taller, straighter, paler hybrid *Hyacinthoides* x *hispanica*. First introduced into Britain by the Victorians, the Spanish bluebell was an ornamental garden plant but soon escaped its domestic boundaries. Like another Victorian import, the American grey squirrel, the Spanish bluebell is more vigorous than its British cousin, outcompeting it for habitat and resources. Unlike grey squirrels, which are unable to breed with the red species, English and Spanish bluebells can hybridise, diluting the native variety's genes. Now, with ash dieback, our bluebells are under further assault.

Seeking shelter from the rain, we headed off the exposed ridge onto a path through tangled woodland, where we took refuge under a fallen ash tree. Around us lay many other fallen trees. Why had so many trees come down here, I wondered as we waited for the rain to abate.

'Trees in the centre of a wood are more likely to be blown over in a gale, as they have greater competition for root space,' Rebecca explained as rain pattered on the leaf canopy, 'whereas trees around the edge have room to spread their roots, and so tend to be better anchored.' It was good, after so many days walking alone, to be in the company of an expert who so evidently loved the Downs as much as I was beginning to, someone who also happened to be a friend from a past life who I'd not seen for so long.

The rain softened, and an ancient, tree-lined track now led us down towards Offham. Known in the Sussex dialect as 'bostals', these trackways were traditionally used to take the sheep from the valley up to the Downs for grazing. By day the sheep would be left to roam the open hills; by night shepherds would drive them down to the lower fields, where they were enclosed and their manure collected as a natural fertiliser. Centuries of feet and hooves have eroded the chalk, creating a deep, water-filled and ultimately unusable gully. Now, the old bostal to Offham is superseded by a parallel track, hugging the edge of the escarpment with views over the wooded Weald below.

Beneath our boots, the chalk had become a rivulet, gathering in white pools of rainwater, the path fringed with the same autumnal colours I'd been seeing all week, with hedgerow leaves now as red as rowan berries. The day was damp, melancholy. I felt melancholy also, knowing I wouldn't be treading the chalk paths and upland tracks of the Downs until another quarter-year had passed, pandemic permitting.

We reached Offham, the Old English for 'Offa's homestead', and the church of St Michael from which exhaled the faint drone of an organ and the hum of hymns. Offham itself was a peaceful, unremarkable place that Sunday morning, yet like so many seemingly peaceful, unremarkable places in this part of England it had a stormier past. This was the birthplace of Jack Straw, one the ringleaders of the 1381 Peasants' Revolt. Jack Straw was a pseudonym, possibly for one of the other ringleaders, Wat Tyler, or a reference to the nearby hamlet of Pepinstraw, where Jack was born. Either way, he is now deeply embedded in English cultural history, the hero of popular stories and poems, though his birthplace lives on only in the name of a housing estate on the edge of the village. Memories are long here, hibernating just beneath the surface and ready to burst forth at any time, like spring bulbs in winter earth.

From Offham another chalk path led down through woodland to the floodplain, where we squelched our way alongside the River Ouse and across a disused railway line. The path led us to South Malling and the church of St Michael the Archangel, tucked away in a kink of the river at the end of a dead-end lane. So tucked away is this little square-towered flint church on the semi-industrial outskirts of Lewes that Rebecca, who had lived in the town for over twenty years, didn't know of its existence.

Legend tells us that the knights who struck down Thomas Becket hid at South Malling after fleeing the scene of the crime. This is not as unlikely as it may appear, as the Collegiate church at South Malling had been rebuilt by Theobald, Archbishop of Canterbury, in 1150 – just twenty years before Thomas's murder. Straying from the historical record, the story goes that when the knights cast their blood-stained cloaks on a table inside the church it broke under the weight of their sin. This stone table is now on display at Anne of Cleves House in Lewes.

A notice on the locked door of the church advertised a churchwardens' meeting by Zoom, a true sign of the times. By all accounts there wasn't much to see inside this plain, seventeenth-century building, even with the twelve continuous centuries of Christian worship on this site. Ealdwulf, a prince of the South Saxons, established a monastery here in around 765, in honour of St Michael, sensibly choosing a site on a promontory above the floodplain. The manor of Malling was subsequently bestowed on the Archbishop of Canterbury by King Baldred of Kent in around 823. Some of the fabric of Theobald's building was incorporated into the later parish church, now standing locked before us.

We rested among fading wildflowers in the churchyard, the faint hum from the A26 the only interruption to the peace of a place yanked unwittingly into the violence of England's history 850 years before.

Leaving the churchyard for the final push into Lewes we crossed the slow-moving, rain-brown Ouse and entered the town via the church of St John Sub-Castro, its wild and wooded Victorian graveyard like so many urban churchyards a haven for nature. Sub Castro means 'beneath the castle', and sure enough the great castle of Lewes loomed above us. St John's is a Victorian edifice, built in 1839 in Early English style on the site of a late-Saxon church, and of little architectural interest except for a blocked archway in the apse, the only vestige of the original church and the likely entrance to an anchorite's cell. A Latin inscription around this doorway has the translation:

> There enters this cell a warrior of Denmark's royal race; Magnus his name, mark of mighty lineage. Casting off his mightiness he takes the Lamb's mildness, and to gain ever-lasting life becomes a lowly anchorite.

As a Dane, Magnus was thought to be a Viking warrior who converted to Christianity and, with the zeal of a convert, opted for the harshest life of piety. Standing before this ancient doorway I couldn't help remembering an afternoon just a few days — and twenty-five miles — earlier when I stumbled upon another dwelling hidden behind a similarly historic church. Not belonging to a Danish warrior called Magnus, but to a homeless Briton called Michael.

We climbed the castle mound, with its views across the Lewes rooftops to the surrounding Downs and the cross carved by the monks of Lewes Priory to commemorate the Battle of Lewes. On the Gough Map, Lewes (or *lewis*) is represented by two buildings, a spired church with a cross and a castle — the same castle on whose mound we were now perched. A lane took us through the flint-walled Barbican, a fourteenth-century gate described by architectural historian Ian Nairn as 'one of the mightiest barbicans in England'. We continued steeply along Cliffe High Street, a thoroughfare of grand facades and a fine Georgian house clad in black-glazed tiles, looking like it belonged in London's Downing Street rather than in Lewes's high street.

Turning off the high street we walked down St Martin's Lane, which became ever narrower, to enter Southover Grange, once the home of the diarist John Evelyn. It wasn't the sixteenth-century house we had come to see but the mulberry tree in the gardens, around which autumn cyclamen now bloomed. As a mother, Rebecca brought her children here, and now also brings her young grandsons. The tree's lineage goes back much further than the past few decades of Rebecca's memory, presumably dating from the construction of the grange. Though, like a churchyard yew, it may be very much older.

From Southover it was a short walk to the edge of town, and the priory of St Pancras. Standing in this field, the traffic on the A27 pounding by just a few dozen metres away, it was hard to believe that St Pancras was once one of England's largest and most powerful monasteries. As a Cluniac house it was linked to the great abbey of Cluny in Burgundy, reinforcing the early medieval relationship between England and France. By all accounts, it was a splendid set of buildings, surrounded by gardens and orchards, and one of the wealthiest in the country, owning 22,000 acres of land in Sussex alone. The church was longer than Chichester Cathedral, and opulently decorated, painted in bright colours, ornamented with stone carvings, floored with patterned tiles.

Built around 1080 on the site of a Saxon church, apart from its brief role as refuge for Henry III during the Battle of Lewes, the priory pretty much kept itself to itself. In its twelfth- and thirteenth-century heyday there were perhaps 100 monks living and working here. For Cluniac monks, the main occupation was prayer and contemplation. Lay workers were enlisted to bake bread from the grain harvested on the priory estates, brew beer from undrinkable water, pluck fruit from the orchards, catch carp from the fishponds and keep pigeons in the pigeonniers (or dove-cotes) to eat. By 1537 the number of monks had dwindled to only twenty-four, although the priory remained the heart and soul of the town.

Then came the Acts of Suppression, and almost 500 years after its construction the priory was torn down by Italian engineer Giovanni Portinari on the instructions of Henry VIII's arch henchman, Thomas Cromwell. An interpretation board in the priory ruins explains how Portinari undermined the priory walls, digging trenches and setting fire to the foundations until they collapsed. Cluniac houses like St Pancras were renowned for their artistic quality, and that Portinari deliberately targeted the sacred buildings can only be seen as an act of spite, an attempt to destroy not just the fabric of the priory but the spirit of the people – the monks and the townsfolk of Lewes – for whom St Pancras was the centre of their world.

St Pancras was briefly owned by Cromwell before becoming a quarry, and later the site of the Lewes to Brighton railway, which now clips the priory precinct. Workmen digging this line in 1845 unearthed lead caskets containing the skeletons of the Norman William de Warenne and his wife, Gundrada, who founded the priory on their safe return from pilgrimage to Rome. Today the priory church lies buried under the railway line, and all that remains above ground are a few sad, lumpen walls and grass-filled trenches.

Such deliberate and brutal destruction of what must have been a magnificent example of medieval architecture and religious faith made for grim viewing. I stood looking at the ruins of the priory, rain splashing onto my hood. A train trundled past on the line built across the grave of the great church of St Pancras, testimony to the destruction of our heritage and landscape that continues to this day.

Clamping my palms over my ears, I tried to imagine how this place might have been for a pilgrim arriving half a millennium ago, on the eve of the Dissolution. Huddled within its bowl of hills, surrounded by meadows and orchards, the summer-green Downs beyond, St Pancras would have been an astonishing sight. Almost a glimpse of heaven.

St Pancras wasn't the final stop of my walk that day. There was one other pilgrim destination I wanted to visit, so I headed back up into town to the twelfth-century church of St Thomas à Becket. As a piece of architecture it's not that interesting, having been scoured of both its plaster and its soul by Victorian restorers, but like most churches of this dedication its origins are late twelfth century, when the cult of St Thomas exploded. I didn't stop long. I was cold and tired, and in need of a hot bath. But it was good to be reminded of why I had walked to this Sussex town at the edge of the chalk downs, on a wet afternoon in autumn so far from home.

I had now completed five stages of the Old Way, and was just over halfway through my walk along the Gough Map. When I next returned to Lewes it would be Imbolc, a year from when I first made the decision to walk in the footsteps of pilgrims to Canterbury. I hoped, perhaps vainly in this age of warming winters, that the South Downs, today shrouded in mist, would then be swathed in snow.

The Testimony of William Thorpe

1407

The Testimony of William Thorpe is a first-person narrative account of the trial of the Lollard chaplain William Thorpe (whose actual existence is not verified), a follower of the 'heretical' teachings of church reformer John Wycliffe. In this extract, from a translation published in 1831, Thorpe is holding forth on the dissolute behaviour of some pilgrims.

Also, sir, I know well that when divers men and women will go thus after their own wills, and finding out, on pilgrimage; they will ordain with them before, to have with them both men and women, that can well sing wanton songs, and some other pilgrims will have with them bagpipes. So that every town that they come through, what with the noise of their singing, and with the sound of their piping, and with the jangling of their Canterbury bells, and with the barking out of dogs after them, they make more noise than if the king came there away with all his clarions, and many other minstrels. And if these men and women are a month out in their pilgrimage, many of them shall be half a year after great janglers, tale-tellers and liars.

IMBOLC REVISITED

LEWES TO WINCHELSEA

Sun spilled from a clear blue sky, glancing through the ring of trees and casting long shadows of their trunks. Within the trees, in a meadow on the threshold of the South Downs, a circle of men, women and children held hands, breath misting in the chill afternoon air. Joining them, just another link in the chain of gloved fingers, was a stranger from the North.

We were a group of around sixty people of all ages, wrapped against the late-January cold, most dressed in fleeces and anoraks, a few in richly embroidered robes. To the west of our circle, on the other side of the village car park, lay the remains of old Wilmington Priory. To the east, just visible in a darkening scoop of hills half a mile away, as if caught in mid-stride and holding a staff in each fist, stood a tall white giant. The giant, rather than the old priory, had drawn the crowd to this spot. Directly under his gaze a Druid ceremony was about to take place, as it does at this time every year, in celebration of Imbolc and the first stirrings of spring.

A lantern lay balanced on the grass in the middle of the circle, a lighted candle inside. Mobile phones had been muted, and a reverential silence settled over the gathering. One of the men, tall with grey flowing hair, stepped forward. This was Damh the Bard of Sussex-based Druids Anderida Gorsedd, Pendragon of the Order of Bards Ovates and Druids, and master of ceremonies for the occasion. Asking us to take a long, slow breath, Damh, who was born Dave Smith, welcomed the goddess Bride, aka Brigid, into our circle. In turn, members of the group faced north, south, east and west, calling for peace from each corner of the earth.

'May the circle be blessed with fire,' announced Damh.

'And may the circle be blessed with water,' answered Cerri, the female Druid standing next to him. From the treetops a crow cawed, and in the adjacent field horses grazed, oblivious of the sacred rite being performed alongside the car park of Wilmington Priory.

Duly blessed with fire and water, we listened as Damh called the spirits from the four corners of the earth into our circle. 'Hail and welcome,' we chanted to each spirit in turn. I stayed silent as the group intoned an unfamiliar verse in unison, feeling like I did at primary school before I'd learned the words of the Lord's Prayer. I joined in again as the group chorused a long 'Awen' to Brigid, the Irish goddess of spring, fertility and life. The main Imbolc ceremony was over, but for the drinking of home-made mead passed round in plastic cups.

I slipped quietly away, leaving the bards to their Eisteddfod in praise of Bride, honoured to have been received so graciously into this sacred rite of spring.

The Imbolc ceremony I'd just witnessed felt ancient, even timeless. Having just arrived from the north of England, after a winter at my desk staring into a computer screen, the scent of the awakening earth and the sensation of wind on my skin were the immersion into nature I craved. No matter that this Druid rite was not quite as timeless as it appeared. While Druidry has its roots in Celtic culture, Neo-Druidry emerged in the late eighteenth century, when poets, artists, musicians and antiquarians turned their creative endeavours to the veneration of nature. For the devotees of the Romantic movement, the Celtic Druids represented an innocent, pre-Christian world where divinity was rooted in the landscape, and in nature in all its forms. Druids' polytheism appealed to the Romantic sentiment, while their egalitarian structure was timely in an age when women's place in society was being debated.

Julius Caesar, when in Gaul, wrote one of the earliest accounts of Druid priests and their practices. Later, in AD 54, the Emperor Claudius outlawed Druidry, and his governor, Gaius Suetonius Paulinus, stormed the Druids' Anglesey nerve-centre in AD 60. With the later Christianisation of Britain, Celtic customs declined, and by the seventh century ancient Druidry had all but died out.

Died out, but never forgotten.

XV

The morning after the ceremony in the car park, many months after my Samhain arrival, I left Lewes on foot. It was the first day of February, and the feast of Imbolc. One of the four major Celtic festivals, Imbolc is a 'cross-quarter' day, halfway between the winter solstice and spring equinox. While meteorological spring begins in March, solar, or astronomical, spring begins on 1 February and ends on May Day, or Beltane, the onset of summer. Imbolc is proto-spring, a transitional season when lambs are born, and when nature returns to life after the long winter. Falling at a time of regeneration, Imbolc is regarded as a women's rite, observed at the opposite side of the wheel of the year from Lughnasa, celebrating Lugh, the male god of Light.

St Brigid, or St Bride as she is known this side of the Irish Sea, is the Christian embodiment of Imbolc. Venerated by the Celts even before the Roman settlement of Britain, she is one of the patron saints of Ireland, along with St Patrick and St Columcille

(St Columba). In English tradition, she is the goddess Brigantia, worshipped by the Brigantes tribe of northern England. The conquering Romans renamed their northernmost province Britannia. Helmeted and holding a trident and shield she is still the emblem of Britain, depicted on coins struck by the Royal Mint in the reign of every monarch since Charles II. When St Augustine introduced Roman Christianity to England in 597 her pagan festival became Candlemas, celebrated forty days after Christmas Day, when parishioners carry lighted candles around their church and receive priestly blessings.

As the patron saint of travellers, sailors and fugitives St Bride was a fitting mascot that morning as I walked out of Lewes via a narrow, steep lane of weatherboard and tile-hung cottages clambering up the hill onto the South Downs. The ground was cold and hard, though the sun warmed my face, the only part of me left exposed within my wrapping of winter-season hiking kit. The South Downs is not the Arctic, or even the Alps, but the hills are bare and a bitter north wind whipped across the sky as I climbed.

I already had three seasons, spring, summer and autumn, Ostara, Lughnasa and Samhain, under my belt. In those three seasons I had walked 112 miles from Southampton to Lewes, vacillating between the hills and the coast, between the chalk and the sea. Now, my destination was Firle. At just eight miles away, it would be a short day's walk to ease myself back into the landscape. The first of seven walks that would lead me along the trajectory of the Gough Map to the ancient, landlocked port of Winchelsea.

For three days I would walk the chalk hills of the South Downs, then cross the waterlogged marshland of the Pevensey Levels to Battle, site of the most momentous conflict in English history. Before arriving in Winchelsea I would pass flint churches and sequestered villages, white figures etched into the hillside and ruined abbeys. Alongside me every step of the way would be Alice of Southwick, my pilgrim companion since leaving Southampton all those months ago.

The Gough Map marks the distance over these next three stages – six, seven and eight – as thirty-three medieval miles, though I estimated it to be double that in modern measurement. The first of these was the hardest. After so many sedentary months my legs howled in indignation as I climbed towards the sun. Chest thumping, I reached the summit of the down and paused for breath. Below, the River Ouse wound towards the sea. On the opposite side of the valley unfolded the western half of the South Downs, landscape of my Samhain walk. The wind plucked at my hair and snagged my rainwear, but the sun was strong and pulled me onwards.

I had reached Southerham Farm, an upland nature reserve protecting this chalk habitat, restoring the grassland lost since the decline of sheep farming in the mid-twentieth century. Scrub and trees, originally cleared by early pastoral farmers who found the soil too shallow for crops, had begun to recolonise the hills, crowding out the wildflowers that thrived here when the grass was grazed by sheep.

'Windy morning!' shouted a wiry, fit-looking man who was skipping down the hill as I was trudging up it. 'Going far?'

'Just to Firle. You?'

'I was going that way as well, but it's so windy this morning I've turned back. Enjoy your walk!' he said, striding briskly down towards the town. I didn't have the option of turning back like him, but this brief exchange cheered me on. There's a camaraderie among walkers, a shared bond. Instinctively you recognise a kindred spirit, because who else on a winter weekday morning would be walking over the windy Downs by choice? Only someone who loves striding out over open hills, sun breaking across the slopes and casting the valleys into shadows as deep as night. Winter in the valleys, the first faint glimmerings of spring up on the hills. Soft sculpted hills, as if they had been blown here like the dunes of Wadi Rum. Chalk down might seem permanent, but it's supple, malleable, constantly shifting and shaping. Like the sea, it feels alive. Over 100 million years ago chalk was made from the sea, and chalk and sea belong together.

A short distance to my left, the first skylark sang on the first day of solar spring. Alone, it performed its aria of high trilling notes, before dropping back down into the grass like a stone. My Imbolc walk was only one hour old, and spring had kick-started. The path dipped towards the valley, into winter once again. I was surrounded by human activity, yet in this valley I was alone. Just the wind, and a buzzard skimming overhead. Gorse clasped the valley sides, pulsating into bloom. Scrub and woodland, hawthorns hung with withered berries, clung on to the higher slopes. Here, the tussle between spring and winter, vernal and hibernal, was at its fiercest.

My OS map showed me ringed with old field systems, the gothic font boasting their antiquity. Over a thousand years ago this was a heavily worked landscape of agricultural importance. Mount Caburn, a wedge-shaped Iron Age hillfort on the summit of the down ahead, was evidence that it was also a landscape of ritual significance. As I approached, the late-winter sun still low in the sky, I could make out its ditches and embankments. Now a nature reserve, it's home to Adonis and chalkhill blue butterflies, meadow pipits, corn buntings, yellowhammers, kestrels and, of course, skylarks.

Did Alice of Southwick walk here also, seven centuries before me? As a devout Christian she may have steered well clear of this pagan spot, even though folk revered these sites of ancient ceremony well after the advent of Christianity. The Imbolc ceremony at Wilmington had proved that they still hold a place in people's hearts, as did the boot-marked track now leading me to Mount Caburn's summit.

At the top I turned and looked west, towards the hills of my Samhain walk. It felt as if I'd been walking there only last week. In a place so geologically and archaeologically old a season is infinitesimally small, just a pinprick of time. As I circumnavigated the hillfort, the wind nearly blowing me off the embankment, I saw not only my past journey but the one ahead. This place was a fulcrum on which the Downs, and my whole pilgrimage, gyrated.

The cold was caustic, so I made my way off the hillfort and down through sheep-grazed meadows and leafless trees to the village of Glynde. At the tail end of winter the scene was like a polaroid photo from the family album, the garish colours now faded to sepia. Russet-roofed, tile-hung and weatherboarded, Glynde clustered around its demure Georgian church, while above the village brooded Mount Caburn, all pagan magic and mystery.

As I descended into the village, the wind in my sails, a group of middle-aged walkers loud with bonhomie puffed up the path.

'You're going in the right direction!' joshed one. I'd only been walking a couple of hours, yet apart from Alice's shadow I'd not met anybody since the lone hiker near Lewes. All winter I'd been sheltered at home, with Richard and my pets. Now, for the first time in months, I was alone, and it felt strange. I hadn't yet reacquainted myself with my own company, let alone with large parties of fellow walkers.

Warmed by a hot coffee from Glynde Post Office and Stores, I walked out of the village centre. Passing the railway station, I imagined the villagers taking trains to London and back each weekday, just as my own father commuted for twenty years from our Buckinghamshire village to London. Two chalk villages, one in the Downs, the other in the Chilterns. Glynde was the doppelgänger of Ashley Green, brick and flint glinting in the sharp winter sun.

The Old Way takes a detour as you leave Glynde, swinging by the settlement of Beddingham. Medieval pilgrims wanted to get to their destination by the safest and straightest route, but they also wished to visit holy sites and interesting churches along the way. Churches like St Andrew's Beddingham, lying in a cleft between the eastern and western halves of the Downs. The path to the church passed through the Ouse Valley, a flatland of luminous green winter wheat. Ploughed-up flints lay scattered along the path and I searched among them for worked flints – arrowheads, axe-heads, scrapers – the tools of Neolithic folk. Not that this was a major Neolithic trading route like the Ridgeway or the Icknield Way, but my Chiltern chalkland gaze couldn't help casting itself downward in search of half-buried history.

The path met a lane of old flint cottages running parallel to the modern A27, which meets the A26 here. The frenzy of traffic alongside me was enervating, and far more arduous to walk than the steep, quiet hills of earlier that morning. Beddingham had better be worth it.

St Andrew's, all chequered flint and ashlar, lay just ahead, severed from the rest of the village by the road. Once at the heart of its community, the church is now dislocated on the wrong side of the carriageway. Crossing the A26, one of the busiest trunk roads in the country, was a nuisance but a small hardship compared with what confronted many medieval pilgrims en route to holy places. As soon as I stepped onto the buff brick pathway into the churchyard a hush descended, muffling the encircling traffic. The brick path led to the porch, where I paused to read a notice:

> For over a thousand years there has been a Christian presence on this site. To start with there was a monastery either here where the church stands or very close by. Some of the stone used to build the church comes from the monastery.

In the ninth century St Andrew's was a minster housing a college of priests, and the Saxon heart of Sussex. Seven centuries later, ashlar from the demolished Lewes Priory was used to rebuild its flint-and-stone-chequered west tower. Standing on the Glynde Reach, a navigable tributary of the River Ouse, in the Middle Ages the church serviced a small port. Now it lies stranded on its island between the Glynde Reach and the River Ouse, the A26 and the A27, its port gone.

Inside, the church is simple and whitewashed under a plain wooden roof. There was no sense of the outside world, so near and moving so fast. I wandered through the nave and approached the chancel. On the underside of the south arcade were faint traces of wall paintings, just red pigment remaining. The church's isolation in the Glynde Valley had protected the murals not only from the Puritan zealots of the seventeenth century but from Victorian restorers 200 years later. What remains today is a delicate scrollwork of rose-like flowers, and an unidentified female saint, probably painted in the thirteenth century. The arches support hefty stone piers, their unusual square capitals of the so-called 'Ouse Valley' type and carved with gargoyles almost heathen in their countenance. It's in these furtive, half-hidden traces you truly encounter the spirit of a place.

You find it also in the memorials set into the walls, spanning the centuries of the building's existence. Memorials to parishioners who died hundreds of years ago, but also to those who have died during my own lifetime, like the plaque dedicated to Roy Eastwood who departed this life 17 November 1979:

> Mr Eastwood of Comps Farm Beddingham loved this church and parish and served God and his neighbours here with simplicity for sixty years. He was organist and choirmaster from 1919 to 1979, and churchwarden at the time of his death.

He had 'served his neighbours with simplicity'. What eloquence, and how apt for this quiet church with its thousand-year history. Beddingham was indeed worth crossing the A26 for.

I ran back over the road, following paths through fields and farmyards that took me to Firle, and the end of my day's walk. The shrieks of schoolchildren in the playground hailed me as I walked, cold and windblown, into the village. Here I stopped at the Ram Inn and ate my supermarket sandwich in the garden, surreptitiously, and feeling more like a vagrant than a pilgrim. It had not been a long day's walk, and in summer I would have walked on further. Imbolc may have arrived, but it was still winter and I was cold. I hadn't yet adjusted to the weather or the landscape, and although only covering a few miles of geography, I had walked through thousands of years of history. It was enough for one day.

Stuffing my sandwich wrapper into my backpack I hopped on one of the few buses that stop at the village, and fifteen minutes later was back in Lewes.

XVI

Firle's schoolchildren welcomed me again the next morning when I returned, feeling like a pilgrim rather than a vagrant, and respectable enough to order a flat white at the Ram Inn and contemplate the walk ahead. Later that afternoon, and ten miles further on, I would arrive at Wilmington, scene of the Imbolc rite two days earlier and home of the Long Man. From the hillforts and effigies of the Downs, to the white cliffs of Dover with all their wartime symbolism, chalk is the rock on which England's story is etched, and I would soon be walking to its heartland.

The Ram Inn sits at one end of the estate village belonging to the adjacent country house, Firle Place. Along the main street jostle cottages of rosy brickwork with steeply pitched roofs, almost edible in their deliciousness. Pausing to stroke a cat called Graham, who brought to mind my own tabby cats back home, I continued along the street towards the church, sheltered beneath the backdrop of the Downs. You could tell by the parked cars – not a Range Rover in sight – that this was a community rare in southern England these days. A community of garden allotments and honesty boxes, home to artists, craftspeople, brewers, even a working blacksmith.

At the end of the street a brick-paved path alongside a beech hedge exploding with sparrow song led to St Peter's Church.

Buried in the churchyard are members of the Bloomsbury Group who, in the early decades of the twentieth century, lived at nearby Charleston Farmhouse. Vanessa Bell lies here, Duncan Grant is next to her, and Angelica Garnett is nearby, their gravestones unremarkable.

St Peter's has the proportions, if not the size, of a cathedral. This building, or incarnations of it, has stood here for 1,000 years, massive flint walls having replaced the original Saxon wooden structure. The church is massive inside also, nave walls pierced by a clerestory through which the morning sunlight spilled. In the Gage Chapel, named after the family who have lived at Firle Place since the reign of Henry VIII, a stained-glass window by John Piper blazed with colour. A Tree of Life grew at its centre, spreading out to the sides of the window. Sheep dozed on the turf beneath the tree, a sun and moon suspended on either side. The window glowed like a jewel set in its whitewashed walls.

I turned to leave, keen to begin my journey to the Long Man, when a newspaper cutting in the corner of the chapel caught my eye. Yellowed and fading, it was the front page of the *Daily Mirror*, dated 8 November 1940. 'SHEPHERD TELLS OF VISION IN SKY' screeched the headline. I stepped over to get a closer look. 'Old Fred Fowler, sixty-six, lifted his weather-beaten face skywards and pointed west way above the highest peak of the Sussex Downs,' the article began. The photo next to the text showed a man with a bowler hat holding a traditional shepherd's crook, gazing into the distance with his hand shielding his eyes. I read on:

> 'It be there when I see it', he said. 'There in the clear blue sky, a vision they calls it – it was the like of something which I never see before.' Then he said, reverently, 'It be

Christ I see.' Fred, who is a shepherd, lives in the village of Firle, near Lewes, Sussex. Yesterday, the *Daily Mirror* told of how he and other villagers claimed to have seen a vision of Christ and six angels. Fred told me the strange story himself. I joined him in his shelter of bracken in the Downs, the biting wind blew round us. His two dogs, Bob and Watch, guarded his 250 sheep. 'I never be one to see things,' said Fred. 'I am alone too much for that. I just have me two dogs, me sheep and me missus way back at the cottage, and I goes to church on a Sunday. That's all I sees or knows of life, that's all I really want to see or know. I'd just rounded up the flock that morning – it be about eleven. I says to meself it's a nice clear day and I looks up west at the sky. Then I sees it.

The unnamed reporter, a 'Special Correspondent', goes on to describe Fred's vision: Christ, his head to one side, nailed to the cross. Six angels surrounding him, wearing white robes that reached to their feet. 'I even saw their toes,' said Fred. He went down to Firle to tell the villagers what he'd seen.

'There were other people who had seen it too. But mine's a simple life – I just got my two dogs, my sheep, and my missus, and I go to church of a Sunday. I forgot', he smiled, 'there's my pint I always have of a night.'

There was a further account of how the angels were dressed, the harps they carried, and the nails in Christ's feet. Two widows evacuated from London, a Mrs Evans and a Mrs Steer, as well as another Firle resident, Mrs Stevens, also witnessed the scene. The story ends with a statement from the vicar, the Rev. A. G. Gregor, who was interviewed by the reporter. 'I saw nothing,' he said, 'and I think the whole thing is nonsense.' Yet visions were not unheard of in these Sussex hills, I remembered, with apparitions of St Thomas and St George hanging above Lewes in the battle of 1264.

Nonsense or not, I found the story both fascinating and moving, particularly given its context. Next to the front-page splash were two shorter pieces. '100 AFS MEN DEAD IN LONDON,' one was headlined. 'APPLY NOW FOR A NEW RATION BOOK,' announced the other. Two worlds, the chillingly urban and the mystically rural, colliding in a time of war.

I looked again at the photo of Fred Fowler with his shepherd's crook. I had seen these crooks before at Pyecombe, on my Samhain walk. Except for the bowler hat, Fred's way of life was little different to that of the Neolithic shepherds who first cleared the land for grazing some 5,000 years ago. The photo was taken in 1940. Five years later, the war was over. The revolution in agriculture that followed, which saw the tractor replace the horse once and for all, was when everything changed for the shepherds of the South Downs. How did Fred Fowler cope with the loss of his old way of life, where visions in the sky were, in his words, 'what they tells me the cinema is like, but I think it be more real'?

Leaving the Gage Chapel I stepped out of the church and into the February sunshine. As I walked down the path, the Reverend Peter Owen-Jones was walking up it. With his chin-length hair, and dressed in a woollen hat and multihued clothes, he was immediately recognisable as the presenter of TV programmes on religion, the South Downs and pilgrimage. I introduced myself, telling him I was walking the Old Way to Canterbury. As a pilgrimage enthusiast he knew about the path, and asked where I was heading that day.

'To Berwick and Alciston, then on to Alfriston and Wilmington,' I told him.

'It's not raining today, so go the high way, over Firle Beacon,' replied the reverend. 'I've just come from up there myself.' This was my planned route anyhow, though a lower way exists along the foot of the Downs that connected the villages, farmhouses and hamlets long before the A27 was built in the mid-twentieth century. We said our farewells, and I went on my way. The Reverend Pilgrim, as Peter Owen-Jones is sometimes known, was a very different character to the Reverend A. G. Gregor, who so bluntly dismissed his parishioners' accounts of the vision of Christ on the Downs. With his informal, dog collar-free attire and easy-going manner, he seemed to me more like Fred Fowler and the old ways of the shepherding life, now all but gone from these hills.

I was now a day into my winter-cum-spring journey. When you've not been on a long walk for some time it can take a full day to acclimatise yourself to the path again, to the rhythm of putting one foot in front of the other, mile after mile, day after day. It also takes time to reconnect with the landscape, for your feet to accustom themselves to the ground beneath them. Before you take that first step, the path isn't real. It exists only in your mind. A day of the wind numbing your face, skylarks trilling above your head and chalk crunching under your boots, and you regain your footing on the path.

These were my thoughts as I left Firle, with its blacksmiths and brewers, its visionaries and pilgrim priests. I was tempted, contrary to Peter-Owen Jones's advice, to walk along the lower lane, a byway known locally as the Old Coach Road. This route would have taken me close to Charleston Farmhouse, home of the Bloomsbury Group, three of whose members I had visited in Firle churchyard that morning. But I also knew this would be my last full day on the South Downs, my last view from open chalk hills swelling into the horizon. It had been a dry winter so far. In wet weather, travellers followed the ridgeway on the top, avoiding the boggy bottom of the valley. So that's what I would do also.

The Old Way followed the byway for a few hundred metres. Cut into the chalk and flint, it evoked *strade bianche*, the unpaved 'white roads' of Tuscany and Umbria along which I walked when leading groups of hikers through central Italy. This was how most roads looked before the opening of the toll roads, or turnpikes, from the late seventeenth century onwards. Until then, roads were dirty, rutted, and poorly maintained. Privately operated turnpike trusts improved the road system, funding the works by charging its users – much like the toll roads of today. With its compacted chalk base, the Old Coach Road along the foot of the Downs was one of the better surfaces Alice and her companions traversed on their journey to Canterbury, if she passed this way.

Alongside the path the bare fields were tawny-grey, clods of silver brown earth as big as rocks. In the battle between spring and winter, the old season was winning this particular skirmish. At 217 metres high it was a steep climb to Firle Beacon. The path became narrower and claggier, and the flints shone from beneath, lighting my way to the top. Catching my breath, I turned to look back at Firle behind its veil of trees. The scene had changed little in hundreds of years, and was one that the Bloomsbury Group would have known a century earlier.

Hooves had imprinted themselves in the clay, alongside human footprints. As a lady of means, Alice of Southwick might have travelled on horseback. From her saddle she would have noted the weather shifting as she rode up from the valley, felt the strengthening wind on her face and the clouds converging over Firle Beacon. She may have observed a buzzard skimming the thermals below her, musing on how strange it felt to be higher than that buzzard, as if nature had turned on its head. She may have looked back west from where she began her journey, and thought of her home in Southampton and her husband, Richard. And she would have looked south where the sun rained into the sea, and east towards Canterbury, where her walk would end.

West winds nudged the clouds along, and splashes of sunlight illuminated the early greens of spring. I breathed in the rich, grassy scent of sheep droppings, and my legs took on a life of their own. After months sitting at home I felt my fitness levels rising, energy racing through my veins, propelling me along effortlessly towards the hill ahead. Firle Beacon is not a mountain, or even a particularly high hill. But it's the highest point for miles around, and it's where the earth meets the sky. Perhaps that's why our ancestors chose to be buried there. My OS map showed Firle Beacon topped with Bronze Age round barrows, and next to them a Neolithic long barrow known locally as the Giant's Grave. Before the great cathedrals were built, hilltops were as near to heaven as most people got.

Long barrows, like the Giant's Grave, are among the oldest surviving architectural monuments in England. They are also some of the largest. Firle Long Barrow is thirty-three metres long, twenty metres wide and over two metres high. Like Christian cathedrals, it has an east–west orientation. Just as an altar faces east, the doorway of this tomb is aligned with the dawn of summer solstice. Again like cathedrals, long barrows had a mix of uses beyond the burial of human remains, perhaps as places of ritual, or where the living communed with their ancestors. This I could believe. I was alone that day, but I didn't feel lonely in this liminal place. If visions of angels are to be seen anywhere, they are seen here on the summit of Firle Beacon.

The Old Way dropped off the ridge and descended through woodland. Autumn's beech leaves littered the path. With its shallow root system, beech is one of the few trees that grow on these steep-sided hills. A holloway, or bostal, cut through the chalk embankment, leading me directly down and off the Beacon. If a holloway deepens by a metre every 300 years, this one, its banks rising high above my head, was at least six centuries old. In this hollowing lane I was back in Tuscany again, walking the Etruscan *vie cave*: 3,000-year-old roads cut so deep into the rock you're walking beneath the ground rather than over it. This sunken lane, along which the farmers of Alciston once took their sheep to the ridgetop, was a Sussex version of an Etruscan road – secretive, mysterious, magical.

The holloway opened out as I approached Alciston over winter fields the colour of ash. A building as large as a church rose from the flatness. As I entered the village a grey wagtail flitted from the wall, radiating sunshine from its lemon breast, a splash of spring on this first day of February. The roof I saw rising above the village belonged to a late-medieval tithe barn built of sparkling flint. I looked inside, beyond the hay bales to the old timbers that had propped up the barn since the sixteenth century, when it stored the local population's tithes and rents. The remains of a medieval dovecote lay beyond the barn, doves or pigeons being an important source of food in the Middle Ages. And beyond the dovecote was the church, perched on its ancient mound just above level ground.

I was now following the Cuckmere Pilgrim Path. Created in 2018, the route encompasses seven rural Sussex churches around the Cuckmere river, and takes you into Alciston Church, encircled within its protective flint walls and mature trees. Unusually, the church has no dedication, though, like so many of its downland siblings, its origins are twelfth-century. Inside, the nameless church is open to its timbered roof, rather like the medieval barn I'd just passed, though the barn is considerably grander than this simple whitewashed building. With elegant understatement, a notice inside the church read:

> The original church was altered in the 13th century and restored in 1853. The restoration has not been kind to the interior of this ancient place.

Ahead lay Berwick, a few flat fields away, its church spire rising over a palisade of woodland and framed by the South Downs. Spiked hawthorn hedgerows edged the track, no hint of the snowy blossom that would, in a few weeks, erupt from the bushes. St Michael and All Angels in Berwick was the treat I'd been looking forward to all morning, with its interior decorated by Bloomsbury artists Duncan Grant, Vanessa Bell and Quentin Bell. Painted in 1942–3 as an expression of hope in wartime, the story goes that having been refused permission to decorate St Peter's in Firle (perhaps by the same grumpy Reverend A. G. Gregor who'd dismissed Fred Fowler's vision), the artists turned their attention, and their paintbrushes, to Berwick instead.

How I love these flint downland churches with their wood-shingled spires silhouetted against the deep blue sky. Snowdrops swathed the churchyard where I sat. They may be the emblem of early spring but snowdrops may not be native to Britain, and were probably introduced into ornamental gardens in the sixteenth century before later escaping into the wild. Native or not, they decorated churches during Candlemas, giving them their alter-native name of Candlemas Bells. I picked my way through the snowdrops to the church. The door was blocked by the cement mixers and trenches of rebuilding works, so I walked around to the back of the building and, standing on tiptoe, peered in at the interior covered in frescos. Full of colour and life, they couldn't be more different from the little whitewashed church at Alciston I'd just walked from.

A straight track through open fields led me towards Alfriston, the Downs beyond brooding darkly, backs turned against the sun. At the village outskirts, where the track became tarmac, a wooden crucifix stood overlooking the lane. For medieval pilgrims, road-side shrines and crucifixes were a familiar sight, as they are still in southern Europe today. This one had been placed there by Alice S. Gregory, and was dated 28 April 1919, the year after the end of the First World War. What was Alice S. Gregory commemorating, or who had she lost?

The lane dipped down to a village buzzing with school-children, traffic, shoppers and, even on this early February day, lots of tourists. Where there are tourists there are tea shops, and Alfriston has tea shops aplenty. I was headed, though, for the Star Inn, a fifteenth-century inn known until at least 1520 as the Star of Bethlehem and now a smart restaurant. Once run by the monks of Battle Abbey, it accommodated friars and pilgrims on their way to the shrine of St Richard at Chichester, and also offered shelter to pilgrims going in the opposite direction, to the shrine of St Thomas at Canterbury. Alice of Southwick may even have stayed here – or so I liked to think as I sipped my flat white in the pub's cosy half-timbered surroundings.

In many ways it was good to be in civilisation again, especially a place as civilised as the Star Inn, Alfriston. Even so, I am always happier striding out over the hills, and was keen to be on my way. My plan was to reach Wilmington and its famous Long Man before the sun dipped over the horizon, but I couldn't leave Alfriston without stopping by the so-called Cathedral of the Downs, and the medieval Clergy House next door. Former home of the village priest, the thatched and timber-framed Clergy House was the first building to be saved by the National Trust, who in 1896 bought it for £10. Sadly it was still shut for the winter season, though St Andrew's was open. Built on the banks of the Cuckmere at the furthest point medieval ships could reach, the great cruciform church stood aloof on the lip of the Downs, exuding antiquity and peace.

The path took me along a footbridge over the River Cuckmere, which empties into the sea at Cuckmere Haven, for centuries a refuge for smugglers. At this point the Old Way diverts from the South Downs long-distance path, continuing along the Cuckmere Pilgrim Route. As a pilgrim myself, this felt more authentic than the South Downs Way ridge path, which bypasses the villages and churches at the foot of the Downs. Churches such as Lullington, halfway up the hill above the Cuckmere river.

A flurry of pigeons burst from the bushes as I approached. Lovely and lonely, Lullington 'half-church' is a miniature, chapel-like flint building with a wooden bellcote and lichened roof. Only the chancel of a once-larger church remains. Like Alciston, it has no known medieval dedication, but its official name since 2000, the church of the Good Shepherd, was appropriate. This is sheep country after all, a country of folklore and legend, of ancient practices reaching far beyond our post-Christian times.

Inside the church I met Judy and David from Lewes, a retired couple who were on a day out. They gave every impression of being pleased to meet me, quickly introducing themselves. Judy had a New Zealand accent.

'But I've lived in Lewes for a few years now,' she said.

'We're friends,' added David, as if keen I shouldn't assume a closer relationship between them. 'You should have been here a few minutes ago,' David continued. 'A girl was playing the harmonium for us, over there.' He nodded towards the instrument in the corner. Judy asked me about my walk, fascinated to hear about the Old Way. We chatted for a few minutes, then they left. I'd expected to have this solitary little church to myself, but meeting David and Judy added to its magic. You meet the loveliest people in places like Lullington.

It was good to be back on the Downs again. This was the first day of solar spring, but it looked like late summer with the light skimming across the hills, throwing the valleys into shadow. The Old Way rejoins the South Downs Way here, on a wide chalk track that led me steeply up, my unused legs wearying as I neared the top. I followed the track up onto the ridge, and the bright chalk hills rolled out ahead like frozen waves. This is what I'd dreamed of, looking out of my study room in the Pennines that long-ago February day. I hopped over a rickety stile and then, below me on a hillside so sheer it made me dizzy, stood the largest human hill figure in Europe.

I couldn't properly see him from the summit of Windover Hill, just his head, shoulders and right arm. Standing seventy metres tall, the Long Man of Wilmington was cut from the turf in elongated form so, when viewed from the valley, he would assume the proportions of a normal human being. To see him in all his full-length glory I would have to go down the hill and look at him from below. For now I just sat on top of the hill, feeling giddy, watching the miniature people in Wilmington, where my day's walk would end.

It's notoriously difficult to date chalk figures accurately. Newly scraped-away turf looks much like turf scraped away two millennia ago, especially if it's been continually re-cut over the intervening centuries. At some 3,000 years old, the Uffington White Horse in Oxfordshire is generally accepted as the earliest chalk-cut figure in Britain, as well as the most charismatic. In Dorset, the formidable Cerne Abbas Giant has confounded archaeologists and historians for decades, with theories over his age (and it definitely is a he) ranging from prehistoric to post-medieval. Only recently have scientists, using state-of-the-art methods to examine soil samples, revealed his true age as late Anglo-Saxon – to the complete surprise of everyone.

There is similar uncertainty about the Long Man's origin. Some historians are convinced he is prehistoric, while others, citing his similarity to figures on contemporary coinage, suggest a Roman date. Still others are convinced he is Anglo-Saxon, like the Cerne Abbas Giant. Given his proximity to Wilmington Priory, one theory goes that he's a late-medieval pilgrim, which might explain his carrying two poles, rather like modern hikers. Twenty years ago, archaeologists concluded he was made in the sixteenth or seventeenth century.

Either way, the first known illustration of the Long Man was made by the surveyor John Rowley in 1710, where he appears as an indentation in the turf rather than a solid outline. By the nineteenth century his profile was so indistinct that he was marked in yellow bricks to preserve it. The Second World War saw him camouflaged in green to prevent enemy aircraft using him as a landmark, before the restoration in 1969, when he was permanently affixed to Windover Hill with whitewashed concrete blocks. And so he remains to this day.

Though preserving the Long Man for posterity, this solidity erases, for me, some of his allure. The charm of chalk is its pliancy, even for effigies carved into the rock. You have to work to keep chalk figures alive, or they soon disappear back into the turf. That's not to say the job of cleaning chalk figures can't be fun. In Uffington, from at least 1677 until the late eighteenth century, a midsummer 'scouring festival' was held every seven years, during which villagers made merry within the adjacent Iron Age hillfort, Uffington Castle. Over in Dorset, the nineteenth-century Osmington White Horse all but faded away over two years of Covid-19, due to lack of maintenance. Said to represent George III on his mount Adonis, he needed urgent action to polish him up.

Chalk figures, as King George and Adonis proved, need continued effort and commitment to preserve them in all their pristine glory, even if it sometimes goes too far. In January 2021, at the height of the pandemic, the villagers of Wilmington woke to discover a giant white surgical mask had been painted across the Long Man's face. Whether in earnest or in jest, we are continually reaffirming our relationship with our cherished chalk figures, be they human, animal or mythological. In a world of flux, there's a touching permanence in our connection to this most ephemeral of rocks.

Following the Countryside and Rights of Way Act of 2000, much of the South Downs was designated access land where the public have the right to roam freely, so I scrambled down the open hillside. Near the bottom I found a path of crushed chalk that led me beneath the Long Man, still standing in shadow. It's said that the sun doesn't fall onto the Long Man until after the spring equinox, still many weeks away. In high summer he would shine white, then in late September he'd be thrown back into darkness for the winter half of the year.

The descent off the hill was so steep it made my ears pop, but soon I was in the valley. The Long Man was at my back as I followed a narrow path towards the village, the spire of Wilmington Priory my guide. It was the end of a long walk and in the lengthening sun I elongated, like the chalk figure on the hillside. A lone Long Woman approaching the end of a long day's journey.

XVII

Sunshine and birdsong greeted me in Wilmington the next morning. Tarmac glistened wet, the sky was cobalt. The sun was rising over the head of the Long Man, still in his winter shadow. All around him, sheep grazed on the steep hillside, clinging on like mountain goats.

I was standing outside the medieval ruins of Wilmington Priory, a cell of the Benedictine abbey at Grestain in Normandy. Dating to 1100, it's a further token of the long ties between southern England and northern France in the centuries following the Norman Conquest. After its closure in around 1414 it became a residence and then a museum of rural life, before it was restored by the Landmark Trust as holiday accommodation. Downhill from the priory I found the church of St Mary and St Peter. A colossal and hoary yew tree bowed across my path as I entered the churchyard, its trunk contorted into human-like shapes, its branches propped up with huge wooden posts like an old man on crutches. At ground level, the yew's girth measures twenty-three feet. Further up, a chain holds the two twisted halves of the tree together, the wood having grown around the huge, rusted links. A sign stood nearby:

The Wilmington Yew, approximately 1,600 years old.
New wooden props were fitted in 2019.

Considerably older, then, than everything around it – the church, the priory and the Long Man – suggesting this was a pre-Christian sacred site, as yews were frequently planted near holy wells or burial mounds.

The canopy above my head trembled with birdsong. Countless generations of birds and animals have made their homes in this yew, nesting in the holes that crater its trunks, sheltering under its evergreen branches, feeding from its berries before discarding the poisonous seeds. Hoary and tottering it may be, but the new wooden props were evidence of the villagers' continued love for this yew. As much a part of the community as the church it stands beside.

Inside St Mary and St Peter I found a simple whitewashed interior, faint traces of a medieval mural on one of the piers. All was silence, but for the rooks calling me into the countryside. So out I went, through the heavy oak door incised with age-old initials, under the timber-framed porch, and out into the churchyard. Before leaving, I placed my hand on one of the yew's twin trunks. The wood was as hard as rock, but under my palm I could feel a vital being. One living thing, touching another.

A track led me away from Wilmington and its one street of impossibly pretty cottages, back into the hills. The track was a byway, open to all vehicles, including four-wheeled ones. Underfoot were the deep ruts of tyres, the imprint of horses' hooves and, of course, human feet, the most ancient mode of transport of all. Skylarks sang over the fields either side of the track. A more perfect morning to set out on what would be my final walk over the South Downs was hard to imagine.

The track deepened and hollowed as it climbed, and I was soon puffing and out of breath. Then I was on top, striding past a herd of Exmoor ponies, brought onto the Downs to graze the longer, coarser grasses, so allowing wildflowers underneath to catch the sun. With their brown coats, shaggy black manes and grey muzzles they looked prehistoric – as indeed they are. Exmoor ponies have lived in Britain for tens of thousands of years, changing little in the intervening millennia. They looked as if they truly belonged in these hills, far more than the graceful racehorses I'd watched galloping across Firle Beacon the previous day.

I was still following the Old Way, which in turn follows the Wealdway linking the North Downs with the South Downs at Eastbourne. My track contoured the side of the hill, scything through beech woods, bronzed leaves still dangling on winter branches. Ahead, the roofs of suburban Eastbourne shimmered in the sunshine. My walk across the South Downs, which I'd begun in Samhain and ended in Imbolc, would soon be over. Once down in Eastbourne, I wouldn't meet chalk again until my final journey into Canterbury, a whole season away.

Eastbourne would have to wait. First there was Folkington with its church of St Peter ad Vincula, another of those small flint churches clinging on to the edge of the Downs. Firle, Berwick, Alfriston, Wilmington and now Folkington. They were like sisters, built in similar style, with patched flint walls and wood-shingled bell towers. Folkington's churchyard had run charmingly wild, with baroque, ivy-covered gravestones half-hidden in the undergrowth. I was nearly on the fringes of Eastbourne, yet this place felt as remote as a Pyrenean mountain church, the most forgotten and atmospheric of the churches on this stretch of the Downs. Around the back, an old wooden-handled spade was propped up against the wall, rusting and sinking into the earth as if the caretaker had gone for lunch fifty years ago and never returned.

The front door was locked, so I strolled around the churchyard soaking up birdsong and looking at the headstones, stumbling unexpectedly on the grave of cookery writer Elizabeth David. 'Her books on cookery brought joy and enlightenment to food lovers all over the world,' was inscribed on her headstone, alongside a cooking pot surrounded by ingredients. Yesterday I'd passed the home of the Bloomsbury Group, near Firle. Now here was Elizabeth David, buried in the village where she grew up. Eastbourne, where I was heading, was the childhood home of Eric Ravilious, whose watercolours of chalk hills are globally renowned. The South Downs is clearly a landscape of inspiration for artists and writers alike.

Perhaps it's the plasticity of chalk that encourages creativity. The Pennines, where I now live, is an unyielding place. Millstone grit, the local rock, is so hard they used it to grind wheat kernels, with Ted Hughes in his poem 'Wild Rock' describing it as a 'soul-grinding sandstone'. The landscape is austere, the climate can be harsh. Emily, Charlotte and Anne Brontë wrote memorably about the wildness of the moors surrounding their home at

Haworth, but there's something about the softness of chalk that makes artists want to leave their mark. Physically, like the Long Man, in paintings, or in the written word.

The Old Way and Wealdway led me along a white chalk track over the final spur of the South Downs, towards Jevington. The winter sun was brilliant, almost Tuscan in its intensity, rebounding off the chalk into my eyes, flints flashing underfoot. This well-trampled track once tethered the settlements lying at the foot of the Downs. It still does, though in place of the travellers, merchants, soldiers and pilgrims that once journeyed this way was a solitary female walker with her imaginary medieval companion. A mountain cyclist whizzed past, but that was it. The hills might have felt empty that February morning, but my map told a different story. It showed a landscape layered with thousands of years of human activity, a living monument. The link between the past and the present is most powerful, most visceral, on the smooth chalk of the Downs.

In Jevington I paused at the church of St Andrew, its Saxon west tower squarely solid. This was a place of worship, but it was also a place of refuge from the Vikings who reportedly landed at Cuckmere Haven, raiding the coastal villages. So peaceful that day, but this quiet corner of southern England has been invaded and attacked through the ages, from the Normans of 1066 to the Luftwaffe of the Second World War.

I climbed out of Jevington onto Combe Hill, the slopes and billows of the Downs a tartan of washed-out winter greens and the deep tawny-browns of ploughed fields. This was the last hurrah of the South Downs, and the last chalk hill on my Imbolc pilgrimage. And what a hurrah it was. Skylarks sang their summer song, hovering in the ether then swooping down to hide themselves in the grass. These skylarks were the outliers. Later in the spring, perhaps a month from now, other breeding birds would join them, including stonechats and corn buntings.

As I approached the brow of the hill Eastbourne incongruously emerged, and beyond the town, the silver-blue sea. You forget, when you're walking deep in the combes and valleys of the South Downs, how close you are to the English Channel.

I stood on the edge of the escarpment, relishing the moment. It's said that on a clear day you can see the Cotswolds, away to the northwest. Today was pretty clear, just light cloud, but I couldn't see the Cotswolds. To the north and east was the Weald, then the North Downs beyond which lay Canterbury. Eastbourne seeped into the valleys, and I could see the farmland and marshes I would cross before reaching Battle. I took one last look back at the South Downs, and descended a steep, chalk-carved path towards Willingdon. Pausing a moment, I grabbed a lump of chalk from the path, and slipped it into my pocket. I would need it to keep me going across the Pevensey Levels and on to Winchelsea, the final destination on my winter–spring walk.

A path between high-fenced back gardens led me into Willingdon. Subsumed now by greater Eastbourne, Willingdon is nevertheless another of those gorgeous downland villages I'd passed during the last few days. A main street, lined with brick and flint houses. A flint church and, in the churchyard, a yew tree, under which I ate my lunch. This truly was the last of the Downs. Ahead now was the main road, and the modern town of Eastbourne.

I continued east, and Eastbourne fizzled out as I walked over quiet farmland where sheep grazed the meadows and sparrows chirped from hedges, and the traffic on the main road faded to silence. Then, a screech of herring gulls. I was now walking parallel to the coast, and the sea was just over my horizon.

Here, the Old Way follows the 1066 Country Walk, a thirty-one-mile trail beginning in Pevensey and ending in Rye, tracing the route taken by William the Conqueror's army when he invaded England in October 1066. It crossed a strange edgeland of railway lines, pylons, electricity cables: the detritus of modern civilisation. Yet this was an old way. You could see it in the hedgerows, the fragments of ancient woodland and the trace of a drover's road. Old paths and tracks lie burrowed beneath the modern thoroughfares, and may well outlive them.

Just to my south was Hampden Park, childhood home of one of Britain's greatest twentieth-century artists. Born in London in 1903, in early boyhood Eric Ravilious moved with his family to this new suburb north of Eastbourne. The South Downs, a mile or so from his new home, was his playground and, when he began painting, his inspiration. As Ravilious himself wrote, the Downs shaped 'my whole outlook and way of painting . . . because the colour of the landscape was so lovely, and the design so beautifully obvious'. A talented wood engraver, the young artist exploited the stark, elemental whiteness of the chalk, producing exquisite engravings of downland scenes alongside his celebrated watercolours.

Throughout his mid-thirties, Ravilious was a frequent guest at Furlongs, a cottage near Beddingham at the foot of the South

Downs near where I'd walked a couple of days before. Here, he painted watercolour after watercolour of the downland scenery: chalk tracks, winter fields, dew ponds, old farmsteads, even industrial scenes and the Wilmington Giant (as he called it). Travelling away from Sussex, Ravilious also explored the chalk landscapes of Wiltshire, Dorset and Oxfordshire, in 1939 painting an abstract of that most iconic of chalk figures, the Uffington White Horse.

Ravilious wasn't the only artist for whom chalk was the pole-star of his work. His contemporary, Paul Nash, also found artistic stimulation in the chalk landscapes around his Chiltern home, and in the ancient monuments of southern England. Wittenham Clumps, the Iron Age hillfort in Oxfordshire, and Avebury's stone circles in Wiltshire were among his subjects. Today, Nash's most famous works are those he produced during the First World War, which brought home, as did the writings of the War Poets, the savagery of the conflict. Ravilious's own career as a war artist during the Second World War was short-lived, and ended more tragically than Nash's. As an Official War Artist he had already painted scenes of the coastal defences at nearby Beachy Head, and on 2 September 1942, aged thirty-nine, was accompanying a rescue mission off Iceland when his plane was lost at sea.

With his love of the chalk landscapes of southern England, and interest in ancient figures like the White Horse and the Wilmington Giant, Ravilious was tapping into a vogue for all things chalk and prehistoric that evolved in England through-out the early twentieth century. Archaeologists like the great Sir Mortimer Wheeler excavated Iron Age hillforts such as Maiden Castle in Dorset. A couple of decades earlier, authors like Edward Thomas were tramping the chalk trackways of southern England, and writing about them. No wonder, perhaps, that the Second

World War saw chalk dragooned as the emblematic landscape for which Britons were fighting. Eighty years on, we still remember the song '(There'll be Bluebirds Over) The White Cliffs of Dover', made famous by Dame Vera Lynn in 1942.

From the early prehistoric peoples who stippled the Downs with earthworks, to the painters, writers and lyricists of the twentieth century, chalk was the canvas *par excellence*. It still is. On 31 January 2021, on the eve of Britain leaving the European Union, an expression of lament by Stephen Goodall and Sidney 'Sid' Daw, two veterans of the Second World War who had fought for peace and unity in Europe, was projected from a boat in the English Channel onto those famous chalk cliffs.

A further scrap of no man's land belonging to neither town nor country took me to Sharnfold, a scrap of rural East Sussex marooned in a sea of highways. A higgledy-piggledy mass of farm buildings, barns and carthouses, Sharnfold Farm's café was where, over a mug of hot chocolate, I ended that day's walk. The day I bid farewell to chalk until the North Downs near Canterbury, nearly one hundred miles from here. To paraphrase another of Dame Vera's wartime songs, we would meet again.

XVIII

A thick vapour had descended over the land when I left Sharnfold the following morning for my walk across the Pevensey Levels. The onset of rain did not bode well as the levels are reclaimed marshland, which soon relapses to its original state in wet weather. Not only had the landscape changed since I'd left the Downs the day previously, but the climate had reverted from spring to winter.

The rain was not heavy but the ground was already saturated. Within a few minutes my supposedly waterproof boots were letting in water, so at Hankham I followed a minor road to Rickney, avoiding the quagmire as Alice would have done. A veil of drizzle hung over the flatlands. The rain was almost invisible, but it was insidious. It sneaked under my hood, up my sleeves, down my trouser legs. I was wearing the latest technical rain gear but this wasn't rain, it was a dense mist that leached in around the edges of my hood, as if from below.

Thick cloud enveloped the summits of the South Downs, still visible to my left. I was glad to have been up there on clear blue days, the whole of Sussex and Kent laid out before me. Even in the drizzle it was pleasant to be walking along this quiet country lane linking isolated cottages, barns and farmsteads with their back-of-beyond vibe. Eastbourne was just a few miles to the south, yet it was as if I was walking through the badlands of the Wild West rather than the fields of the Mild East. That's what marshlands do to the imagination, I guess. As if to confirm my fantasy a large sign confronted me on the approach to Rickney:

Warning: Surveillance cameras operating in this area

Since the Middle Ages, the Pevensey Levels have been the refuge of vagabonds and smugglers who came ashore unseen at remote Pevensey Bay and hid in the mists and marshes of the hinterland. The hinterland I was now crossing, alone and in the rain, passing hedgerows with thick trunks bent sideways. These hawthorn hedgerows had clearly been pleached, decades or even centuries earlier. From the Latin *plectere*, to plait, a pleached (or plashed) hedge formed an impenetrable, livestock-proof barrier of thickly interwoven stems and branches. In the eighteenth century, at the height of the enclosures, some 200,000 miles of new hedges were planted to break up common and private land; 100,000 of these have been lost since the mechanisation of farming. The pleached hedge approaching Rickney had grown out now, returning to trees, but it was confirmation that under the modern tarmac where I now walked there lay a very old way indeed.

I'd now reached the banks of the Yotham, one of the many rivers, streams and channels cutting through the Pevensey Levels. In 1066, when William of Normandy's men marched from Pevensey to confront Harold Godwinson, this area was a shallow lagoon. Since then, the sea has receded by over a mile, leaving a maze of ditches and streams crossing meadows and marsh.

The drizzle had dissipated by the time I reached the riverbank, but it doesn't take much water to soak ground that is sea kept at bay. You become a sponge, wetness soaking through the soles of your boots, wicking up your socks. I was tempted to avoid the sponge by taking the lane running parallel to the Yotham, but opted to take my chances and follow the riverside walk, hoping to see the birds for which the area is renowned: kingfishers, herons, peregrines and egrets.

Even though they're now drained, there's little human settlement on the levels. You have the landscape to yourself. Just you and the wildlife, and miles of yellow-green flatness, the clouds coalescing where water and sky meet.

My next waypoint was Herstmonceux, just a couple of miles away but invisible in the marsh and the mist. Two miles on boggy terrain is hard going though, and with every step your boot slips back a little. Herstmonceux's domed observatory lay ahead, yet there were no shortcuts over the marsh. It would have been easier walking on a dry summer's day, but the weather suited the ambiguity of a landscape uncertain whether it was land or water. Sunshine bathed the fields ahead, yet I was walking in rain. Clouds hung above me, but over Herstmonceux stretched a band of blue sky.

I saw no kingfishers, herons, egrets or peregrine falcons that day, just a few magpies and pigeons, and a flock of bemused sheep, who stood up and shook their fleeces as I passed. The sun was out now and the observatory's dome glowed ahead. If anything it seemed to be getting further away, mirage-like, as the riverbank path meandered through the marsh. I felt lonely, aware of my solitude out there on the levels. On the Downs there were always other walkers shouting cheery greetings as they passed. Here the sheep offered the only companionship, except for a lone skylark, singing far away over the marsh.

At last, the path wrenched itself away from the river towards Herstmonceux, following a ditch hidden under wool-snagged hawthorns, the dense thicket a habitat for birds and other wildlife. I didn't stop at Herstmonceux, despite its magnificent moated castle. It had begun drizzling again and I wanted to reach Wartling before dark. The track was slightly elevated above the levels now, and the terrain drier, although by this time my boots were so sodden it made little difference. A secretive, hedge-lined path took me off the mud to the edge of Wartling. Here I did see wildlife: robins, blackbirds, a flash of yellow that may have been a great tit. I was happy to reach Wartling, where the church of St Mary Magdalene was a refuge for this wet and weary pilgrim.

Wiping my boots, I went inside and sat down in one of the box pews, acclimatising to my new surroundings. The bedrock had changed since I'd left the Downs, and so had the architecture. No flint and weatherboard here; Wealden houses are timber-framed, and have vast, hipped roofs, or they are built of sandstone, also named greensand by pioneering geologist William 'Strata' Smith

(1769–1839) for its greenish tinge. Like chalk, greensand is sedimentary, laid down between fifty and 140 million years ago and divided into Upper and Lower. I'd already met the clays of the Low Weald, wooded and watery and wrapped by its greensand ridge, crossing the Pevensey Levels. Greensand underpins the High Weald, the landscape of wooded hills and sandstone outcrops, small – often medieval – fields and isolated farmsteads through which I was now walking.

In Old English, *wald* meant 'forest'. Dense woodland once cloaked the greensand, largely cleared by Neolithic settlers and later tribes to leave the rich farmland of East Sussex, Surrey and Kent. For the Anglo-Saxons, this was 'Andredesweald', or 'the forest of Andred', from *Anderida*, the Roman name for Pevensey. It was also the name of the Druid group with whom I'd celebrated Imbolc a few days earlier, in the meadow next to Wilmington Priory.

The sun had come out again when I left St Mary Magdalene. I looked back at the Downs, now just blue shadows on the horizon, white clouds cleaving to their tops. Wartling was a natural place to finish my day's walk, but it was just a couple of miles on to Boreham Street, where the Gough Map makes an unscheduled stop. So I strode out along a lane edged with mature oaks and thick hazel hedgerow hung with pale-yellow catkins, the westering sunshine warming my back. It felt good to be walking on solid ground again. I just don't do mud.

Boreham Street is the only place on the Gough Map's itinerary that doesn't have a holy site associated with it, though settlements with the suffix 'street' were often situated on ancient thoroughfares, such as Roman roads. In 1086, the year of the Domesday survey, Boreham Street had a population of 280, land able to support eighteen ploughs, woodland for 200 pigs, three salt workings

and a chapel, and is depicted on the Gough Map as a single building. Today, it sits halfway between Hailsham and Battle, a village
of weatherboard houses and saggy-tiled roofs, and cleft by the
A271 – the 'street' that gave the village its name and which took
me, via a circuitous bus route, to my bed for the night.

Where Alice and her companions slept, I never knew.

XIX

The next morning I was back in Boreham Street and, with a
vengeance, so was the rain. The Gough Map's next stop was
Battle, as was mine. Mushy fields and sodden paths lay ahead, so
like any sensible medieval pilgrim I took the drier route, avoiding
the waterlogged valley bottom.

Tilley Lane was another of those scooped-out holloways that
wayfarers have used for centuries, hollowing and deepening as it
descended the hill towards Nunningham Stream. Tree roots dug
into the clay banks as if clinging on for dear life. Up it climbed
again, through brown bare fields, the Wealden landscape evaporating into the mist. On Brown Bread Lane I passed isolated
farmhouses, weatherboarded and rickety, turning their backs to
the rain and passers-by. Even the Ash Tree Inn was barred to this
wet traveller, craving a cup of hot coffee.

I was now back on the 1066 Country Walk, and my destination was the hamlet of Penhurst and then Battle – around ten miles
in all. Rain was still falling when I arrived at Penhurst, so I took
refuge in the ancient porch of St Michael's Church, under timbers
greyed and wood-wormed and inscribed with medieval carvings.
In the graveyard, snowdrops had forced their heads through the
turf and glistened in the easing rain. Across from the porch was

Penhurst Manor, now Penhurst Retreat Centre, and as peaceful a spot as you could wish for. It was hard to leave the shelter of the porch, and the serenity of the view, and move on. But move on I did, down a lane where snowdrops smothered the banks, to Ashburnham Forge.

At least the rain had stopped, and although the clouds had lifted, my spirits had not. This was the lowest point in my journey so far, psychologically at least. For two days I'd had an exhilarating walk over the Downs, where the light was crystalline and the vistas endless. Now I was down in the valleys, drenched and disheartened. Winchelsea, although now only two days' walk away, still felt far off. And I was lonely. Walking on the Downs, even in winter, you meet the occasional walker, a companion-in-arms. Here on the Weald, trudging through waterlogged fields and leafless woods, I felt bleak. I missed home, I missed Richard and I missed my cats.

Low spirits must have afflicted pilgrims throughout the ages, too. You set off with high hopes, but there comes a point when you wonder why you're putting yourself through this ordeal. Just as I was now. The end of my journey seemed as far off as its beginning, but here I was, in its muddy midst, hundreds of miles from home. There was nothing for it but to continue putting one sodden foot in front of another, head down. Pressed into the mud underfoot were the boot prints of fellow walkers who had passed this way not long before me, and they gave me comfort.

Once they'd left home, medieval pilgrims would have had no word from their loved ones for weeks, months, or years. I could at least speak to Richard and my parents. This easy connectivity had its downsides – the emails and WhatsApp messages that kept pinging into my phone. I had turned off sound notifications, but every time I looked at my phone to check the digital map against my soggy paper one, those insistent icons popped up on the screen that I just couldn't ignore. Were we really that much better off than our medieval forebears?

My head was as low as my mood as I watched the path disappear under my feet. I forced myself to look up to the sky, at the gunmetal clouds suspended above the woods, the trees bare and bony. In full summer leaf, trees are shelter from the sun and rain. They're a traveller's friend. In winter they're almost hostile, with their strange, contorted forms and rooks gyrating above. Or maybe it was just my imagination that wet February day.

I squelched on, over fields and through woodland. As I neared the road the sky split, and a thin sliver of turquoise burst through the cloud. I peeled back my hood, the rustle of Gore-tex ebbed away and I heard the world again. 'Tea-cher tea-cher tea-cher,' called a lone great tit from the tree canopy, serenading me through the woodland until I reached a dry track leading across the Normanhurst Estate to Catsfield. At last, I could stride out over the landscape rather than slipping and sliding through it.

Like so many of the East Sussex churches I'd visited, St Laurence lies a short distance outside its village. Buttressed, and buffeted by wind, St Laurence had been here 1,000 years and wasn't going anywhere soon. Inside, the atmosphere was medieval, hushed and enchanted. I wanted to sit there and rest, but it was cold and to keep warm I had to keep moving.

So on I walked, through woodland and pasture where horses grazed and gorse unfurled. A buzzard lifted from the ground, perching on a branch to watch me pass. I met no one else that afternoon, yet a millennium ago this innocent, pastoral setting witnessed the most momentous conflict in English history. The clues were there, in the landscape. To my right was Saxon Wood. In front, Senlac Hill, where, one October day in 1066, tens of thousands of men were slaughtered. History was made on this hill, and it was history I trod under my feet as I trudged up the slope towards Battle.

Ahead was the great gatehouse of Battle Abbey, about to shut its doors for the night. I was too late, but I didn't mind. It had stood there for nearly 700 years and it would still be standing there tomorrow.

XX

The morning started cold, bright and fresh. I had dried off and warmed up overnight, and the previous day's mud was only encrusted onto my trousers rather than soaking through them. I was now five days into my week's walk, and had another two to go. Depending on the weather and the state of the ground underfoot, I would walk on to Westfield, and then to Doleham eight miles away.

I was keen to get underway before the weather turned again, but leaving Battle without visiting the abbey was unthinkable. Entering through the gatehouse I walked around the precinct walls, begun in 1338 when the Crown granted the abbey permission to fortify itself against French raids during the Hundred Years' War (1337–1453). Religious buildings were particularly vulnerable to attack, and fortifying them offered protection and refuge to the town's citizens as well as to their own inhabitants.

Seven centuries on not much of the abbey remains, having been given the *coup de grâce* by Henry VIII in 1538, along with the rest of England's religious houses. I walked over the grass to where the chancel of the abbey church once stood, and where a large stone plaque is set into the ground.

Between the Chalk and the Sea

*The traditional site of
the high altar of Battle Abbey
founded to commemorate
the victory of Duke William
on 14 October 1066
the high altar was placed to mark
the spot where King Harold died*

History, as the adage goes, is written by the winners. This was true of the Romans, who, on taking power from the Etruscans in central Italy, hijacked many of their innovations and reinvented them as their own. It is also true of the Battle of Hastings. The Bayeux Tapestry is the most celebrated of the battle's accounts, while written chronicles include those of William of Poitiers (1020–90), Duke William's chaplain and author of *Gesta Guillelmi*, the *Deeds of William*. Both tell the same, one-sided story.

In 1051, King Edward the Confessor, whose mother, Emma, was Norman, appointed William, Duke of Normandy, as his heir. Thirteen years later the Saxon earl Harold Godwinson, Edward's brother-in-law, swore an oath of fealty to William at Bonneville-sur-Touques following his shipwreck off the Normandy coast. On Edward's death in January 1066, Harold broke his oath and assumed the English throne, an act which William took as a personal insult. On 28 September that year, and accompanied by 700 ships, William landed in Pevensey, intending to take the Anglo-Saxon kingdom by force.

As William was massing his armies, Harold Godwinson was at Stamford Bridge in Yorkshire, where he had just defeated Harald Hardrada, king of Norway, who, adding to the complexity, also had a claim to the English throne. Arriving in London on 6 October, Harold marched with his exhausted troops directly to Sussex to challenge the Norman Duke. William meanwhile, who had learned of Harold's advance, chose to confront Harold at his camp at Senlac Hill, on a spur of the South Downs near Hastings. As the *Anglo-Saxon Chronicle* relates, on 14 October 'William came against [Harold] unawares, before his people were set in order'.

William of Poitiers takes up the story. He tells how the English soldiers, 'descended from the ancient Saxons (the fiercest of men), are always by nature eager for battle'. The Duke and his men, 'in no way dismayed by the difficulty of the ground, came slowly up the hill and the terrible sound of trumpets on both sides signalled the beginning of the battle'. At first the Normans, with the element of surprise, had the advantage. The English, meanwhile, 'resisted valiantly, each man according to his strength, and they hurled back spears and javelins and weapons of all kinds together with axes and stones fastened to pieces of wood'. The battle raged, and the 'shouts both of the Normans and of the barbarians were drowned in the clash of arms and by the cries of the dying'. The English, on higher ground, remained in position and 'inflicted losses upon the men who were shooting missiles at them from a distance'.

The battle, which had begun in the morning, continued throughout the day with large losses on both sides. Nine hours later there was stalemate. The Normans, believing William had been killed, began to flee. The Duke, still very much alive, rallied his troops to attack once again. The decisive blow came, as every schoolchild knows and the Bayeux Tapestry portrays, when Harold was shot in the eye by a Norman arrow. Or was he? The monk William of Jumièges, another chronicler of the battle, describes his death differently: 'Harold himself, fighting amid the front rank of his army, fell covered with deadly wounds.' In other words, he was hacked to pieces. Either way, the battle was decided. Leaderless, the English resistance soon collapsed, and the fleeing English troops were butchered by pursuing Norman soldiers.

Up to 10,000 men are believed to have died that day. The *Anglo-Saxon Chronicle* speaks of 'great slaughter on both sides', while William of Poitiers wrote that 'far and wide, the earth was covered with the flower of the English nobility and youth, drenched in blood'. Recently, some historians have speculated their bodies may be buried in Malfosse ditch at the bottom of Caldbec Hill, to the east of the town and around a mile from the official battleground, throwing into doubt the true site of the conflict.

Whatever the battle's exact location, the upshot was that on 25 December 1066 William was crowned king of England in Westminster, and the course of English history swivelled on its axis. Within a generation a new ruling class had taken hold, and Norman laws, architecture, language and customs were adopted – although strong resistance remained in the north of the country. In 1070, William, overcome with remorse at the bloodshed, ordered a great abbey to be built. Its high altar occupied the spot where Harold fell.

All that violence was hard to swallow that benevolent February morning as I strolled through the abbey grounds, the birds chirping peaceably. The violence didn't even end in 1066. Within 500 years, one of William's direct descendants ordered the complete destruction of the abbey church, and most of its monastic buildings. The best preserved of what remains today is the thirteenth-century dormitory, now roofless, where the monks slept in beds arranged along the side walls. Under open skies I walked to its southern end, where, through gaping lancet windows, I saw the Weald pitching and rolling towards the sea.

Most of the other monastic buildings have gone. There are the ruins of the refectory where monks took their midday meal, sitting on long benches and eating in silence while listening to readings from the pulpit. Of the chapter house, the focal point of monastic life, nothing remains except its foundations and a wall where I read this notice:

> *This stone has been set in this place to*
> *commemorate the fusion of the English*
> *and Norman peoples, which resulted from*
> *the great battle fought here in 1066.*

Nearly 1,000 years on from the battle, after a millennium of uneasy peace punctuated by periods of intense hostility, we were again separating from our continental neighbours. I pondered this as families wandered through the ruins, enjoying the early spring sunshine. The buildings might be relics, but history is still alive, lying dormant beneath our feet.

It was almost time to go. On my way out I climbed a steep spiral staircase onto the upper floors of the gatehouse from where there's a 360-degree view of the countryside. The upper room houses a museum of objects found in the abbey grounds. Fragments of stained glass, painted floor tiles, pottery urns and pieces of sculpture are all that remain of one of England's richest monasteries.

Wealthy and powerful perhaps, but monasteries were the lifeblood of the towns that grew around them, delivering medical treatment, education and refuge, as well as accommodation for passing pilgrims. The relationship between a medieval town and its abbey was deep-seated and symbiotic, and lasts until this day, 500 years after the Dissolution. Twenty-first century Battle is a tourist destination, the shops, pubs and tea rooms supplying the goods and services to the abbey's visitors that they would have once done for the monks. To witness this relationship at its most visceral, visit the town in early October, when a re-enactment of the Battle of Hastings takes place in the same field where King Harold and Duke William fought so fiercely in 1066.

I climbed a further flight of stairs, and looked over the parapet to Battle's high street of red-tiled roofs and jumble of pretty facades. The parish church of St Mary, built by Abbot Ralph for the townsfolk in the twelfth century, was to my right. Below stood the fifteenth-century timber-framed abbey guesthouse where Alice might have lodged, now a wedding venue renamed Pilgrim's Rest. Beyond lay the fields and woodland of the Weald. Much of the country surrounding the town was owned by the abbey after William the Conqueror granted it all the land within a radius of one and a half miles of the high altar.

Yesterday's rain and despondency now forgotten, I left the abbey and set off under blue skies, renewed. There was one last church to visit before leaving Battle, and I found it on the Old Way out of town.

St Mary's, standing by the north wall of the abbey, is a large, buttressed church built of local greensand. By the time it was founded in the twelfth century, the Normans had well and truly embedded themselves into English life, and although Latin remained the language of most legal documents, Anglo-Norman French was used by royalty and nobility, and for trade. Until Geoffrey Chaucer popularised it as a literary language, only uneducated people spoke the vernacular, the idiom we now call Middle English. Even so, most ordinary folk were illiterate, and parishioners relied on pictures, stained in glass or painted on walls, to relate the biblical narratives and lives of the saints. St Mary's was no exception, and above the arches are faded traces of St Margaret of Antioch among the murals that in 1300 would have covered these walls.

I wandered through the nave to the Lady Chapel, and the gilded alabaster tomb of Sir Anthony Browne, 1548, beneficiary of the abbey on its suppression ten years earlier. As I was standing there, musing on the irony of this turn of events, a smiling dark-haired woman approached. She introduced herself as Angie, the wife of the Dean of Battle.

'Have you seen the Crusader crosses?' Angie asked me in a soft South African accent. I hadn't. She led me over to a side chapel at the end of the south aisle and pointed to some small crosses incised into one of the stone pillars. 'This is where the Crusaders came back and blunted their swords in penance for the bloodshed they'd caused,' she said, referring to the series of religious wars involving Christians and Muslims between 1096 and 1291. One of the Christians' avowed aims was to protect pilgrims travelling to the Holy Land, giving rise to the noble orders of the Knights Hospitaller and Knights Templar.

'How do they know they're Crusader crosses, and not made by other people?' I asked, squinting into the shadows.

'Well, it's information that's been passed down through generations in the church's history,' replied Angie.

Three centuries after the religious fervour that saw knights and knaves throughout Europe leave their homes to wage war in a far-off continent, Henry VIII renounced the Church in Rome and, with it, medieval ideology. In 1534, using the pretext of Protestantism, he declared himself the Supreme Head of the Church in England, and set about destroying every one of England and

Wales's 800 abbeys, priories and nunneries at a time when royal finances needed a boost. While he was about it, Henry outlawed pilgrimage, and although little physical evidence of pilgrim routes like the Old Way survive, they remain incised in our collective memory. Just like the little crusader crosses carved into the masonry of St Mary's Church so many centuries before.

Angie was from South Africa, not from Battle. Yet these stones spoke as powerfully to her as if she had been born and bred in this small East Sussex town rather than in a faraway country in the southern hemisphere.

It was late morning when I finally left the church, passing Lake Field on my way out of town. The National Trust, who in 1938 bought the field to preserve the view north to Caldbec Hill, had placed a plaque by the gate showing a handful of significant places and their distance from Battle. Two hundred and twenty miles north was Stamford Bridge, where Harold Godwinson defeated Harald Hardrada before marching south to confront Duke William. Saint-Valery-sur-Somme, where William assembled his fleet before sailing to Pevensey, was seventy-one miles to the south. Sussex is not only closer geographically to France than to much of England, it is also closer geologically. Connected by chalk, and divided by the narrowest of seas.

I was still following the 1066 Country Walk through Battle Great Wood, on a bridleway clogged with hoof prints. Alice of Southwick, if she passed this way, would have been used to the mud and mire. After the Roman occupation and before toll roads, travelling was a mucky affair. At least this was a straight, wide track, and easy to follow. Once the property of the abbey, Battle Great Wood has always been a managed woodland. Between the sixteenth and nineteenth centuries its timber supplied the local shipbuilding industry, and its sweet chestnuts are still coppiced, continuing the wood's links with the area that have lasted seven centuries.

A buzzard spun overhead, keening. I was not her intended prey, but when you see a raptor with a one-metre wingspan eyeing you as you walk alone through a dark forest, it sends a shiver down your spine. As soon as it began, the ancient wood ended and I found myself walking through the middle of Sedlescombe Golf and Country Club. I passed by, unheeded by the golfers. Nobody looked up, or acknowledged my presence in the way a fellow walker might. I was a ghost, drifting silently between the bunkers. The golfers were so engrossed in their game they didn't see me walking across the middle of a putting green as flat and lifeless as a billiard table. Two worlds, the walker and the golfer, each invisible to the other, passing like supertankers in the night.

The track entered woodland once again, and I walked on past banks popping with snowdrops, their heads the colour of the snow that never arrived that winter. Along the valley bottom I trudged, through a wetland of thicket and bog and hazel trees, pale catkins unfurling from their branches. The wetland had a wild, untamed, primeval atmosphere, as if the dinosaurs that roamed here when this part of Sussex was closer to the Equator than the North

Pole might reappear at any moment to nibble, giraffe-like, at the vegetation.

The wild wetland valley wound round to Westfield, and the church of St John the Baptist on the fringes of the village. Two yew trees stood sentinel across the brick churchyard path, which led to a square, solid, castle-like structure. The Normans again, declaring through their macho architecture, 'we're here to stay.'

I entered St John's via its nail-studded door, the date 1542 hammered on in iron. Inside, the church is just as virile as its exterior, with scalloped piers and round arches, the capitals of its chancel arch decorated with foliage. How powerful the presence of the Normans was on my Wealden walk. You feel them watching over you all along this stretch of coast, but as you near Kent, where French shores are just thirty miles away, it's visceral.

The Old Way leaves Westfield along ancient, hollowed paths and heads east, over wood-crested hills, past sandstone outcrops, across open heaths and through hedged fields. In 1993 the High Weald was designated an Area of Outstanding Natural Beauty for its medieval landscape, virtually unaltered since the four-teenth century and one of the best-preserved in Northern Europe – very different from the open, Iron Age South Downs, where my winter walk began. Now, six days later, I was nearing its end, past brambles that, in late summer, would be drooping with blackberries.

Crossing a railway line I reached a quiet lane which led me to Doleham station. Here, if you're lucky, the train will whisk you from its tiny platform on the Marshlink line to Hastings, and your bed for the night, for there is nothing at Doleham village except a row of terraced cottages spilling down the hillside into the lonely valley below. I sat for a while inside the one platform's Lilliputian wooden waiting room. The sky was darkening once again, and I smelled rain in the wind. The one train that day was not due for another few hours, so I pulled my phone out of my jacket pocket and dialled a taxi. It's what Alice would have done, after all.

XXI

A week earlier I had been standing in a human circle next to Wilmington car park, under still skies and the gaze of the Long Man, celebrating the Druid rite of Imbolc. Snowdrops corralled us, soft winds blew through the tree canopy and spring seemed to have arrived. Now, walking from Doleham that Sunday morning, the season had backtracked to winter. Overnight rain had soaked the ground, and clouds flung showers from above. But I was not downcast, for this was the final leg of my walk to the medieval town of Winchelsea, the next waypoint on the Gough Map and now just a few miles away.

A quiet lane led me east along the Old Way, high above the River Brede. Below, Brede Level fringed the Romney Marshes, the enigmatic flatland of water and mists, empty skies, isolated churches and remote hamlets that I would cross on the final leg to Canterbury. From the hedgerow a robin chirped, eventually showing himself, hopping among the bare-leaved branches. I'd seen robins throughout my week's walk. It was as though the same one had been following me all the way from Lewes, popping out of the hedges as I passed, then fluttering back in again. Like Alice, he was my constant companion.

A tractor-rutted track, gloopy after the night's rain, contoured downhill through pasture. Alice, I thought a little uncharitably, did not have tractor ruts to contend with, though cartwheels chewed up the ground nearly as effectively. No one was about that blustery morning, no joggers, no dog-walkers, no cyclists. A path through moor, interlaced with dykes and crossed by wooden bridges, led me down to Lower Snailham on the edge of the floodplain. It's never easy to find your bearings in flatlands such as this, particularly in bad weather, though the 1066 Country Walk markers kept pointing me in the right direction, towards Icklesham.

Walking on the Downs a few days before I had never felt lonely. Not only because more people were enjoying the well-trodden paths of England's newest National Park, but because my horizon stretched so far in each direction. Wherever I looked, I saw the hills rippling away, and each hilltop revealed the evidence of humankind – the tumuli, long barrows and hillforts that studded the landscape for miles. Here in the Brede Valley, even though I was never further than a mile or two from a village, I felt so alone. If I fell into one of these watery dykes and drowned, I thought gloomily, nobody would find me until some archaeologist dug up my remains aeons later, like Boxgrove Woman.

In spring, summer or autumn, or even a dry day in winter, this would be a beautiful walk. I would see the lapwings and herons – maybe even the cuckoos – that live in this empty water-land of reeds and carrs, springs and ditches. If I didn't fall into a dyke and drown I would come back and walk here when I could look up at the skies, instead of down, doggedly, at the path disappearing under my boots.

It felt endless, this wet, wetland walk. I couldn't change my mind and turn back. Winchelsea was only three miles further on, but it might have been a hundred, so dispirited was I by the mud and the rain. I just had to forget Winchelsea, and keep putting one foot in front of the other until, step by soggy step, I would reach my destination. Wasn't this true of life, as well as walking? This, surely, was how pilgrimage differed from an ordinary walk.

Pilgrimage was an allegory for life. You cannot turn back however bad the weather, and however difficult the path.

Then, a miracle. I was climbing on a gravel track out of the levels and the gloom, up onto the hills. Dryish underfoot, protected by old and twisting hedgerows, with views all around – even though they were mostly of mist. This was my kind of Old Way. The rain had stopped and fields glistened, great clods of tawny earth thrown up by the plough in deep, mechanically scoured furrows. Anglo-Saxon farmers once worked this landscape, their scratch-ploughs pulled by pairs of oxen, sowing the barley and rye, oats, beans and peas that made up their diet. Could they have imagined that their lighter-touch ploughing, and their system of rotating crops rather than drenching them in chemical fertiliser, was best? Or that farmers are now turning to 'no-till' cultivation as a means to minimise soil erosion and nutrient depletion? Soil scientists warn that with modern industrialised farming methods, soil health is becoming compromised. Time, perhaps, for the Anglo-Saxons to return to the Weald with their scratch ploughs.

I reached the last summit before Icklesham. The clouds parted and the Romney Marshes opened out in a canvas of watercolour greys and greens towards the North Downs, where my feet would, on the next leg of my journey, meet chalk once again. The sun had beaten away the gloom, and the pasture through which I now walked glittered after the rain. The Old Way was taking me through a hidden valley where blackbirds sang, the sun sprinkled watery rays onto my face, and glorious green meadow tingled in anticipation of spring.

Strategically located on a peninsula on the once-broad, once-navigable River Brede, Icklesham was managed by Fécamp Abbey in Normandy even before the Conquest, and deemed by Duke

William a legitimate target. Two centuries after his invasion, the great storm of 9 February 1287 transformed Icklesham from an important port with an expensively rebuilt Norman church to a quiet village marooned a couple of miles inland. This was one of two 'great storms' that year. The other, on the east coast, killed hundreds of people and drowned thousands more on the opposite shores of the North Sea.

This was just how I found Icklesham nearly eight centuries later, when I climbed up the slope to the church of All Saints and St Nicolas – the 'Nicolas' added after Henry VIII's objection to 'all saints'. When I pushed open the doors, Sunday Eucharist had just ended and the church had recently emptied. A churchwarden was busying herself turning off lights, and was clearly perturbed by my unexpected arrival.

'I'm just locking up,' she said as I peeped in at the massive early Norman piers of Caen stone with their delicately carved scallop capitals. Icklesham was a waypoint on the route to the ports for France and Spain, and I'd read about the crosses chiselled into the columns by medieval pilgrims travelling to Santiago de Compostela, and doubtless to Canterbury also, and was looking forward to seeing them.

'Can I just have a brief look around?' I asked. 'I'll only be a few moments and I've walked a long way to get here.' It was true – I had walked a long way to get there. Not just from Doleham that morning, or even from Lewes a week ago, but from Southampton many months and 170 miles ago.

'I've got other churches to lock up this morning, sorry,' said the churchwarden. 'There's a nice church at Winchelsea, though. That should be open today.' She wasn't going to soften, and I wasn't in the mood to argue, so I left her to finish turning off the lights and went on my way. This had been the first church on my pilgrimage so far where I hadn't felt welcome, but I wasn't going to let it spoil my day. And she was right: there is a nice church at Winchelsea. Not only a nice church, but one of the most magnificent in East Sussex.

The Old Way led me up Hogg Hill, where, at the summit, I found a traditional weatherboard windmill, its great white wooden sails still attached. Originally built in nearby Pett, it was moved to Icklesham in 1790 and was operated by wind until 1920. Its chief claim to fame today is as the recording studios of Paul McCartney, who bought the mill in 1981.

Here I paused, and looked back for the last time to the Downs, which had almost disappeared behind the High Weald. Ahead, fewer than two miles away, was the sea. I'd left the chalk behind, and was now approaching the coastline that had shaped English history. The Norman Conquest, the French raids of the Hundred Years' War, when England contested the succession to the French throne, the Napoleonic threat of the early 1800s, the airborne Battle of Britain in 1940 – they all transpired along this slender stretch of shore.

This coast still shapes events. In place of French soldiers or German bombers, migrants are crossing the Channel everyday, risking their lives in the hope of a better one. This shoreline stands at the frontline of our island story, and Winchelsea, now so near, tells that story better than anywhere on my journey so far.

Watching the sea, even the English Channel on a grey day, is always uplifting. It was the sea that drove me the final few miles towards Winchelsea. I climbed a last hilltop, past a concrete pillbox, and looked out over the Channel. There was nothing that day, not even a boat on this, the busiest shipping lane in the world. Yet somewhere below the pewter sea lay the submerged town of Old Winchelsea. An English Atlantis, dramatically lost under the

'No one has avenged me'

The next flashpoint came with the coronation of the king's eldest son – also called Henry – as the Young King, or king-in-waiting. With Becket out of the country, the Archbishop of York and the bishops of London and Salisbury officiated. Becket retaliated by excommunicating all three, sending Henry into a rage. The one-time friends had become sworn enemies.

At this point, the Pope interceded by encouraging a meeting between the two men. This led to an uneasy truce, and Becket made plans to return to England, arriving back in Canterbury on 2 December 1170. On Christmas Day he preached a sermon in the cathedral prophesying that the time of his death was close at hand.

Around this time, the three excommunicated bishops made their way to the king, then in Normandy, to seek his support against Becket.

Henry's rage was well known. His precise words are not, but Becket's biographer Edward Grim, a clerk who was also injured at his martyrdom, recorded him as saying:

'What miserable drones and traitors have I nourished and promoted in my household who would let their lord be treated with such shameful contempt by a low-born clerk.'

Another version has him saying:

'A man . . . who has eaten my bread, who came to my court poor, and I have raised him high – now he draws up his heel to kick me in the teeth! He has shamed my kin, shamed my realm; the grief goes to my heart, and no-one has avenged me.'

Among those present were four knights: Hugh de Morville, Richard Brito, William de Tracy and Reginald Fitzurse. Together they hatched a plan to travel to Canterbury, apparently to arrest Becket on the king's behalf and bring him to trial at the royal court. By doing this they hoped to curry royal favour. What might have been an official arrest party appears instead to have been a scheme concocted on their own initiative.

waves nearly 800 years ago, never to be seen again. Way beyond, on its shingle spit in the brown-grey water, white breakers pushing towards the coast, was Dungeness nuclear power station. One millennium of history on a windswept hill swooping down to the levels and the sea.

Just ahead, and screened by woodland, was Winchelsea, marked on the Gough Map as *wynchelsee*. I followed the Old Way along a lane verged with sunshine-yellow aconites, precursor to the daffodils that would appear later that month, and across sheep pasture to Wickham Manor. This great stone house, its tiled roof interrupted by huge chimney stacks, has stood here in various incarnations since the twelfth century. Now owned by the National Trust, it's a working farm and vineyard, and also a bed and breakfast – an ideal stopover for footsore pilgrims. Winchelsea, the final destination of my Imbolc journey, was just a sheep-cropped pasture away and I wasn't going to stop now.

I entered what remains of the old town through the New Gate. The late thirteenth-century gate is not that new, and though it's lost its roof it retains much of its walls, pierced by a tall archway. A defensive ditch called the Town Dyke once crossed the front, spanned by a bridge. Nearing the gate today, you sense how forbidding it must have been to those approaching the town in the Middle Ages. Not forbidding enough, though, to deter the French forces who raided Winchelsea in 1380, ransacking the town.

Today, the New Gate is stranded half a mile from the centre of Winchelsea, a clue to the ambitions for this medieval planned town. A last steep push uphill, and I was following an oak-lined lane high above the marsh past the ruins of St John's Hospital, where the elderly, infirm and passing pilgrims stayed. No traces remain of Winchelsea's two other hospitals, Holy Rood and St Bartholomew.

I walked on until I reached the church of St Thomas the Martyr – the martyr, of course, being Thomas Becket. I had now completed three quarters of my journey, and Canterbury was within arm's reach. Only another week's walk across marsh, weald and down separated us.

In the churchyard I sat a while among the gravestones and snowdrops. Half a church stood in front of me. When it was founded in 1288 by King Edward I, St Thomas was to be a much larger building, a magnificent church befitting the great planned town. Today, it stands only part-built, testament to Winchelsea's sudden and catastrophic decline. How did this happen? I wanted to find out, but I was cold, muddy and wet. I was delighted to have reached Winchelsea, but I wanted to go home. Proper home, not just a hotel bedroom. For a perennially rootless person who has spent a lifetime hankering after new places, this was an unaccustomed feeling.

I walked over to the shelter from where, I hoped, the No. 100 bus would soon carry me back to Hastings. It had started raining again. A week ago, I had begun my walk at Imbolc, the first day of solar spring. Now I was ending it back in winter.

The tale of two cities, Old and New Winchelsea, would have to wait for another walk, and another season.

Pilgrimages to Saint Mary of Walsingham and Saint Thomas of Canterbury

Desiderius Erasmus, *c*.1511

Desiderius Erasmus (1469–1536) was a Dutch theologian, philosopher and humanist, and editor of the New Testament. He was committed to the reform of the Catholic Church, and wrote this satirical 'colloquy' (dialogue) about his expedition to England's two principal shrines. This version is from an edition published in 1849.

OGYGIUS: Know, then, that those who journey to London, not long after leaving Canterbury, find themselves in a road at once very hollow and narrow, and besides the banks on either side are so steep and abrupt, that you cannot escape; nor can you possibly make your journey in any other direction. On the left hand of this road is a hospital of a few old men (60), one of whom runs out as soon as they perceive any horseman approaching; he sprinkles his holy water, and presently offers the upper part of a shoe, bound with a brazen rim, in which is a piece of glass resembling a jewel. Those that kiss it give some small coin.

ME: In the same road I would rather meet with a hospital of old men than a band of valiant robbers.

OGYGIUS: Gratian rode on my left hand, next to the hospital. He was covered with water; however, he endured that. When the shoe was stretched out, he asked the man what he wanted. He said that it was the shoe of St Thomas. On that my friend was irritated, and turning to me he said,

'What, do these brutes imagine that we must kiss every good man's shoe? Why, by the same rule they would offer his spittle to be kissed, or other bodily excrements.' I pitied the old man, and by the gift of a small coin I comforted his trouble.

BELTANE

*'An ancient Celtic festival celebrated on May Day,
marked by bonfires being kindled on the hills'*

WINCHELSEA TO CANTERBURY

XXII

It was the last day of April, and the day before Beltane, when I found myself back in Winchelsea. The sun was hot on my face, spilling through clouds that thickened and threatened rain, or worse. Tomorrow would be May Day, the ancient festival and modern bank holiday observing the onset of solar summer, and another cross-quarter day, halfway between the spring equinox and summer solstice, or Ostara and Litha in the Celtic calendar.

Summer seemed far off that Beltane eve as one of the coldest Aprils on record drew to a chilly close. In Celtic mythology, the deity Bel ('bright one') is united with *teine* (fire), and folk celebrated May Day with fire in honour of the sun. Indoors, the hearths that had burned all winter were extinguished, and new ones lit. Outdoors, celebrants danced around bonfires, and cattle on their way to summer pastures were purified by their smoke. Beltane was the occasion to rejoice in the fertility of the land, and a time of courtship when couples went 'a-Maying' in the countryside, canoodling and gathering greenery to decorate their homes.

It was too cold to go a-Maying that morning in Winchelsea, and although the season had changed since I was last in East Sussex, the broad view over the Brede Valley to the hills beyond had not. The view had, though, altered dramatically since Saxon times, when the Brede was the 'broad waterway' which gave the river its name. Until the Middle Ages this was a wide tidal estuary. At low tide it shrunk to a network of creeks. At high tide the water spread across the valley floor to the Udimore Ridge and Rye, my next waypoint on the Old Way.

From Rye I would leave the sea and cross Romney Marsh, one of the most bewitching landscapes in southern England, then climb for the final time onto chalk down before walking along riverbanks and through ancient woodlands into the heart of Canterbury. The city, and the cathedral where St Thomas was martyred, lay sixty miles from where I now stood, in the former port of New Winchelsea.

My half-day in Winchelsea would be an excuse to pause, gather my thoughts and gird my mental loins before embarking on the final two Gough Map stages to Canterbury. This was a moment to cherish. Over a year ago I'd begun my pilgrimage in search of a lost path, and my own topography within southern England's chalk landscapes. Each time I returned from my northern home, I needed to recalibrate, reset my internal compass. Find my feet. This would be the last time I'd set off, hills ahead, the sea at my back. At the end of the week and sixty-five miles later, all being well, I'd be in Canterbury.

There was no one that day to wish me 'Godspeed', the customary farewell at the onset of a lengthy journey where arrival was by no means guaranteed. For medieval travellers, excursions away from the safety of home were unpredictable, and often perilous, especially for lone women. As they are for modern lone women, as I was soon to find out. I put that thought to the back of my mind as I got off the bus in the centre of Winchelsea.

The once great town of New Winchelsea is now no more than a sleepy village. Yet, walking its quiet streets of pastel-painted houses, you touch the ghosts of its former grandeur. Its parish church is on a cathedral scale, filling one block of the planned town and dedicated to the saint whose trail I was following to

Canterbury. St Thomas's was begun at the same time as the rest of the town, in 1290, around the time the Gough Map was first made. Today only the chancel and chapels remain. The transepts are in ruins, there's no tower and no evidence of a nave. It's likely the nave was never even begun, as the church's ambitions were soon rendered unnecessary by a change in Winchelsea's fortunes that saw the town decline, and its population diminish, almost as soon as the chancel was finished.

In 1288, when New Winchelsea was founded on a hilltop above the sea, its harbour lay along the narrow strip of land between the base of the hill and the edge of the estuary. As its name suggests, this was not the earliest metropolis to be called Winchelsea. The town I'd arrived in that morning is a replacement of the original settlement now lying under Rye Bay, near the present village of Camber. Old Winchelsea's position on a shingle spit of land extending out to sea was its undoing. Originally called *Gwent-chesel-ey*, or 'Shingle Isle on the Level', the clue to its downfall is in its name.

A millennium ago, Old Winchelsea was home to thousands of people, with an estimated 700 houses, two churches and fifty taverns. It was still thriving on the arrival of the Normans in 1066, who renamed it *Wincenesel*. By then, the writing was largely on its seawalls. In February 1287, around the time that Alice of Southwick made her pilgrimage to Canterbury, the sea finally swallowed the town, realigning the shoreline and altering the entire geography of this coast. Tremendous storms had already turned the shingle spit into an island, redrawing the coastline and altering course of the River Rother to the advantage of the neighbouring port of Rye. On a map of 1616, Winchelsea's watery grave is commemorated with the poignant words *Old Winchelsey, Drowned*.

So important to trade was the first Winchelsea that, in 1288, Edward I commissioned a new harbour on the navigable River Brede, and a new town above on Ilham Hill, to replace the original. Inspired by the *bastides* of southwestern France, the new town was laid out in a grid pattern, like a medieval Manhattan.

For its first century, New Winchelsea prospered. Along with Rye, it joined the Confederation of Cinque Ports, uniting with Hastings, Romney, Hythe, Dover and Sandwich. By the fourteenth century Winchelsea had become a major Channel port, where goods from the Continent – chief among them wine from Gascony – were offloaded. At its peak, the medieval equivalent of a million bottles of wine a year are thought to have entered the harbour and been rolled up the hill in barrels to be stored in the dozens of medieval cellars that you can still see today. With an estimated population of 6,000, New Winchelsea had three churches, two monasteries and two weekly markets. An affluent and civilised metropolis, where most of the inhabitants spoke French.

Unlike its namesake under Rye Bay, it wasn't only the weather to blame for New Winchelsea's misfortune. Throughout the Hundred Years' War the town, like its coastal neighbours, was raided by French forces, depleting its prosperity. The sea then finished what the French had started. While business was booming up in New Winchelsea, the harbour below was running into problems. Upstream, the estuary was being drained for farmland. Dams were laid across the valley floor and the river channel was artificially narrowed, reducing the force with which the river flushed silt from the bay. Meanwhile, ships were growing in size, making navigation to Winchelsea's harbour more difficult.

Without its port the town's fortunes soon declined, and the last merchant departed at the end of the fifteenth century. By the mid-sixteenth century, just 300 years after it was built, the harbour had completely silted up. Further decline was inexorable. The Methodist John Wesley, who preached his last open-air sermon here on 7 October 1790, described the town as 'that poor skeleton Ancient Winchelsea'. Wesley died a few months later, aged eighty-seven. His visit is remembered by a worn plaque set at the base of the Wesley Tree, a successor of the original ash under which he preached, opposite the church of St Thomas the Martyr.

Now, seven centuries after the church of St Thomas was founded, I pushed open its doors. The chancel, which acts as a nave, is lined with elaborate tombs commemorating the great and the good of medieval Winchelsea. The usual aristocratic suspects are represented, their Purbeck marble effigies sitting alongside memorials to Winchelsea's new money: the Alard family, wealthy merchants engaged in the wine trade with Gascony. On the wall above the tombs is a list of rectors, dating back to 1170, and the murder of Becket. After St Thomas's church in Old Winchelsea was lost in the great storm of 1287, the new St Thomas was founded on Ilham Hill, and by 1294 it had its first rector, Adam of *Agmondesham* (Amersham). Nothing much happened for a few centuries until 1529, when the rector, Edmund Atkynson, was 'jailed for revelry'. By this time the town was in steep decline, and a century later the church was described as 'a forlorn ruin'.

Happily, St Thomas the Martyr still has a rector today, installed in 2018, and the church continues to be cherished and polished by its parishioners. The churchyard is also cared for, with specimen trees blossoming in the cold sunshine, a few faded daffodils drooping beneath. Mingled among the old gravestones, some dating back 300 years and smothered in lichen, there are the recent ones of townsfolk buried just a few months before. The church might have lost its importance, and half its intended size, but it hasn't lost its significance for the people who live and die here. I wandered through the churchyard, looking for the grave of comedy genius Spike Milligan. 'Terence Alan (Spike) Milligan 1918–2002, Writer, Artist, Musician, Humanitarian, Comedian', the gravestone read. And in Gaelic underneath: '*Dúirt mé leat go raibh mé breoite*' (I told you I was ill).

I left the graveyard and its centuries of dead, and explored the streets of old New Winchelsea. Following its post-medieval demise the town languished for three centuries. There were attempts at a revival. In the 1760s weavers from Cambrai settled in the town, planting the mulberry trees which still thrive in some Winchelsea gardens. Wellington's troops were garrisoned here in the 1790s, in anticipation of a Napoleonic invasion, though they didn't deter the smugglers, who hid contraband in the town's medieval cellars.

From the early nineteenth century, Winchelsea's romantic charm attracted writers, artists, actors and historians. I stopped at a white weatherboard house, looking like it belonged in New England rather than in 'good old Sussex by the sea'. Ford Maddox Ford, poet and author, lived here, said the plaque. Thackeray, Conrad, Turner and Millais were also inspired by the town, and the most celebrated actress of the Victorian era, Ellen Terry, lived in New Winchelsea from 1896 until 1906, in a house once occupied by the Duke of Wellington.

Between the lanes I walked along that morning, flower-filled gardens commingled with well-tended allotments. Everywhere, nature was encroaching, climbing the garden walls, creeping along the verges and colonising the hedgerows. Civilisation and wilderness, rubbing along in a town forgotten by time.

Before leaving Winchelsea to its memories, I walked northwest to the crest of the sandstone ridge where, so say historians and archaeologists, existed the Saxon settlement of Ilham. Named after the Old English for 'high fields', there's nothing left of Ilham above ground. The last building to stand on this gusty hilltop was a windmill, blown down in the Great Storm of 1987 – seven centuries after the storm that consumed Old Winchelsea – and leaving nothing but a 360-degree panorama over the hills of East Sussex and Kent. A noticeboard informed the visitor that the windmill stood on the site of the Saxon church of St Leonard, its surrounding village once serving a port at the bottom of the ridge. Although the thirteenth-century city walls of New Winchelsea encircled the Saxon village, it did not form part of Edward I's grid-planned town and eventually disappeared under the turf.

I drank in a last view from Ilham Hill. Further back up the ridge, to my left, was the village of Icklesham, and beyond, Pett Level Marsh. Further away still, a glimpse of the English Channel.

To my right, across the Brede Valley, was Udimore Ridge, with Winchelsea's sister port of Rye at its tip. Udimore means *O'er de mer*, or 'over the sea', a clue that the marsh below was once a tidal estuary. In the Middle Ages, boats navigated up the River Brede as far as Sedlescombe, near Battle, carrying lead for the abbey roof. Brede means 'broad' in Old English, though today it's not easy to pick out the narrow river in its valley. Apart from the river itself, most of the waterways you now see are channels dug to drain the reclaimed farmland, known locally as sewers or drains.

Ahead was the High Weald. Hills of sandstone and clay pitching and rolling, separating the wide river valleys formed during the last Ice Age when silt from meltwater scoured into the bedrock. As I stood there that morning surrounded by pastures grazed silently by sheep, the thin ribbon of river wove its way through the marsh below. It wasn't easy to reconcile this bucolic scene with the tidal estuary and noisy seaport of 800 years ago. The coastline of this country has been changing for millennia – shifting, receding, silting up. Nothing is permanent, as much as we might wish it so.

On the edge of the hill I followed a sunken trackway that once took villagers from Ilham down to shore, as it once was. The track led me on a loop back up to New Winchelsea, and I exited the town via one of its three surviving medieval gateways. Built in 1300, shortly after the founding of New Winchelsea, the Strand Gate stands at the top of Strand Hill, a hundred metres above the former harbour at the bottom. In its heyday the harbour was a busy commercial and military port, and the gate was a third taller than it is today, with a porter's lodge inside the northeastern tower and a portcullis. The road still passes straight through the middle. Seven hundred years ago, horses and carts clanked and clattered through this arch. That day, as I walked down the hill, a man in a Panama hat was pushing his bike noiselessly up. I was heading south towards the sea, now fully retreated from the town and stranding it a mile inland. As I walked, I saw in my mind's eye the ships jostling on the waters below, and heard the shouts of the sailors offloading their goods.

At the bottom of the hill I turned and looked back at Winchelsea. Where I stood was once an inlet of the English Channel. The late-April morning air was chilly, but the sun was warm, and ewes basked with their lambs as I set out across the marshes towards Camber Castle, shimmering ahead. A buzzard skimmed and shrieked over the marsh. If I'd been here nine centuries ago, I'd have been walking towards Old Winchelsea on its shingle spit, before the sea came to reclaim it that night in 1287.

The salt marsh I was now walking through was Rye Harbour Nature Reserve, over 1,000 acres of low-lying ground and shingle ridges, forged by millennia of tides and storms. In recent decades, sea defences have shielded the land from the sea, lowering the water table to allow grazing, and today the reserve hosts breeding colonies of terns, avocets, oystercatchers, lapwings, redshanks, ringed plovers and wheatears, with many other wading birds joining the fray in winter. The coastal shingle habitat encourages sea kale, viper's bugloss, sea campion and the unappealing-sounding stinking hawksbeard. These in turn attract butterflies like the swallowtail, Britain's largest, and until recently found only in the Norfolk Broads, breeding here for the first time in 2020.

I followed a stony track over the marsh, inhaling the familiar ovine odour of lanolin and sheep poo. Inland, the hills rose towards the High Weald, and to my right, though I couldn't see it, was the sea. I could sense it, though, the light echoing off the waves onto this empty marshland where the only sound was the wind, and lambs bleating for their mothers.

Under my boots the ground was parched. It had been one of the driest and coldest Aprils on record, with only 10 per cent of the usual rainfall, and the grass was already yellowing. It felt like late July rather than late April. The only token of spring was the gorse in full flower circling the stony remains of Camber Castle as I approached. A Friday morning, and all around me, unseen and unheard, people were getting on with their lives. I was walking alone through empty marsh, accompanied only by grazing ewes and dozing lambs.

In 1538, when a treaty between France and Spain left the southern coast vulnerable to French attack, Henry VIII ordered the construction of Camber Castle. Five years later the building was completed, financed in part by the plunder of the country's monastic houses. Forty-two men were garrisoned in the castle, but by 1600 the River Camber had silted up and the sea had receded so far that the coast was out of range of the royal cannons. Shingle ridges built up in front of the castle, reducing its access to the sea, and in 1637, less than a century after the foundations were laid, the garrison was disbanded and the castle ransacked for its stone and timber.

If I'd been a buzzard floating over Camber Castle that morning rather than a woman walking past it, I'd have beheld a five-towered edifice with a round tower in its centre, resembling a Tudor rose. The original ashlar facade is now gone, and only roofless rubble walls remain, deserted except for a few oblivious sheep. The gate was padlocked, so I peeped through a doorway to the massive central tower. A notice on the door read:

The Rural Crime Team patrols here – Sussex Police

An unexpected warning for a remote and ruined castle deserted in the middle of the marsh.

And what a marsh. With the delayed spring I was too early for the orchids and vetches, and for the singing marsh frogs and hovering dragonflies of summer. A few weeks on and I would witness whimbrel pausing on their migration north, and I might have heard the bittern, Britain's loudest bird, booming out its unearthly call across the marsh like a foghorn. Chaucer's Wife of Bath described how bitterns 'bombleth in the myre', but five centuries on they almost vanished, with just eleven breeding pairs left by 1997. A concerted conservation programme has saved them from local extinction, with around 200 pairs now thriving in Britain's wetlands. Even so, you're more likely to hear than see this famously secretive bird, especially if you're around at dawn or dusk. This was still April, and it was too cold for booming bitterns. They, and the orchids and dragonflies, would have to wait for another journey.

I picked my way through sheep droppings, dandelions and diminutive pink common stork's-bill as I neared Rye, its silhouette carved into the sunshine. The path led me alongside a stretch of the now shrunken River Brede, where moorhens bobbed, following the trajectory of the Royal Military Canal. Dug by hand in the early nineteenth century, the canal was designed as a defence barrier on the low-lying Romney Marsh when the possibility of Napoleonic invasion was very real. A biplane buzzed overhead, a faint ricochet of those air battles in the Kent skies in the summer and autumn of 1940.

It was the last day of April, and the florets of cow parsley along the lane into Rye were still green, as if waiting for May Day's permission to burst into summer flower.

Rye was the only town on the Old Way I'd previously visited. It was before the pandemic, and the streets were crammed with tourists visiting craft shops, cafés, antique stores and boutiques, and admiring the tile-hung facades, elegant brickwork and cobbled lanes of this ancient harbour town. Another of the Cinque Ports, it's much larger than present-day Winchelsea, whose trade it appropriated when Winchelsea's declined. Nearly every building in its centre is a gem of vernacular architecture and an idyll of English cosiness, although in its prime as a major trading town Rye, like Winchelsea, had more in common with France than its English hinterland. On an April weekday in semi-lockdown, it was a place of calm and serenity.

When Alice of Southwick passed through Rye in the late thirteenth century it had recently received its charter from Edward I and was one of the busiest ports in England, ringing with shouts and rank with smells. Centuries of estuary silt put paid to that, as it did New Winchelsea, and today I had the town to myself. I'd seen the pyramidal spire of St Mary's Church from the marsh. Like St Andrew's in Steyning, in the early twelfth century the church was held by the abbey of Fécamp in Normandy, explaining the magnificence of a building known as 'the Cathedral of East Sussex'. In 1377, French troops set the church on fire, taking the bells to Normandy as war booty. The following year they were recaptured by raiders from Rye and Winchelsea, who set fire to two Norman towns in retaliation.

Next to St Mary's is Ypres Tower. This was Rye's original castle, built in 1249, later becoming the town prison. It's now a museum. From its curtain wall, cannons still pointing towards the coast, I saw the English Channel. Between us was Rye harbour, the River Rother rolling through the marsh and, beyond, a gleaming sliver of sea.

I turned my back to the sea and walked inland, towards Canterbury.

XXIII

In the footsteps of uncounted pilgrims, I left Rye by the Landgate. Erected in the early fourteenth century when Edward III further fortified this important Cinque Ports town, of the four original gateways this is the only one still standing. It may have now lost its portcullis and drawbridge but it's still a formidable sight, with its crenellations and two bulky towers. The Landgate doesn't appear on the Gough Map, which presents standardised symbols of each town in accordance with its size and chief function rather than an accurate representation of its architecture. So *Rye* (spelled the same as today) is indicated by a spired church with a cross, demonstrating its importance as a religious centre.

Rye was getting ready for the bank holiday weekend as I left that morning, and stepping through Landgate's mysterious medieval arch was an apposite way to bid the town farewell. My aim was to find the Royal Military Canal, and follow it as it hugged the escarpment before reaching Appledore, on the northern edge of Romney Marsh some eight miles from Rye. A variant of the Old Way would lead me to the remote church of St Thomas à Becket, alone out on the marsh. The closer I got to Canterbury the more Becket's presence became manifest. If not the man himself, then the religious and political reverberations arising from his martyrdom and the swell of devotion that followed.

A few wrong turns later I found the path out of Rye's suburbs and followed the River Rother as it meandered through the marsh. If I'd been here five centuries earlier, and the tide had been in, I'd have been swimming now rather than walking. Alice of Southwick, on her way to Canterbury in the 1280s, might have sailed to Appledore, then the furthest navigable reach of the river before storms and silt altered its course.

Luckily, I was on dry land that morning, my only company a pair of skylarks, swooping and diving into the marsh. My first skylarks of solar summer. This was, after all, May Morning. When living in Oxford, I got up at dawn to hear the choristers sing the medieval melody 'Sumer is icumen in' from Magdalen College tower, and join in the revelries of students and citizens as they celebrated Beltane in true pagan fashion. Today, on the tipping point of spring and summer, it was chilly and overcast and the air was thick with a salty, muddy estuary aroma. I was happy to be here rather than in Oxford at the threshold of seasons, black-headed gulls circling overhead.

Two centuries earlier, in 1803, it was Napoleon's eyes rather than mine that were set on Romney Marsh. 'I only want for a favourable wind,' Bonaparte proclaimed, 'to plant the Imperial Eagle on the Tower of London.' As in the Middle Ages, the Kent coast was vulnerable to French attack, and something had to be done to defend the land. Plan A was to flood the marsh if Napoleon invaded. This was discounted, as a false alarm would drown the reclaimed pasture and farmland on which so many people relied. So plan B was implemented. Travelling 'navigators' (or navvies) were hired to create a physical barrier across the marsh, complementing the seventy-four Martello Towers already built along the southern English coast. Beginning in 1804 and taking five years to complete, the navvies dug the canal by hand, all twenty-eight miles of it from Hastings to Folkestone, using the excavated soil to create an embankment on which defending English soldiers could patrol.

As it happened, the French never invaded and Napoleon was defeated at the Battle of Waterloo in 1815, though the Royal Military

Canal proved effective in the war against smugglers, who transported their cargo inland along the many waterways. For the twenty-first century walker, it is the perfect way to cross miles of soggy terrain. The spring had been particularly dry, but this was still marshland where the water is never far from your feet.

Marshland metamorphosed into farmland, and still I followed the Royal Military Canal north, away from the sea. I was now walking along a stretch of the Sussex Border Path, separating the counties of Sussex and Kent and shadowed by the Old Way. Farmland reverted to marshland once again and still I walked on, through pastures and past bramble hedges snagged with strands of lanolin-scented fleece. The stretch of marsh I was walking through felt vast and endless. I could have been in Texas, or the Russian steppe, rather than on the fringes of southern England where, on the map at least, the topography is on a miniature scale. It's only when you're walking deep inside the English landscape, views expanding for miles, that you're conned into a sense of immensity.

Now, as I headed towards the swell of the Kent Downs, it felt as if I'd been walking for eternity, and would be walking across this ancient and mysterious marshland until the end of my days.

It was only the beginning of May and a haze of mosquitoes hovered over the mire. Five centuries earlier the inhabitants of Romney Marsh suffered from marsh fever, or ague, the affliction later known as malaria, from the Italian for bad air. On Romney Marsh malaria was a major problem, with mortality rates twice as high as in nearby villages. In the late eighteenth century, the antiquarian Edward Hasted wrote that 'the airs and waters of the Romney Marsh are both foul and fatal'. Malarial mosquitoes likely arrived at the end of the last glacial period, when the temperatures in southern England rose. Only with the improved drainage of the

Royal Military Canal did malaria subside here, along with the discovery that its cause was mosquitoes, and the parasites they carry, rather than putrid air and stagnant waters. With today's warming climate, and the recreation of coastal wetlands, malaria might yet return to Romney Marsh.

To my left rose Broom Hill, gilded with gorse. Grass glowed a lime green, hawthorns and willows sprouted into leaf. Also known as the May tree, it's the hawthorn rather than the month that is alluded to in the old adage, 'Ne'er cast a clout till May be out.' The May tree was not out, and I hadn't yet cast a clout. Instead, I was wrapped in a fleece, rain jacket and lined trousers as if it were still midwinter.

Earlier, I had been walking between the chalk and the sea. Now I was walking upon the sea, as it had once been. The sky thickened, spitting raindrops at me before the sun forced the clouds apart again. The day wasn't warm, yet following the canal was a sweaty, swampy affair. Pale-gold reeds swayed in heavy air, and my T-shirt stuck to my back. Just like walking along the banks of the River Jordan as it trickles into the profundity of the Dead Sea.

Here, the Old Way diverges. One route takes you to the top of Broom Hill, and the site of a temple dedicated to the Roman god Mithras, supposedly lying under the church in Stone in Oxney, its *-ey* suffix revealing that this village was once an island. I decided to stay off the hill and follow the alternative route to the church of St Thomas à Becket, standing alone in the marsh. So off I swung, across pasture speckled with dandelions, towards the hamlet of Fairfield.

In the 1800s author Thomas Ingoldsby wrote that 'the World, according to the best geographers, is divided into Europe, Asia, Africa, America, and Romney Marsh', inspiring the marsh's sobriquet 'the fifth continent'. Today it still has a desolate, other-worldly atmosphere like nowhere else I've been. Enormous skies domed the flatness, moving the horizon ever out of reach, so though my map told me St Thomas's Church was only a mile or so away, it still felt impossibly far.

Paths pitched through plains of wheat and pungent oilseed rape, a crop devoid of any discernible wildlife – no bees, no birds, no butterflies. Just regimented rows of acid-yellow, marshalling me towards Fairfield.

Fairfield is a hamlet that has not forgotten St Thomas after nearly 1,000 years. First I passed Becket's Court and Becket Barn Farm, both isolated in the moor, and later I would cross Becket's Bridge on my way into Appledore. Now, though, I would traverse the marsh to the church named after the saint. As I walked through sheep pasture, lambs calling for their mothers, the spire of St Thomas à Becket rose from the reeds like a sail of a galleon.

My map told me I had now crossed into Kent, the final shire on my walk across four counties, although there was no sign of the boundary on this endless, timeless marsh. Ahead, the church stood alone on its island surrounded by 100 square miles of marshland. Nothing else, just infinite flatness. Apart from the few outlying farms I'd passed, the village it served has disappeared, as if swallowed by the marsh.

This is a landscape of loss, a waterland of mists, myths and legends. One such tale involves the saint himself. When travelling across Romney Marsh on his way to Canterbury, Thomas fell into one of the hundreds of dykes, drains and sewers that lattice the marsh. Desperate, he prayed to his biblical namesake, Thomas the Apostle. Just as he was about to drown, a local farmer arrived and pulled him from the water. In gratitude at the intervention of the saint and the farmer, Thomas built the church where he so nearly lost his life and which still stands here today.

To visit the church, I had to collect a large, medieval-looking key that hung on the wall of a nearby farmhouse. The old iron key with its four-leaf clover bow was heavy and cold in my hand as I approached the church, its mossy tiled roof like an upturned ship. Bordered by the busy seaports, resorts and fishing towns of the south coast, this deserted place felt lost in time. There was no sense of the modern world encircling the marsh, just an aura of emptiness and peace.

With only the rasp of wind through the reeds as company, I crossed a wooden footbridge, skirting the sheep lounging by the iron-studded porch door. The key slid into the lock. The porch led via another ancient iron-studded door into a room that felt more like a barn than a church. Originally timber-framed, the building was encased in brick in the eighteenth century, retaining its medieval crown-post roof, low beams and braced trusses inside. The sensitive restoration of 1912 left this plain, rural church clear but for its Georgian box pews and profoundly medieval atmosphere.

Sitting in one of the box pews, I heard the rain that had pursued me all morning begin to pound on the roof. Miraculously, I'd reached the sanctuary of this beautiful, lonely church just in time to avoid a heavy spring shower. There's no electricity – the church is lit by candles hanging from old chandeliers, and by the windows cut into its plain limewashed walls. Wood, plaster, brick, tile and stone converge, and from every window I saw nothing but miles of flat marsh where sheep plucked at the grass. It's not only in the great cathedrals of Chichester or Canterbury, Winchester or Westminster, that you encounter holiness. It's in these simple churches that seem to have grown out of the landscape, and are as much a part of it as the sky and the marsh and the rain.

Clock time all but vanished, replaced by a moment of eternity, a sense of the church, the marsh and me coalescing, becoming one. I wanted to sit there forever but I had a walk to finish, so went out to the porch to eat my sandwich. It had been a shower of hail bouncing off the roof, not rain. The sheep didn't seem to mind the hailstorm, their bleats still floating across the marsh.

The hail stopped, and the grass glistened in the sunshine. Returning the iron key to the farmhouse I struck north across the marsh again towards Appledore, leaving Fairfield. In *Piers Plowman*, the fourteenth-century poet William Langland describes, with characteristic medieval alliteration, a 'fair field full of folk'. This particular fair field was empty of folk that afternoon. I met no humans as I walked across the marsh, but the marsh wasn't empty of life. There were the skylarks, the sheep, and the living, breathing church of St Thomas à Becket on its lonely island.

Another rain shower, great fat drops of water staining the cracked ground beneath my feet, saw me into Appledore. It may be a small, out-of-the-way village now, but on the Gough Map it's *appeldre*, the 'place at the apple tree', and a busy port on a tidal branch of the River Rother. The red line of the Old Way runs alongside its icon: a single building with a red roof.

In the garden of the Black Lion, I paused for a cup of tea and to warm up. There was no accommodation available in Appledore that night, even at the inn. When Alice of Southwick was on pilgrimage to Canterbury, she may have stayed in inns such as this if no other accommodation was available, although not if she was alone. Like Margery Kempe a century later, as a wealthy woman she travelled with her maidservant or an escort, and often in the reluctant company of fellow pilgrims.

My plan was to walk the mile along the road to Appledore station, and catch the train back to Rye. I was tired and cold, my feet ached, and the rain was not letting up. I asked the waitress if there were any taxi companies nearby. There weren't. The waitress, her dark hair pulled into a ponytail, regarded me for a moment.

'Look, if you wait a bit I'll be having my lunch break soon, and I'll take you to the station.'

Half an hour later and we were on our way. Tracy, as the waitress was called, chatted to me as we drove. When she dropped me off at the station I offered to pay for petrol, but she declined.

'I always think if you do nice things, good things happen to you,' she said. 'It's karma.' It was one of those encounters that only happen when you're travelling alone. As a solitary pilgrim, particularly if you're walking, you're not a threat. You're exposed, and people warm to you. If I'd been driving or travelling with others, I may never have got to know Tracy during those fifteen minutes of her precious lunch break when she drove me to Appledore station.

As it happened, the train was to be replaced by a bus that day. According to the timetable it was due in a few minutes, so I waited. And waited. The bus's allotted time came and went. It would be an hour until the next bus, which might also not arrive, and I didn't fancy walking all the way back to Rye in the rain. Next to the station was an old brick barn which had been turned into an antiques shop. The owner was locking up for the day, so I asked him if the bus was normally on time, as it certainly wasn't that afternoon. He was wearing shorts and a polo shirt, though the afternoon had turned cold and wet.

'Where are you off to?' he asked, walking over to his van.

'Rye.'

'I can take you as I'm going that way. Hop in.'

I hopped in, and off we drove, all the way back to Rye.

As we rode, Graham, as the antiques shop owner was called, told me something of his life. He'd moved twenty years ago from London to near Dungeness, and as well as running Station Antiques worked in the film industry. We talked about how atmospheric Romney Marsh was, and he told me he was constantly fascinated by it even after two decades living here. 'The marsh speaks to you,' he said, as we pushed on through the rain.

XXIV

I remembered Graham's words as I travelled by train back across Romney Marsh the following morning. It was Sunday, a chill sunshine strained through the clouds and all was peaceful in Appledore. The village is strung along its main street, a patchwork of old weatherboard houses, Georgian brick mansions and Victorian villas, front gardens spilling with roses. And everywhere blossom, including on the apple trees after which the village is named.

A notice outside the church of St Peter and Paul told how the French sailed upriver to Appledore and burned the church and the village in the devastating raid of 1380. A year later, its villagers joined Wat Tyler's men in the Peasants' Revolt (now renamed the Great Revolt). A fair, first established by Edward III, ensured

Appledore's prosperity, with fairs held in front of the church until the end of the nineteenth century. I walked up the path to the church door. Sunday worship had just begun, so I continued my walk along the Old Way. On the Gough Map the red line passes arrow-straight 'XVII' (seventeen) old miles to Canterbury, but the modern Old Way meanders through a string of Kentish villages.

A lane aptly called Old Way led me back out onto the marsh, just as it took generations of villagers to their fields and pastures, their crops and their sheep. Alongside the modern rectory stood a 'community mask tree', inviting visitors to take one of the homemade face masks pegged to its branches in return for a small donation. Today's Appledore may be a picture-postcard village rather than the bustling port it was before the Rother changed course, but it's one with a communal spirit uniting its inhabitants in times of crisis – whether medieval French raiders or the twenty-first century version of the Great Pestilence.

A few minutes later I was back on the Royal Military Canal, where a handful of sheep were shading themselves under an oak tree, its canopy vibrating with birdsong. This was International Dawn Chorus Day and although it was well past dawn, the chorus was ongoing. My path followed the embankment of the canal, lined with hawthorn trees in leaf but not yet in bloom after the cold

April. A chiffchaff sang from deep inside the thicket – one of the first returning migrants of spring still in full-throat in early May.

The path swung off the Royal Military Canal, and crossed the area of marsh and bog called Appledore Heath. I was on my way to visit Horne's Place, a seventeenth-century Wealden farmhouse – timber-framed, tile-hung, topped by tall chimney stacks and set in glorious gardens. Attached to the manor house was a medieval chapel, visible over a wall. Such domestic chapels allowed high-status families to attend religious services without sitting among the hoi polloi in the village church. When Wat Tyler's men arrived in Appledore in 1381 they raided the manor house, then belonging to William Horne, stealing goods to the value of £10 (equivalent to around £6,000 today). Unfortunately for the rebels, William Horne was a Justice of the Peace, responsible for crushing the uprising in Kent. Wat Tyler marched from Appledore to Canterbury, then to London, where he demanded a raft of socio-economic reforms. He was killed by Richard II's officers at Smithfield, near London, in June of that year.

It was the bank holiday weekend, and for the first time that week I was among others. People walking their dogs of course, but also 'serious' hikers, kitted up in boots and Gore-tex. Pilgrimage can be a solitary activity but it can also be a communal one. Walkers on the Camino de Santiago regularly fall into companionable step with fellow pilgrims, and although I'd not yet met anyone else walking the Old Way, it was good to exchange pleasantries with other people when you've been on your own.

This camaraderie was something that medieval pilgrims, travelling in the safety of groups, also experienced. For Chaucer's fictional pilgrims, the journey was enlivened by a storytelling competition, each of the thirty characters striving to outperform the others, with Harry Bailly, host of the Tabard Inn in Southwark, the master of ceremonies. Pilgrimage was one of those rare occasions when people from all walks of life mingled. In *The Canterbury Tales*, as well as the innkeeper there were a prioress, knight, scholar, miller, reeve, pardoner, merchant (like Richard of Southwick) and, most famously, Alisoun, a widow from Bath who had already seen off five husbands and was working on acquiring a sixth. Alice, our Wife of Southampton, was perhaps less ribald than her West Country counterpart, but I like to think she joined in with the companionship of a shared journey.

Paths led me through vineyards of the Gusbourne Estate, whose lands date back to 1410, when John de Goosebourne, a nobleman, owned 143 acres here. Its position, on a south-facing slope above Romney Marsh, protects and warms the Chardonnay, Pinot Noir and Pinot Meunier grapes used to make their sparkling wines. Crossing its dried clay *terroir* that day was like walking through the *Crete* of Siena rather than the Weald of Kent. With the warming climate, the Garden of England is also fast becoming its vineyard.

The Old Way now traces the Saxon Shore Way, a long-distance path following the former Kent shoreline where the Romans built forts to defend England against new invaders: Jutes, Angles and Saxons. When Alice travelled to Canterbury, she may have sailed around the coast rather than travelled overland here, bypassing some of the settlements that lay ahead. As ever, the Gough Map shows the most direct route, leaping straight across the water to Canterbury.

The Saxon Shore Way, marked by yellow signs showing a horned helmet, led me across the fertile farmland of the Weald to the church of St Mary's in Kenardington, set back from its village. In the churchyard a magnolia tree dropped its petals like confetti, and a huge old oak stood sentinel.

Lightning struck St Mary's in 1559, destroying the nave, chancel and north aisle of a much bigger church, leaving only the tower and south aisle. I sat for a moment in the porch studying the jamb of a fine oak door. Medieval worshippers, possibly pilgrims, had etched symbols into the wood. Such porch engravings are not uncommon. Pilgrims bedded down in church porches, and porches hosted liturgical functions such as weddings, with the Wife of Bath marrying her five husbands 'at the church door'. One of the symbols in St Mary's porch was particularly curious, showing what looked like a cross rising from a bishop's mitre. Was this *grafitto* a sign of devotion to Thomas Becket? And did Alice, perhaps pausing in the porch, see these etchings as well?

With its church tower a beacon ahead, I climbed hills and crossed meadows to Warehorne, where a raincloud swept over the hill, pelting drops onto my sunhat. Paths through sheep pastures and past oasthouses – most now converted into comfortable homes – led me to Hamstreet. This was the home patch of Will Parsons, co-founder of the Old Way, who lives near Canterbury. He had offered to walk with me for the final stretch of the day to Bilsington.

I met Will at the entrance to Ham Street Woods Nature Reserve, just north of the village. Wood anemones, which thrive in deciduous woodland, carpeted the ground beneath our feet. Spreading only six feet every hundred years, anemones multiply via their rhizomes in undisturbed earth, rather than through the dispersal of its seeds, and are a useful measure of a wood's age. On banks and in hedgerows they are a sure sign of vanished woodland, lingering centuries after they first grew under broadleaved trees. Their white flowers like stars, wood anemones only open fully in sunshine, and grow alongside bluebells and celandine, flowers that love the dappled half-light of spring before the leaf canopy blots out the sun.

Will and I had met once before, and it was good to see him again. Tall and straight like the hazel staff he was carrying, lockdown locks bound into a man bun, he was accompanied that day by his dog, Holly. Will presented me with a hazel staff, which he'd cut himself and chosen to suit my height. I'd ditched my telescopic aluminium pole after my first walk out of Southampton, preferring to keep my hands free, and was touched by the gift.

Will had been out the previous night in his local woods, singing with the nightingales.

'What time do nightingales start singing?' I asked Will as we set off on our walk.

'After the pubs close,' he replied, not missing a beat. He played me the recording on his phone, Will singing a traditional May love song called 'Searching for Lambs', about a man falling for a woman feeding her sheep. The male nightingale, Will said, also sings to woo a female, she choosing the best singer to pair up with. In the recording Will sang a phrase, and the nightingale responded. A duet, and the combined song of bird and man was magical.

It was through his voice that I first discovered Will, around ten years earlier when he and two friends spent years walking and singing their way around Britain. They had slept under hedges, reconnecting with the landscape through song and posting their adventures on YouTube. These lengthy journeys on foot led Will to his discovery of the Old Way.

'When I was making my singing journeys, before I got into pilgrimage, we generally walked from east Kent,' Will told me as we followed paths through Ham Street Woods. 'And if you're walking from east Kent, where I live, there's only one direction to go, which is west. So I was always looking for these east–west paths, to and from Canterbury.' Most major routes radiate out of London, following Roman roads such as Watling Street, now the A2 to Dover, Ermine Street north to Lincoln and Stone (or Stane) Street to Chichester which I'd partly walked the previous summer.

'When I first set off walking I had no maps,' Will continued. 'I thought, let the wind blow and see where I end up. But that leads to cul-de-sacs and motorways, and I quickly discovered the benefits of public footpaths.' At first, in 2004, he walked the Pilgrims' Way. This was the path rediscovered by Hilaire Belloc a century earlier, which runs from Winchester to Canterbury along the North Downs, and was named by Belloc the Old Road.

'I walked back and forth from Canterbury on the Pilgrims' Way, and was so disappointed by that route,' Will said. 'It's very close to the M20 and M25, with all the noise, pollution and danger of those roads. I just remember thinking, is this the best Britain can offer?'

'Especially as there are so many wonderful public footpaths,' I said. 'Every path is in some way special and unique, and they cover the whole country. We're so lucky to have them.' And so we are. Public footpaths not only allow us to walk across the landscape, they validate it. Walking paths that have existed for centuries or longer, we reaffirm our right to rove the country-side. The Ramblers Association was founded in 1935 to assert this right, leading to the legal protection of public footpaths with the National Parks and Access to the Countryside Act of 1949.

For ten years Will hunted for a better way from the west to Canterbury, the great centre of British pilgrimage, exploring routes that threaded together churches and other holy places, away from busy roads. He knew any ancient route leading to Canterbury would have had its roots in pilgrimage as this was the *raison d'être* of the town, and he had now found one that worked.

'I thought of calling it the South Downs Pilgrims' Way to distinguish it from Hilaire Belloc's route over the North Downs,' Will said. He also wanted to find historic proof of the path, but a certain king stood in his way.

'As you know, Henry VIII was thorough in erasing all traces of Thomas Becket because he really hated him,' continued Will. Becket had defied the Plantagenet King Henry II in 1170, just as the Church defied his Tudor successor nearly four centuries later. 'Apparently, Henry had Becket's bones put on trial, declared guilty, burned, and shot out of a cannon,' said Will. Henry also destroyed Becket's magnificent shrine in Canterbury, reportedly using twenty-three carts to carry away all the gold and jewels to his treasury in London. Later that year Becket was proclaimed an 'enemy of the Crown' (a sentiment echoed centuries later in the notorious 2016 *Daily Mail* headline naming three British judges as 'enemies of the people' during the prolonged and heated Brexit debate). On Henry's orders all images of Becket throughout the country were destroyed or covered up. The Royal Proclamation of 16 November 1538 commanded: 'from henceforth the said Thomas Becket shall not be esteemed, named, reputed nor called a saint, but Bishop Becket, and that his images and pictures through the whole realm shall be put down.'

We had now reached a crossroads in the woods, where every path looked the same, and had stopped to check out some initials carved into the bark of a beech tree.

'Did you know that the word for "book" comes from the Old English word for beech, which is *boece*?' asked Will, always a fount of knowledge. I did not know that, though I did know that likewise the word Bible comes from Byblos, in Lebanon, where they made the paper from which the bible was produced. 'Beech is the tree that everyone always writes on, as though it's still in folk memory,' Will said, contemplating the maze of paths ahead. 'I think we'll go this way.'

We walked on, out of the wood and along a holloway between high embankments thick with hawthorn, branches frosting green. This was another of those hedgerows that had become trees, their handwoven trunks forgotten and left to go their own way. A solitary bluebell huddled into the grassy bank, either the first or the last of the spring's crop. The light tilted across the landscape, igniting the vivid greens of spring.

'Anyway,' continued Will, 'I wanted to find a justification for the path. With the Camino de Santiago, its authenticity comes directly from the *Codex Calixtinas*, which gives its exact itinerary.' This was similar to the Via Francigena, the pilgrimage route from Canterbury to Rome which passed through France, Switzerland and Italy. When, in 990, Archbishop Sigeric 'the Serious' travelled along this route from Canterbury to Rome to receive the customary *pallium* from the Pope, he recorded the places he stayed on the way. This was the kind of evidence Will was searching for, and a decade after starting his search for a pilgrim route to Canterbury he had a breakthrough. He looked a little sheepish as he told me the story.

'I got caught by an old *Daily Mail* headline – "Britain's oldest roadmap!"' he told me. 'So I clicked on the story, and this lightbulb went off.' Inspired, Will studied the Gough Map, now digitised and online, and spotted the thin red line from Southampton terminating in Canterbury. 'To me, this pretty much implied pilgrimage,' he said.

'Because . . . what else would end at Canterbury?'

'Quite. If it had continued to Dover you could say it was a trade or military road.' Will then followed the course of the red line on foot, and realised how many buildings and historical clues en route related to pilgrimage. A eureka moment. In Will's mind, there was no doubt that the red line on the Gough Map, the physical landmarks and the written history confirmed that this was a lost pilgrimage trail. It was then that he set up the British Pilgrimage Trust to promote the Old Way, and other pilgrim routes.

We passed a hawthorn hedge flailed of its leaves, shorn into straight lines and neat angles. This was high spring, the day after May Day and the dawn of summer, but no sounds emanated from the hedge. So many birds could have nested in it, yet it was as listless as if it were January rather than May. Organisations such as Hedgerow Defenders are now lobbying to protect hedgerow habitats from this annual savage, mechanical flailing which destroys berry, nut or seed harvests. As most hedgerow plants fruit only in the second year of growth, campaigners want hedgerows adjacent to fields to be granted a full three-year growth cycle before cutting.

Below us, Romney Marsh glowed in the afternoon sun. Soon, we reached the tiny village of Ruckinge, which in the Middle Ages and at high tide sat just above the sea. We passed the church of St Mary Magdelene, set in a haze of forget-me-nots, and pushed on to Bilsington. Here, a medieval moated manor, a former priory, marked the site of Odo's house. Odo was the Bishop of Bayeux, the half-brother of William the Conqueror. Historians generally now agree that the Bayeux Tapestry was created here, by English embroiderers, rather than in the Norman town where it's now displayed.

At Bilsington, the end of our day's journey, we paused at the church of St Peter and Paul, where the medieval bell hangs outside the building, the timber church tower thought too feeble to bear its weight. Will struck the bell with his staff, and it released a deep, satisfying clang that reverberated into the afternoon.

'Do parishioners still ring this bell to announce church services?' I wondered.

'I don't think so – only annoying pilgrims,' replied Will.

Will led me to a hidden patch of the churchyard where a wooden plank – a poor man's tombstone – marked the nineteenth-century grave of five young members of the Law family. The inscription on the worn plank, set above the ground on rusty stakes, was still legible and recorded the deaths of the six children, alongside their ages. They'd all died within the space of four years, between 1865 and 1869.

Inside the church, the atmosphere was heavy with age and silence. We stood by the altar, thinking about the everyday tragedy of the Law family. After a few moments, Will broke into song. The church resonated with the Irish folksong 'What is the Life of a Man?' sung to the melody of 'Lord of All Hopefulness'. This hymn, so familiar from school assembly, in turn derives from a traditional folksong, completing the circle of song and hymn, life and death.

I had first heard Will singing on YouTube. Now, I was listening to his voice resounding inside a village church perched above Romney Marsh since at least 1086, when the Domesday Book first recorded its presence. As Will finished the song his voice faded, absorbed into the fabric of these ancient walls. Just like all hymns sung here for the past 1,000 years.

XXV

It was a blustery morning when I returned, alone, to Bilsington. I was now twenty-five miles into the last leg of my walk, and had another forty to go before I reached Canterbury. Westerly winds were thrusting clouds across the skies and heavy rain – the delayed showers of April – was forecast for later that afternoon. Beltane might be the point when spring tips over into summer, but spring had the upper hand as I set off east along the Saxon Shore Way towards Lympne.

Woolly sheep grazed the banks of the canal, the wind pushing the water into little waves, and in the field opposite a skylark sang. The wind pushed me along also, towards the tiny church of St Rumwold, huddling beside the banks of the Royal Military Canal. This path contours the edge of two very different landscapes. To my right spread the vast, flat expanse of Romney Marsh. To my left swelled the chalk hills of the Kent Downs – the eastern ridge of the North Downs. Once again I found myself walking between the chalk and the sea, even though the sea had now become marsh.

When the great storm of 1287 silted up New Romney's harbour, diverting the river away from the town and leaving it landlocked, its hinterland fell into neglect. In 1804, when Lieutenant Colonel Brown of the Royal Staff Corps had the idea of the Royal Military Canal, he envisaged not only a defence against Napoleon but a means to drain the marsh, so improving conditions for local people. The new canal may not have been tested against Napoleon's troops but it created the fertile, prosperous countryside I walked through that morning, where fat sheep lounged in the sunshine chewing the cud.

I had now reached Bonnington, and spied the village at the top of the escarpment, though its church was at the bottom by the Royal Military Canal. St Rumwold is another of those remote parish churches along the edge of Romney Marsh that seems to have unhitched from its village and slid down the hill. Perhaps it felt at home here, down among the sheep of the marshes, rather than among the farming folk above.

There are only eight churches in England dedicated to the Saxon St Rumwold. Little is known of his life, except that it was extremely short – he was born in Buckingham in around 650 and only lived for three days. He was a precocious baby. At one day old he proclaimed, 'I am a Christian!' and asked to be baptised. On the second day he preached a sermon, extolling Christian virtues. On his third, and last, day he declared that he was going to die, which he duly did. Rumwold's baptismal font can still be seen at King's Sutton church in Northamptonshire, with his shrine in Buckingham a focus of medieval pilgrimage – much to the delight of medieval innkeepers.

There's been a church in Bonnington since at least the twelfth century. The current St Rumwold's is chiefly a fourteenth-century rebuilding of the Norman original, with walls of Kentish rag – the stone used to build London's city walls. I sensed the spirit of the place – its holiness, if you like – outside in the churchyard, where I walked around the building's perimeter, finding bluebells and daffodils, daisies and dandelions, and a windswept harmony. I explored the gravestones, struck again by the continuity of these ancient churchyards. The most recent headstone was dated January 2019, but I also found one smothered with lichen that seemed to be of 1745. People have been buried here for hundreds of years. They still are, and I couldn't think of a nicer place to rest than this churchyard on the edge of Romney Marsh, interred in the earth beneath the sheep and the skylarks.

The sea had long ago retreated, yet there was still a perception of the sea here, an impression of being on the very edge of the land. Romney Marsh is now drained and farmed, but the sea's spectre is ever present, and its light fills the sky. Unlike in the South Downs, where the villages are at the foot of the hill, on the Kent Downs it's the opposite. Apart from the occasional church, such as St Thomas à Becket at Fairfield, there are few settlements in the marsh itself. Instead, you have to climb to the top of the escarpment each time you want to see something, which was why I now found myself walking up through pasture to the remains of a tiny medieval chapel dedicated to Sister Elizabeth Barton, known as the Nun of Kent. Or, less flatteringly, the Mad Maid of Kent.

A sixteenth-century prophetess and visionary, Elizabeth Barton was a strong-willed woman, unafraid to speak her mind at a time when this was not encouraged. For Elizabeth, speaking her mind included warning Henry VIII against his divorce from Katherine of Aragon, which the Pope had refused to grant, leading to a charge of treason. Inevitably in those tempestuous times, her story ended in 1534 with her head on a spike on London Bridge – the only woman to have undergone this dishonour. A chapel was built here in her memory, alongside a holy well, and this is where her followers thronged.

All that remains of the pilgrim chapel today are roofless walls with a blocked-in doorway. Ancient willows encircle the ruin, where you still find the sacred spring, more muddy than holy. It's a forgotten, unmarked spot next to a Second World War pillbox. It's also a romantic spot, perched on the lip of the Kent Downs overlooking Romney Marsh, the sea in the distance. This is a heavily populated part of the country, yet there are places like this where there's nothing for miles. Just the sea and the sky and the wind.

The wind blew me towards Lympne, passing the remains of a Roman castle just up from the shoreline of the Kent Downs, when this was the sea. Bidding a final farewell to the Royal Military Canal, I climbed steeply up through woodland to Lympne, past the stony remains of *Portus Lemanis*, also known as *Lemanae*,

'Where is Thomas Becket, traitor to the king and the kingdom?'

On 28 December 1170, the four knights Hugh de Morville, Richard Brito, William de Tracy and Reginald Fitzurse landed in England and made their way to Saltwood Castle in Kent, where they were guests of the de Broc family. The de Brocs were enemies of Becket, after he as Chancellor had unearthed documents proving their estate should belong to the See of Canterbury.

They arrived in Canterbury on 29 December. Five eye-witnesses recorded what happened next, all agreeing on the key facts – though it should be said all five were supporters of Becket. It was late afternoon when the knights arrived at the archbishop's palace in the cathedral precinct, close to where the Deanery stands today. Becket was finishing dinner; the knights were dressed for battle, though they had removed their armour before entering the palace.

There was a heated argument and the knights left the palace to retrieve their armour and weapons. Those around Becket encouraged him to flee to the sanctuary of the cathedral, entering into the north transept. Becket ordered the doors to be unbarred. Once again he refused to take any step that might have avoided further confrontation.

He began to ascend the stairs to the choir where the monks were singing Vespers. The knights made their way from the palace to the cathedral, calling out 'Where is Thomas Becket, traitor to the king and the kingdom?'

Becket came back down the stairs to confront the knights. They attempted to carry him away but he resisted. Becket was on his knees at the time of the fatal attack, publicly commending his soul to God, the Virgin Mary, St Denis and – according to one account - St Alphege, a former archbishop murdered by Danes. Some argue he had staged his own martyrdom. He certainly did nothing to preserve his safety, just as he had avoided all opportunities for compromise with the king.

The sheer force of the first blow cut into the top of Becket's head and injured the arm of Edward Grim, a clerk from Cambridge, who had come to Becket's defence. The final strike by Brito sliced off the crown of Becket's head, spilling blood and brains onto the floor.

which gave its name to the settlement. Lympne Castle sits at the top of the hill, built in the twelfth century to defend the coast from French attack. Just how close to France you are here is evident in a plinth showing distances from the Roman civitas of *Cantiaci*, or Kent. Lympne lies only thirty-six miles from France, and *Durovernum Cantiacorum*, Canterbury, is only sixteen miles away – though this was as the Roman marched, rather than the pilgrim walked.

I sat down on a bench dedicated to a lost loved one and looked down onto Romney Marsh, the sea beyond. On the rim of that flat edgeland I understood just how near the sea was a few hundred years ago. Now, my path lay inland, all the way to Canterbury. So I followed lanes out of Lympne onto the fertile farmland of the Kent Downs, through wheat-sown fields into the tiny hamlet of Pedlinge. Paths through pastures where sheep basked led me to Brockhill Country Park, then into the village of Saltwood, known for its great castle.

Like Lympne, Saltwood's origins lie with the Romans, who the Saxon Osric defeated in 488. In 1026, and in the presence of the Danish king Cnut, the Saxon earl Haldane gave the manor of Saltwood to the monks of Christchurch, Canterbury. This was the Norman castle where, 150 years later, the plot was hatched to kidnap Thomas Becket.

I made my customary perambulation around the churchyard of St Peter and St Paul, where birds were still singing that chilly afternoon, the wind snatching blossom from the cherry trees, then walked on across pasture towards Saltwood Castle. With its gnarled curtain walls and crenellations, it is every schoolchild's impression of a medieval fortress, and a suitably menacing venue for the plot to assassinate Becket. Now a private house, it was the former home of art historian Sir Kenneth Clark and his son, the MP and diarist Alan Clark.

I was at the end of my day's journey, less than thirty miles from Canterbury and only three days' walk from Saltwood, where the history surrounding the seismic events of 1,000 years ago is palpable.

XXVI

It was more like early March than early May when I set out from Saltwood the following morning. The rain that had drenched the rest of England the previous day had arrived in the southeast overnight, and left by the time I started out on my walk. A cold northeasterly wind bit through my rainwear but soon the sun came out from behind the cloud, warming my skin.

I left Saltwood by a tiny country lane. The Old Way here comes close to Kent's new ways – the M20 and the Eurostar. Yet on this lane leading up towards the Kent Downs, where buzzards skimmed and blossom dropped onto the road like drifts of snow, I was walking through the silence of centuries past.

It felt good to be on chalk again, the crunch of flint beneath my boots as I returned to the landscape of my Samhain and Imbolc walks. Cow parsley and bluebells hemmed the banks of the lane as I plodded uphill to the rock where my feet felt most at home. I crossed a bridge over the Eurostar tracks. HS1, or High Speed 1, connecting London St Pancras with the Channel Tunnel at Folkestone, has created a huge gash in the landscape, still raw after almost twenty years. My thoughts, as often on the Downs, returned to the Chilterns, where I grew up and where HS2 is now gouging through its chalk hills and ancient woodlands.

Still the path rose steeply onto the down, banks arching above my head, deep purple bluebells nodding as I passed. This was now the Elham Valley Way, which runs over the Kent Downs to the coast at Hythe, and shadows the Old Way into Canterbury. Strawberries-and-cream hawthorn blossom and golden gorse edged the holloway. I was glad of Will's hazel staff to power me up the slope. At the top of Tolsford Hill I turned and looked back towards the coast. This would be my last view of the sea, first glimpsed on a Southampton spring day over a year earlier.

It was bleak and lonely up there, no company but the wind. And what a wind. I held on to my rain jacket with one hand to stop it blowing off my back, clinging on to my staff with the other. My map showed that high, gusty Tolsford Hill was the crossroads of three long-distance walking routes. There was the Saxon Shore Way, which I'd been following along the Royal Military Canal for the past couple of days, the Elham Valley Way heading north, and the North Downs Way from Winchester to Canterbury. The Pilgrims' Way, as rediscovered by Hilaire Belloc, also runs near here, but is lower down in the valley, following the route of the springlines as medieval pilgrims did. All old ways, it seemed, led to Canterbury.

A hawthorn-fringed track took me off the Downs, through sheepless pasture, towards Etchinghill. A skylark trilled somewhere to my left. You hear skylarks more readily than you see them, and when you do see them they are often nothing but a speck fluttering way above before parachuting back to earth. So much sound from such an inconsequential-looking bird.

There's a continuity to chalklands, and whether you're on the Dorset Downs or the Yorkshire Wolds, you're walking on the same rock. Unlike 'hard rocks' such as granite and slate, formed suddenly by volcanic, or igneous, activity, chalk is what geologists call 'soft', laid down over millions of years. Chalk is not only a soft rock, but it's a slow rock too. The Cretaceous was the longest ever period in geological time, ending around sixty-six million years ago, when the African tectonic plate collided with Europe, buckling our continent like a car bonnet. The Alps and the Pyrenees are the biggest of these buckles, while in Britain and Northern Europe, at the time one landmass, the ructions caused the chalk to rise from its watery grave. Later accretions of mud and sandstone eroded away until white chalk remained, largely in southern England and northern France, although outposts also emerged in northern England, Scandinavia, Germany and the Netherlands. Chalk connects us, only politics divides us.

Confused by the multiplicity of paths on Tolsford Hill, I'd taken a wrong turn and diverged slightly from the official route. My unofficial route cut through Etchinghill Golf Club. Trees that had been growing here for centuries lined the path, a corridor of wildness, life and birdsong, in the barren setting of the golf course. A deep, tree-sheltered track through the chalk, trunks of tangled oaks creaking in the wind, led me into Lyminge. Official or not, this was a very old way indeed.

The track led me to the church of St Mary and St Ethelburga, said to stand on the site of a Roman basilica. I went inside. A couple of women in face masks were talking quietly in one of the pews, so I looked for a pew a few metres away to socially distance. When the women saw me, they got up to leave.

'Enjoy your contemplation, and your walk,' said one. They had seen my staff, and assuming I was a pilgrim rather than someone just taking a stroll wanted to leave me in peace. They needn't have, but it was a lovely moment – as if in our cultural memory pilgrimage has never entirely disappeared, five centuries after Henry VIII's ban. Carrying Will's hazel staff also felt different to the aluminium walking pole I'd abandoned at the beginning of my journey. My hand comfortably clasped its top, and the wood was warm to the touch. The hazel felt alive, unlike the cold metal and indifferent rubber of a modern hiking pole. Holding the staff, from the Old English *stæf*, just felt right. Like the scrip, the staff had symbolic significance as one of the *signi peregrinationis*, or signs of pilgrimage, and was buried with the pilgrim as testament of their journey.

The Old Way guide mentions that the church is of Saxon origins, and the churchyard has recently been excavated by the University of Reading. These excavations uncovered the remains of a much earlier building: one of the first stone churches in England, built using techniques lost at the end of Roman rule. Archaeologists now believe that the church was founded around 634 by Ethelburga (or *Æthelburga*), a princess of Kent and Queen of Northumbria, whose Christian beliefs led to the conversion of the pagan North. They also saw that the pink mortar was made from crushed Roman brick and lime, indicating the church's masons had come from France, where this technique was widely used. A seamless continuity from Roman to Saxon, pagan to Christian, lying just beneath my feet.

Nearby was St Ethelburga's Well, another of the many springs I'd found on my pilgrimage with sacred associations. This was the source of the River Nailbourne, a stream with a legendary ability to prophesy, by flooding, ill fortune for the nation. From the Old English *brunna* for brook (or 'burn' in northern England and Scotland), most bournes flow only after heavy rainfall, or in winter. They are signposted by placenames with *bourne* as a prefix or suffix, such as Bourne End in Buckinghamshire or Winterbourne on Salisbury Plain, and commonly emanate from porous chalk bedrock.

A timber-framed well-house, dated 1898, shelters the Nailbourne's spring, which is said to have supplied the village from Roman times until 1905, when mains water was installed. An iron pump allowed villagers to pump water from the spring to road level. A notice on the well-house read:

This Well was sunk in the 7th century AD by St Ethelburga, daughter of Ethelbert of Kent and wife of King Edwin of Northumbria. She founded the Abbey of Lyminge after her husband had been killed at the Battle of Heathfield in 633 AD. She was Abbess until her death.

Through a grill underneath the handpump, among the Dr Pepper bottles, was the clear water of the chalk bourne. Eighty-five per cent of the world's 200 chalk streams, home to increasingly rare water voles and white-clawed crayfish, are found in England. Many are under threat from abstraction and pollution, so I was pleased to see the rivulet, blinking in the sunshine after its journey through the chalk.

I left Lyminge and its holy well via the Elham Valley Line, a Victorian railway once connecting Canterbury with Folkestone. There's no sign of the line now, just the flat valley bottom along which flows the Nailbourne. I followed the stream northeast, towards the village of Elham. Willow trees drooped over the banks. One old, hollowed trunk stood right by the stream, a few sheep droppings and tufts of wool around its twisted roots. This tree must have sheltered animals for aeons. So old, but still alive, still in leaf, still offering a home to local wildlife. A rusted roller lay half sunk in the pasture nearby, encircled by daisies and dandelions. It could have been lying there for a century, forgotten, abandoned, supplanted.

There was a spring in my step as I trod the sheep-cropped turf over the Downs, following the clear chalk stream from settlement to settlement, my path edged with hawthorns – some in blossom, some still only in leaf. The Nailbourne looked clean enough to drink. Will had recommended carrying purifying tablets so I could drink from springs and streams along the way. I didn't have any with me, but how lovely to drink water from the earth over which you are walking, binding you with it more tightly.

The chalk stream followed – or perhaps led – me all the way into Elham. I walked up Duck Street, and entered the District of Shepway. In the Middle Ages a *shepweye* was a route for sheep, creatures that had been my companions every day of my walk since Winchelsea. Duck Street took me to Elham's perfect, peaceful village square, fronted with houses whose Georgian facades, judging by the pitch of their roofs, hid much older buildings. Now that I was back on chalk downland, I was back to flint churches, and St Mary's was a flint church *par excellence* with its curvaceous gabled north porch giving it an almost Dutch feel. How close this part of the country is to mainland Europe, despite the thin strip of sea that now divides us.

XXVII

Canterbury was now just twenty seductive miles away. I could reach it that evening, but to honour the spirit of my year-long journey I resolved to walk it over two days. After all, I'd been walking for more than a year now, through plague, pestilence, sunshine, wind and rain, so what was the hurry?

Leaving Elham that cold, bright May day, I rejoined the Nailbourne. A stately procession of poplars, flanking the stream as if to protect her, escorted me out of the village. It had rained the previous evening but the chalk path beneath my boots was dry and fissured, and drew me up towards the Downs. From a hawthorn hedge brimming with blossom, a great tit piped its two-tone song. The collage of arable fields, pasture, copses, thickets, woodland and rounded hills evoked the Chilterns of my childhood, and I was very much at home in the landscape that morning.

BELTANE

My path hugged the hillside, an old way between the soggy valley bottom and the hilltop, halfway up and halfway down. You could see it had been trodden for centuries, feel yourself walking in the footsteps of wayfarers and soldiers, peasants and pilgrims. Among sunny yellow daisies, dandelions, cowslips and wild violets quivered. Technically this was 'unimproved' meadow, but in my eyes vastly improved by being allowed to get on with the business of being a meadow, with all the flowers and plants and insects it sustained. Even the dead-nettles were blooming a deep pink. I'd never thought of nettles as attractive before, but they were as beautiful as any other flower I saw that morning.

I diverged from the Nailbourne, though I still saw her in the valley bottom, escorting me step by step. I climbed steeply up through coppiced woodland and a haze of deep-purple bluebells, then out into fields again and across ploughed farmland stippled with crystalline flints. The swallows swooped and dived, hoovering up insects feeding on the meadow's dandelions. Without the dandelions there wouldn't be the insects, and without the insects there wouldn't be the swallows.

Down again into one of those steep-sided, secluded valleys so characteristic of chalk down. No roads passed through here, just tracks. The valley was softly scooped out – nothing hard, nothing jagged, just smooth and scooped and silent.

I entered Bedlam Wood, overflowing with primroses and violets and my first orchid of the year, an early purple (*Orchis mascula*), right beside the path. A lover of both chalk downland and ancient woodland, it had found the perfect habitat here. A pilgrim walking this way in the Middle Ages will not have called it an early purple orchid, let alone *Orchis mascula,* but is likely to have used one of its local nicknames. Goosey ganders, kecklegs, bloody butchers, adder's meat and kettle cases are some of the other colourful names for this flower. Gethsemane, another of its names, arises from the legend that it bloomed under Christ's cross. A not impossible scenario, as the flower is found throughout Europe, North Africa and Southwest Asia.

As I walked on through Bedlam Wood, other common-or-garden flowers with enchanting names multiplied ahead. Red campion, lesser celandine, wood anemone, bird's-eye speedwell and, among the bluebells, star of Bethlehem – also known as Jack-go-to-bed-at-noon, sleepy Dick and, from its habit of opening late in the morning, eleven o'clock lady. Dove's dung and summer snowflake are among its other picturesque names. Folklore has it that the star of Bethlehem, as followed by the biblical Three Kings, fell to earth, splintering into millions of miniature white stars. Perhaps it was this flower that gave the wood its name, Bedlam being a corruption of the word Bethlehem. The present connotation with pandemonium originated with the medieval hospital of St Mary of Bethlehem in London, which treated mentally ill patients. There was no mayhem in Bedlam Wood that morning, only a feast of flowers, the canopy letting just enough sunlight through for them to bloom.

Bedlam Wood was not only a feast for the eyes, but for the nose also as I breathed in that distinctive May aroma of wild garlic, spiky blooms as white as snowdrops hidden within their leaves. I picked off a leaf to chew, its taste transporting me to the scents and flavours of the warm south. Further orchids fringed my path. If the wildflowers were an orchestra of muted yellows, whites, blues and pinks, the deep rich colour of the early purple orchid was its great clashing cymbal, a brash show-off demanding my full attention.

The walk through Bedlam Wood was half an hour of pure magic before a monoculture of arable, a prairie of garish green wheat with not one flower to disrupt the monotony. My path through the wheat field was only around half a kilometre long, but it felt as much of a slog as walking along tarmac. Walking through Bedlam Wood, I had covered three times the distance in what seemed no time at all.

An unremarkable path through thicket of blackthorn and bramble, the sort of path that has served England's communities for centuries, led me down to the village of Barham. I love these commonplace paths, used by ordinary folk to travel between hamlets and villages, towns and fields. Every type of path had its own name. A bypath (what we would today call a byway) was a seldom used path. A rack took you steeply uphill, while a loke was a narrow, grassy path. A trodgate was a trampled footpath and a mudpike an unpaved track before the advent of paved turnpikes. Unlike their prestigious long-distance cousins – the Ridgeway, the Pennine Way, the South West Coast Path – these are the workhorses of the country's public footpath system. Unlovely, sometimes overgrown, and in the age of the car often unused, but for pilgrims like me, invaluable.

There's an almost Venetian feel to Barham, where the Nail-bourne oozes through the middle of the village and across the road, as it has done forever. I crossed a footbridge and followed a path named The Causeway, then up a winding lane with weatherboard and brick-fronted houses, to the church of St John the Baptist. Here I sat in the lychgate to eat my sandwich, trying not to think about the thousands of corpses that had passed this way on their final journey to the cemetery. Lingering on in church terminology, the Saxon word for corpse, *lic*, has fallen out of use in English now, although it continues its old meaning in Germanic languages and in the Lyke Wake Walk, a forty-mile trail on the old coffin route across the North York Moors.

East Kent villages, like those over the county border in East Sussex, are almost edible in their gorgeousness: all burnished brick, bronze-brown tiles cascading from the roof nearly to the ground, exuberant cottage gardens. Barham was hard to leave, but eventually I left to climb up onto Heart's Delight Hill, its gradient taxing rather than delighting my heart. Paths bordered with bluebells led me over fields of slender-legged horses, through garlic-scented woodland and past apple orchards bubbling with blossom, and rejoined the Nailbourne down in her valley.

On my way through Long Ruffett Wood, birds singing in the canopy like choristers in the gallery, I passed a young man in running shorts and earphones, cheery and waving, emerging from the woodland as I entered. How lovely to be that young man, fit and strong, not worried about who you might meet on the path through the woods.

When walking alone in woodland, I am attentive though not afraid. But a few days earlier, just before I arrived in Winchelsea, Julia James, fifty-three, a Police Community Support Officer, was murdered in a random attack while walking her dog in woodland only two miles from where I now was. The TV news each night covered the search for the attacker, not yet identified and still on the run. Police were warning women not to go out walking alone, advising them to tell someone when they were expected home. I was walking alone, and home was 270 miles away. I would not be expected there for another week. Should I cut short my walk and return home, even though I was now within touching distance of Canterbury? Like medieval women pilgrims before me, perhaps even Alice of Southwick herself, I was vulnerable, and nervous. Even more than this, I was angry. Angry that a woman could not go out alone without her life being cut violently short, and those of her family, friends and close-knit community, who never before even locked their front doors, marred forever.

I pushed my fears to the back of my mind and paused at St Giles' Church in the hamlet of Kingston. In 1771 the rector, the Reverend Bryan Faussett, unearthed a brooch dating from the seventh century in a burial mound on Kingston Down. The Kingston Brooch, as it was named, is the largest ever composite Anglo-Saxon brooch discovered, fashioned of gold and inlaid with garnets and blue glass. It's now kept in the Museum of Liverpool, but it put Kingston, and the tumuli of the surrounding Downs, firmly on the map of Anglo-Saxon Kent. I made my customary circuit of the flint building in search of peace, and inspiration. The plain village churches I'd visited throughout my journey hold so much history in their thousand-year old stones, witnessed endless war and turbulence, yet still they stand, as solid and rooted as oaks.

A hawthorn-lined path led me out of Kingston, where I reunited with the Nailbourne. She looked less lively now, her water stiller and laced with grass, winding her way through Charlton Park between beeches, oaks and horse chestnuts. I've never been there, but it was almost Serengeti-like in its yellowing grassland and lone scattered trees. Only the wildlife was different. In place of lions, giraffes and wildebeest, here in Kent fat sheep nibbled on grass. And no wildebeest were drinking at a muddy watering hole, just a few ducks swimming round the ornamental lake.

Charlton Park met Bishopsbourne, then morphed into Bourne Park. I was still following the course of the Nailbourne, through parkland the map called The Wilderness. If this was wilderness, it was a very English kind: benign, peaceful, a Queen Anne country house stuck in the middle. I was near some of the busiest road and rail routes in the country, yet all I heard were birds and sheep, and the soft trickle of the River Nailbourne, leading me all the way to Bridge.

XXVIII

I returned to Bridge the following morning on a high of anticipation. Today would be the final walk of my 240-mile pilgrimage to Canterbury, over a year after I first strode out of Southampton the previous, innocent spring. The world had changed since then, and so had I.

The sun shone, the air was crisp and cool, the birds sang as I began walking from Bridge towards Canterbury. Lying on Watling Street, the Roman road between London and Dover, excavations at nearby Bourne House have revealed Roman coins and pottery. Further digs have uncovered a Roman burial ground near the village itself, which is probably named after the bridge (OE *brycge*) that crossed the Nailbourne here. Canterbury was only a couple of miles further along Watling Street, but the Old Way takes you on a more circuitous route, along the Nailbourne Valley to Patrixbourne. So I left Bridge and struck off into the countryside. After a solid week of walking my legs were feeling the miles, but the staff Will had given me powered me on towards Canterbury.

Through Bifrons Park I walked, the grass dewy and less Serengeti-like after last night's rain. A great procession of lime trees marched across the park. One had a trunk that had split in two, just wide enough for a pilgrim without a backpack and the extra pounds of middle age to squeeze through.

In Patrixbourne I met up with the Nailbourne, healthy and full after the rain. Violets in the churchyard and a yew-lined pathway led to the magnificent south door of St Mary's Church, with its elaborate Norman carving in the tympanum and east 'wheel' window. Above the priest's door was a carved figure, said to be Thomas Becket, now headless. As Patrixbourne was on the pilgrim route to Canterbury, and so close to the city, it's likely this is our saint, mutilated in the Reformation. They might have disfigured his effigy, but devotion to Thomas continued, though in secret.

A heron, which had stopped to feed in the river, glided over-head. The Nailbourne only flows for around six months every five to seven years, but in the winter of 2000 to 2001 flooded many buildings along its course. Will had said that the river was known as 'a woo-mere', or a 'woe-water', whose unpredictable flooding brought inauspicious tidings for England.

'The last time it flooded was in 2016,' he'd told me – a tumul-tuous year in British politics.

I was sad that the church was closed that day, but it was a reminder that we were living in difficult times.

My medieval pilgrim forebears faced enormous problems too. Life was tough, with waves of pandemic, famine, floods and failed harvests, especially in the fourteenth century. Covid had been a wake-up call that we are not always masters, or mistresses, of our own lives, even with the advantages of living in the twenty-first century rather than the fourteenth. Yet the plague had brought benefits. If everything had gone to plan, I wouldn't have encountered those who had so enhanced my journey – Tom in Southwick, the gravedigger in Warblington, the hermit Michael in Steyning, Tracy and Graham in Appledore. And those moments of peace and birdsong in the churchyards when the church doors were locked.

A lane alongside woodland thick with birdsong, a cacophony of sound, led me up Keepers Hill. I recognised a chiffchaff, which was singing loudest of all, and a blackbird hopped among the branches. The direct route into Canterbury from Patrixbourne follows the North Downs Way, but I didn't want to finish my walk before I had to. Following the Old Way guide's recommendation, and the practice of medieval pilgrims, I would make a semicircle around the city and visit some of the holy wells and churches for which this corner of Kent is renowned.

Once out into open farmland skylarks serenaded me, their song full of hope and joy. They weren't serenading me of course, but it felt so that sunny morning, walking along Old Palace Road into Bekesbourne. Archbishop Thomas Cranmer penned the *Book of Common Prayer* here, though only the brick gatehouse remains of his original palace, the initials 'T C 1552' carved over the doorway, after the rest was demolished in the Civil War. A Tudor-style mansion was built on its site, at one time occupied by James Bond author Ian Fleming and his socialite wife, Ann, who was reportedly upset by ghostly goings-on in the house.

Old Palace Road led me across the Nailbourne, still in full and vigorous flow, to St Peter's Church and alongside willows and poplars to Well Chapel. Not much remains of the building today. It's not even recognisable as a chapel, just a few stretches of flint wall protruding from the ground like snaggled teeth, overgrown with bramble and ivy. Yet wells and springs were holy places, and holy places were honoured with holy buildings, such as this.

A narrow path dived through the thicket to a pool of water – the well for which the chapel was built. Will had suggested a swim, but a tractor was driving up and down the vineyard nearby so instead I dipped my hazel staff into the pool, soaking up the magic of this scrap of ancient woodland where mayflies skimmed over the water.

The Old Way then took me through Howletts Wild Animal Park, where the chorus of birdsong was joined by the grunts of wild boar, before it returned to the usual Kent scenery of apple orchards. Wild boar, a species native to Britain, once roamed freely before being hunted to extinction during the Middle Ages. Controversially, as they have no natural predators, wild boar escaped from farms are roving wild in the Weald of Kent and East Sussex, the Forest of Dean and West Dorset, where they are believed to have a positive impact on woodland biodiversity.

Apples, on the other hand and in spite of their connotations of rural Englishness, are not native to England. Originating from Southwest Asia some four millennia ago, and growing from pips discarded along the Silk Road, apples were first cultivated in Britain during the Roman occupation. The Black Death and decades of poor harvests led to the fruit's decline, before its revival by Henry VIII. Until Victorian times apples were a luxury, transported from Kent and sold in the London fruit markets. Only the windfalls and rejects were sold to local people.

I entered woodland, looking for traces of the Roman road marked on my map. Beginning in Sandwich on the coast, this was the road along which St Augustine may have journeyed to Canterbury when he brought Roman Christianity to England in 597, although it's likely he travelled to Fordwich from Thanet by boat, rather than on foot. Christians, though, had worshipped in these islands since the fourth century, particularly in the Celtic north and west. It took another seven decades after Augustine became Canterbury's first archbishop for the Synod of Whitby to vote to follow Roman regulations, rather than those of the Celtic Church, in 664.

The Roman road was now buried under woodland, so I found forest paths that led through bluebells and wood anemones, birch and beech, gorse and heath. After the night's rain the chalk path was less fractured, yielding as I walked. A final country lane took me through pasture and woodland into Fordwich. My map placed me on the outer reaches of modern Canterbury, though I didn't sense it as I walked alone down a sunken lane used by travellers since the Middle Ages, and perhaps by Alice herself.

Fordwich lies at a crossing over the River Stour. This is the waterway that flows through Canterbury, nine centuries ago bringing stone from Caen in Normandy to build the cathedral. With its oast house and street of half-timbered and weatherboard buildings leading into fields and pastures, Fordwich is an archetypal Kent village – though it was hard to enjoy it as I desperately needed the loo. The only prospect was the Fordwich Arms, a pub restaurant with Range Rovers parked outside and one star in the Michelin Guide. I went inside, shabby, sweaty and bedraggled from days of walking.

'Excuse me,' I said to the smartly dressed waitress behind the bar. 'I'm walking to Canterbury. Can I use your loo?' She appraised me for a moment as I stood there with my rucksack and staff. Not a vagrant, but a pilgrim.

'Of course!' she said, ushering me inside and showing me to the facilities. As I left, my hands scented with sandalwood lotion, I thanked her and promised I'd return to eat in the restaurant when I passed this way again, more suitably attired. And I meant it. I went outside, thankful for the waitress's generosity. I didn't resemble the restaurant's usual clientele, but pilgrims have passed this way for centuries, and perhaps subconsciously she understood I was on a mission. Just like St Augustine, crossing the River Stour at Fordwich 1,500 years earlier on his way to Canterbury.

I sat down outside the Town Hall to eat my usual sandwich. The Town Hall is a grand name for a modest timber-framed building, but it's been the town hall since 1544 and is still very much in use. Nearby was St Mary the Virgin, the last village church on my walk, its churchyard full of birds and bluebells. Auspiciously, it was open. Inside I found a remarkable carved stone monument, Norman or even earlier, and thought to be a shrine made for the relics of a saint – maybe even St Augustine himself.

The Old Way exits Fordwich parallel to the main road into Canterbury. But first, before the suburbs, one last, magical wood. Thick and dark, its entrance like a tunnel, a tiny patch of wilderness. Untethered nature, so close to the edge of the city.

After what felt like hours in the enchanted wood I found myself on the first urban fringes of Canterbury. The wilderness had ended. There would be no more woods, pastures, downland, no more ancient tracks coiling over chalk hills. It felt good to reach my destination, but part of me wanted to walk on forever – to the coast at Sandwich, perhaps even to Rome, from where St Augustine hailed.

'This fellow won't get up again'

As Thomas lay dying, Hugh of Horsea, a clerk accompanying the knights said: 'Let's get out of here . . . this fellow won't get up again.' The knights fled chanting 'We are the king's men' – but not before ransacking the archbishop's palace, perhaps looking for incriminating correspondence that could excuse their act.

For hours, Becket's body lay where it had fallen. After a while, some monks came forward to collect samples of his blood. The Canterbury monks, suspicious of Becket for his earlier life of luxury, were surprised to discover that under his robes he wore a hair shirt. This was taken as further evidence of his sanctity.

The first recorded miracle came almost immediately. A townsperson took some of Becket's blood mixed with water to his wife; on drinking this her paralysis was cured. Others were said to have been healed of their leprosy and blindness, in echoes of the Gospel miracles. There was a concerted campaign by the monks to have Becket canonised. As well as describing his saintly life, parallels were drawn with the life and death of Christ.

News of the murder of an archbishop in his own cathedral caused widespread shock and horror as it spread throughout Europe. The Pope excommunicated the four knights, but took no action against Henry. For around a year, the four knights remained in Knaresborough Castle in Yorkshire, where they'd sought refuge. Henry made little effort to punish them. It's not clear what became of them afterwards, but it's assumed they would have travelled to Rome to receive penance from the Pope, who may have sent them to the Holy Land. All four are presumed to have died in Jerusalem or on the way.

King Henry, meanwhile, put on a public show of grief, fasting on bread and water for forty days. Yet he was said to have been unapologetic for about a year and a half following Becket's death, before displaying signs of genuine remorse.

When he first arrived in Canterbury in 597, and before founding his own cathedral, St Augustine set up his headquarters in a church that already existed here. Thought to be the oldest parish church in the English-speaking world, St Martin's has been in continuous use since at least the sixth century. Bede wrote that the building was the private chapel of Queen Bertha of Kent, and historians believe it may have been a mortuary chapel when Canterbury was the Roman settlement of *Durovernum Cantiacorum*. Patches of Roman brickwork are still visible in the flint walls.

It was a peaceful spot, an island of nature above the old city. I sat on the church steps and ahead, for the first time, saw the towers and spires of the cathedral rising above the town. On the Gough Map, where the red line of the Old Way ends, *Cantuar* is given the full treatment: city walls pierced by a gate, a castle, a spired church with two crosses and roofs decorated with stripes. It dominates the surrounding settlements, with Dover on the coast and Rochester on the Thames the only similar-sized towns. Whether arriving from Southampton, or from London, or any of the other roads that led medieval pilgrims to the shrine of St Thomas, this cathedral was larger than anything they had seen in their lives. Even today, surrounded by buildings of two, three or four storeys, it still towers above the old city. It still tears your breath away.

I lingered a while in the churchyard among the twisted yews and tilting gravestones, listening to the birds. I was in no hurry to complete the last few hundred metres to the cathedral, after walking so far and for so long.

After days of walking and visiting tiny villages and churches, I was with Alice of Southwick as she entered Canterbury. The old Roman road to Dover took us past St Augustine's Abbey on the edge of the old city centre. Founded in 598, the abbey predates the present Norman cathedral by some five centuries, and lasted 1,000 years before its suppression by Henry VIII. Alice and I didn't linger at the abbey for long. I had an appointment with Will Parsons, who had offered to welcome me to Canterbury at the end of my pilgrimage.

Will and I had agreed to meet in the cathedral precinct. Huge walls, perhaps forty feet high with round crenellated towers enclosed the precinct, looking more like the ramparts of a castle than a place of worship. These were the original fortifications of *Durovernum Cantiacorum*, built by the Romans in 270–90.

After wandering about for a while I tracked down Will at the back of the cathedral, accompanied by his dog, Holly, and young daughter, Felicity. After a few celebratory photos of me walking into the cloisters, Will led me to the supposed site of the well over which the cathedral had been built. It had been discovered on a twelfth-century plan of the cathedral's waterworks drawn up by Prior Wilbert in around 1165. Historians note that this waterworks and drainage system was the first to have been installed in Britain since the Roman occupation, and is clearly marked on the plan with the Latin word *Puteus*, with a drawing of a well underneath. Prior Wilbert had designed a system whereby water from outside the city was pumped one mile to the priory (as it was then), supplying fresh water for the monks, their 'ponds, conduits and fishpools', said his 1167 obituary.

The well was underground, and not many people seemed aware of its existence, Will told me as we stood on the stone flags near Prior Wilbert's water tower, which still, amazingly, survives.

'Becket was only twenty years after Wilbert,' Will said, 'so it's absolutely contemporary with him. And it's the only place on the plan marked *Puteus*, so one can assume that it's the only well within the cathedral precincts.' As I'd discovered, many churches were built around pre-Christian holy places. Pope Gregory 'the Great' even wrote letters recommending this as official policy to help convert the pagan tribes to the new religion. In all likelihood, this was the pre-Christian well around which the cathedral was built, and which the monks would use if the piped water ran dry. This was also the well, Will reminded me, that famously ran red with Becket's blood. Mixed with water, it became Canterbury (or Thomas) Water, filling the ampules of medieval pilgrims such as Alice of Southwick who arrived in their hundreds of thousands and took them home as holy souvenirs.

'It was a bit dodgy,' Will said, 'because Leviticus is quite clear – don't drink human blood. When Henry VIII's commissioners demolished the shrine of Becket, they took down the well too. I've tasted this water many times now – I drink it whenever I come – and it's naturally iron-rich, so it really does taste like blood. Can I borrow your staff for a moment?'

'Of course. It's been the ideal staff for me, by the way. Perfect size and shape.'

Will took my staff and began to pound the stone flags around our feet. 'The first time I found the well was at the end of my first journey on the Old Way,' he said, still thudding the ground with the hazel staff. 'I knew from my map that it was somewhere around here . . .' After a few further moments of thumping the sound changed, becoming deeper.

'It's hollow!'

'Yes. This is the site of the ancient well of St Thomas. You're standing on the water.' I looked down at my feet. 'In the driest summers, such as in 2018 when it didn't rain for a month and a half, there was still absolutely the same amount of water under here.'

'So to find it you just walked around and bashed the ground with your stick?'

'Yes, and I've had it confirmed since. It's rising from the ground under here.'

Will reached into his pocket and took out a tiny glass bottle, stopped with a cork. Inside was a dark red liquid, just like blood.

'What's that?'

'This is the "blood" of St Thomas. It's just water from the well, which I mixed with red ochre, like the monks did. Here, you can put it on your mantelpiece and it will settle and go clear. Just give it a shake and it will become blood again.'

That's incredible! So you got the water out of here?'

'Yes, and we purified it with a really good purifier, so you can drink it if you want to.'

'How did you get the water out?'

'I have a pump filter, a purifier, in my bag.' Will carries a water purifier on his long walking journeys so he can drink from springs along the way rather than carrying bottled water. He lifted the drain cover as I kept watch, unconvinced the cathedral authorities would be too pleased if they saw what we were up to. Inside, the water was running a few inches below the surface.

'No wonder people believed it was the blood of St Thomas,' I said. 'I'm going to treasure this. I'm not going to drink it.'

'England's saint'

After Becket's murder the cathedral was reopened from April 1171 and many more miracles were reported. Becket was not yet a saint, but the site of his burial was gaining shrine-like status. For the monks of Christ Church, Canterbury, Becket's murder was transformational. In life, he had been absent for many years; in death, he drew great crowds of pilgrims, a source of revenue for the priory. St Thomas, or Canterbury, Water – a tincture of his blood mixed with water – was sold to pilgrims. In 1171 alone, historians estimate, 100,000 people visited Becket's shrine.

Becket was canonised as St Thomas of Canterbury on 21 February 1173 (Ash Wednesday). It was one of the fastest canonisations in history. His murder was an internationally significant event, promoting Canterbury Cathedral as one of Europe's main pilgrimage destinations. Within ten years of his murder 703 miracles associated with the saint were recorded, and news of his miracles spread throughout Europe, where churches are dedicated to him in countries as far apart as France, Italy and Norway. Pilgrims flocked to his shrine at Canterbury, many of these following the Old Way from Southampton.

Becket became England's saint. So popular and powerful was the cult of Thomas that his backstory was elaborated within the next century. In one popular version, his merchant father Gilbert became a crusader who married a Saracen's daughter, who gave birth to Thomas.

In the ten years following his death, ten biographies were written about Becket, and more miracles were claimed for him than were ascribed to the Virgin Mary.

'You can do whatever you want with it. They say you can put it on the fields, or on thresholds, or use it when someone gets ill.' Like the pilgrims who bought souvenir phials of Canterbury Water had done, centuries earlier. Like Alice did.

'Where did you get the little glass bottle from?'

Will gave a small smile. 'Amazon.'

I took a photo of my phial of blood, and of Will, Felicity and Holly.

'There's one more thing before we go,' Will said, turning to Felicity. 'Shall we let Gail make the silver?' Felicity nodded. 'You know the tradition with wishing wells, where we chuck in coins? In the Druidic tradition, they throw silver in the great holy lakes, so my thinking is that silver in holy water comes from that pre-Roman, pre-Christian tradition.' He turned again to his daughter. 'Can you give it to Gail as she's going to do it?' Felicity handed me a tiny silver disc, as small as an old farthing. 'This is 99.9 percent pure silver, the purest silver you can buy. You can even eat it as a food additive: E174. It's not like modern sterling, with seven and a half per cent copper and nickel.'

'Where do you get it from? Amazon again?'

'From Cookson's – it's brilliant.'

'So, you buy bullion online?'

'Yes, I buy silver and I throw it into wells. I like adding value to Britain, putting some treasure back into the ground. If you've made the journey here, and if you're going to take the blessing, then you've got to give something back.'

Will told me that it's considered good pilgrim practice, at the end of your pilgrimage, to take the staff that has been with you the whole way, and throw it into water. You give your staff back to the land, even though you've become emotionally attached to it on your journey. *Because* you've become emotionally attached to it on your journey. 'It's good practice for when you have to give your body back at the end of your life,' he said.

'I can't give my stick back because the well's not deep enough, but I can dip it into the holy water.'

'That's a great idea!'

'And I've put some daisies in there too,' said Felicity.

'And we're all going to make a wish,' said Will.

And we did.

Cold, tired and euphoric, I walked the final few minutes to the Premier Inn. My third-floor window faced south, and overlooked the cathedral. Lying on my bed, I watched as the sun set over the towers and spires, floodlights illuminating them from below. Like an optical illusion, the cathedral floated above the darkening city.

XXIX

I woke up the next morning, reborn, and flung open the curtains. The cathedral was still there, washed in sunshine and casting its immense shadow over the roofs of Canterbury. The building was still not fully open for visitors, but private prayer was allowed for a few hours in the middle of the day, so I pulled on my boots once again and walked to the centre of town, into the cathedral precinct and through the doorway.

'Not as a king but as a beggar'

King Henry's authority was weakened by his association with Becket's murder, and was one reason his wife, Eleanor of Aquitaine, encouraged three of their sons – Henry, Richard 'the Lionheart' and Geoffrey – to rebel against their father.

Facing civil war, Henry arrived at Canterbury on 12 July 1174 to atone for his part in Becket's murder. He arrived on horseback but proceeded from Harbledown, around two miles from the cathedral, on foot. From St Dunstan's Church, now the site of Canterbury West railway station, he removed most of his outer garments and continued barefoot. As one chronicler put it, he came 'not as a king but as a beggar'.

At Becket's tomb, the monks scourged Henry with reeds, and he prayed at the shrine overnight. Through this penance, Henry aligned himself with the cult of St Thomas. The next day, William the Lion, king of Scotland, was defeated and imprisoned at Alnwick by Henry's forces. Had Thomas intervened on the king of England's side?

Henry II made nine separate pilgrimages to Becket's tomb between 1174 and his death in 1189. In September 1174 a fire broke out in the city, spreading to the cathedral. The destruction was an opportunity to rebuild the east end of the church.

In July 1220, Becket's body was 'translated' to the new shrine, an event witnessed by many international dignitaries, including the thirteen-year-old Henry III. The miracle windows around the location of the shrine, an astonishing survival given the Reformation and Henry's hatred of Thomas, tell the story of Becket's life and miracles. One panel shows pilgrims travelling to Canterbury in the 1180s.

Every king of England, from Henry II up to, ironically, Henry VIII, visited the shrine. Edward III made the journey annually.

By the time of *The Canterbury Tales*, Becket had become England's most celebrated saint.

There was only one other person in the area of the nave where the public were currently allowed. Awestruck, I stood looking up at the fourteenth-century pillars, imagining how my forebears must have felt as they entered this holy place after a long and arduous pilgrimage. Stone columns, cleaned now of their original paint, soared towards heaven, and sunlight gushed in through clear glass windows once coloured like jewels. Beyond the rood screen the choir was dark and Romanesque, with much of the original twelfth-century glass miraculously intact. In a chapel on the north side, and today hidden from view, was the place where Archbishop Thomas Becket was murdered on 29 December 1170. It was a different experience to that of medieval pilgrims. Quieter, lighter, calmer. But just as sublime.

I sat myself down on one of the socially distanced wooden chairs. Cathedrals like this are holy places, but as I'd discovered on my walks over four seasons, it's not only in buildings you find the sacred. You find it all around you, if only you slow down enough to look. Churches might offer spaces for contemplation and silence, but so do woods, meadows, hills, rivers, marshes, sea and chalk downland. Nature is a holy place too.

After a few moments a member of the cathedral staff, to whom I'd mentioned that I'd walked 240 miles to Canterbury, came over to where I was sitting.

'Would you like a blessing?' she asked me. I said I would, very much. 'The Archdeacon will be along in a few minutes. She's in a meeting now, but shouldn't be long.' I waited, then a woman wearing ecclesiastical robes and a warm smile approached.

'Hi, I'm Jo. I'm the Archdeacon. Lovely to meet you. Welcome to the mother church.' She had a bobbed haircut and a New Zealand accent. 'So, you've walked to Canterbury?' I told her I had, though it had taken over a year since I'd started out in Southampton.

'Well done you! I understand you'd like a blessing. Just follow me.' I picked up my rucksack and staff, and followed Jo beyond the roped-off area towards the choir. As we walked I asked her about her life here. She told me that she'd been Archdeacon for over four years now, after her role as Dean of Auckland. Before that she'd worked as a solicitor, both in New Zealand and in London. She led me down into the cathedral crypt, the largest of its age in England, which lay under the choir.

The crypt was dark and atmospheric, a forest of Norman columns with an apse and chapels radiating from its centre. Pevsner describes the carved capitals as the best-preserved Early Romanesque sculpture in England, and they were already a century old when Becket was murdered. At the end of the crypt is the site where his body was originally buried.

In 1220, Becket's body was moved into a magnificent, jewel-encrusted shrine in the main body of the cathedral, where it was revered for over three centuries until its destruction in 1538. Our steps echoed on the stone-flagged floors, worn and shiny after a thousand years of pilgrims' feet and knees as they knelt to pray.

'This is the oldest part of the cathedral,' Jo told me. 'It's survived fires, wars, famines, plagues – everything. These stones tell a story.'

Jo suggested we stand in silence for a few moments. I put down my rucksack and staff, and we stood side by side. The ambience of profound peace in the crypt of this great cathedral was the same as I'd found in all the tiny, isolated pilgrim churches throughout my walk along the Old Way. Jo said a short prayer of blessing for my pilgrimage. The prayer was personal and moving, and I did indeed feel blessed to be here in this crypt: a pilgrim who had reached the end of a long journey between the chalk and the sea.

HOMEGOING

NOUN, mid-seventeenth century: The action of returning to one's home, household, or native land; a return home.

It was in the quietude of the crypt of Christ Church Cathedral that Alice and I finally parted ways. My journey along the Old Way was done. For my companion of four seasons and 240 miles of chalk, turf, shingle, sand, mud, sun, rain, drizzle, hail and wind (lots of wind), it was far from over.

More than seven centuries have passed since Alice, the imaginary wife I have fashioned for the very real Richard of Southwick, carried out her pilgrimage. The only hard evidence we have that one or more members of Richard's household made the journey to Canterbury is the two pewter ampules recovered from the cesspit of the house in Southampton. The rest is conjecture.

With the hindsight of contemporary accounts, we can guess what happened when Alice reached the cathedral. First, there were religious duties to perform. No private blessing in the crypt for Alice; she would have elbowed her way through the crowd of fellow pilgrims jostling to reach the tomb of the saint, one of the finest in Europe. Once at the shrine, she offered a prayer of supplication or thanksgiving, making a votive offering of a candle, a silver coin or a wax image of an afflicted body part if sickness was the purpose of her pilgrimage. A document dated 1428, and held by the British Library, describes the scene that awaited pilgrims arriving at the cathedral:

> The shrine-keepers open the doors to the people who have kept a devoted watch throughout the night and let them enter. Many of them arrive with great devotion, eager to hear the life and works of the glorious martyr Thomas which

are usually read in the mother tongue, and they store them up in their attentive minds and pious hearts. This having finished, the two clerks serve the people, who may be wearied by toil, drawing them to the heat of the fire that they have prepared, soothing them, and serving them sufficient bread, cheese, and ale.

After completing her devotions Alice left the cathedral, buying her pewter ampule of Canterbury Water, embossed with an image of the sainted archbishop, on the way out. Canterbury Water, like all relics associated with St Thomas, was renowned for its miraculous healing properties, so perhaps she bought it for Richard, languishing at home in Southampton, to drink or rub on his skin. Archaeologists excavating their house in Cuckoo Lane in 1966 found two ampules, so it may be Alice bought one for herself as a talisman, to wear around her neck or sew on her clothes, and another for Richard. Or perhaps Richard, healthy and in fine fettle after all, accompanied Alice on pilgrimage to Canterbury, each of them buying a souvenir of the visit.

Before returning home, Alice spent a few more days at Canterbury, resting and sightseeing. She might have stayed in Eastbridge Hospital, built in 1180 by merchant Edward Fitzbold ('son of Odbold') as accommodation for the torrent of pilgrims arriving after Thomas's martyrdom. It's still there today. Probably she returned to the cathedral, visited the church of St Martin (then 700 years old) and toured some of the other city churches, particularly if one was dedicated to her favourite saint.

Eventually, though, she will have gone home. Unless she managed to hitch a lift on a vessel sailing back to Southampton, Alice turned round and re-walked, or re-rode, each one of those 240 miles. Only when she reached her house in Cuckoo Lane a few weeks later, bearing ampules of Thomas's blood as proof of her journey, was her pilgrimage fulfilled. After regaling her household and friends with tales from the road, she may have sought blessings from her parish priest, and given thanks for her safe return. Only then will she have resumed her ordinary life as mistress of a wealthy Southampton household, her memories and the ampules of Thomas's blood the only traces of her journey to Canterbury.

We can presume Alice did arrive home safely. Canterbury was not Jerusalem after all, and the two ampules found in her house confirm it. Like Alice, I too returned home safely. Unlike Alice, I did not walk home. My journey began in Southampton, like hers, but my home was in North Yorkshire, a distance Google Maps estimates as 264 miles as the crow flies.

But walking is not flying. It would have taken many more weeks for me to emulate Alice, and cross the country on foot to reach home. Hers was a pilgrimage in its truest, medieval sense: a circular and self-propelled journey of departure and, God willing, return. My own pilgrimage was an approximation of Alice's, a modern version constrained by modern pressures. In the Middle Ages, pilgrimage was a valid and respected reason to take weeks, or even months, out of one's ordinary routine. Not so in twenty-first century Britain. I had my work to get back to, and my Richard, unlike Alice's, did not have servants to help him run the household.

Back home, major upheavals were happening in our lives. Between beginning and ending my pilgrimage, and amid the various lockdowns, we moved house. Our new home is not far from the sturdy gritstone farmhouse where I first envisioned my walk between the chalk and the sea, but the landscape is more forgiving, with velvety green hedges fringing the lanes instead of rugged stone walls. We even have four pet sheep. Whether this house will ever feel like home, only time will tell. Under its foundations lies sandstone, not my bedrock. Chalk is where my roots are buried, and I still miss it. On the wall of our new sitting room hangs a framed copy of Ravilious's *The Vale of the White Horse*, depicting the Uffington White Horse high on its chalky hilltop just twenty miles from my former Oxford home. If I can't live near chalk, at least I can bring chalk, if only in painted form, home to me.

My modern pilgrimage diverged from Alice's medieval one in other ways. I hadn't met the trials and tribulations faced by Alice and her companions on the road, the injuries and diseases, the bandits and swindlers that threatened their progress, and sometimes their lives. The murder of Julia James, so near to where I walked as I approached Canterbury, was the closest I came to understanding those perils.

My mobile phone, as essential a piece of kit today as a pair of good walking boots, never fully allowed me to switch off from my work or domestic life. Unlike Alice's family and friends, mine could contact me at any time to check my progress, though I tried not to engage with that implacable luminous screen until the end of each day's walk.

There were similarities to medieval pilgrimage, as well as differences. I started my walk just before the Covid-19 pandemic took hold, and my four seasonal journeys through the Celtic calendar evaded three national lockdowns. Just like my medieval forebears whose lives were shaped by the Black Death and other devastating pandemics, I discovered that we too, despite our technological and medical advances, are at the mercy of events far greater than ourselves.

More revelations. With the notable exception of its feet, my body, in the autumnal equinox of my life, was as capable of a long walk as it was in its spring. We humans are made to walk, and if we continue walking we'll stay fit and agile into old age, as the many white-haired people I met climbing the hills between Southampton and Canterbury proved. This was as true 600 years ago, with Margery Kempe still walking at the then ripe old age of sixty – to the amazement of her fellow pilgrims:

> It was a great marvel and miracle that a woman unused to walking and about three score years of age should each day keep her pace with a vigorous and lusty man.
>
> (*The Book of Margery Kempe*)

But walking is far more than a physical act, a way of keeping fit. Above all, it offers a deep connection with the landscape, a serenity that comes from journeying across a terrain on foot.

My pilgrimage was not all serenity, of course. There were times, especially given the events of 2020 and 2021, when it would have been easier, justifiable even, to give up. After all, reaching the shrine of the 'holy blessed martyr', as Chaucer called St Thomas, was less important to me in this secular age than it was to Alice in her more devout one. Unlike a medieval pilgrimage where the objective, whether Jerusalem or Rome, Santiago or Canterbury, was the primary purpose, a modern pilgrimage is less focused on the destination.

Many people still travel to shrines for reasons of faith today, but faith – at least of a religious kind – is now not compulsory. As the British Pilgrimage Trust puts it, you can bring your own beliefs. My faith was in the act of walking itself: the earth beneath my feet, the nature around me and the people, both present and departed, I encountered on the path. My pilgrimage had become more than a long walk. It had become an affirmation of my love of the landscape, and my rootedness within it.

When I reached Canterbury there was no jewel-encrusted shrine awaiting me as once awaited Alice. Henry VIII saw to that. So comprehensively had Becket's shrine been annihilated that one of the only surviving remnants is a marble fragment. Fished out of the River Stour in 1984, over 500 years since it was tossed in, it's now on display in the British Museum. Other than my sorrow at the sheer nihilism of the act, for which Henry was finally excommunicated by an exasperated Pope Paul III, I didn't mind. The path was my shrine.

In 1538, when King Henry VIII outlawed shrine veneration, he struck at the heart of medieval religion and the economy it supported. Within a few decades, the infrastructure of pilgrimage had been largely dismantled. Shrines, such as Becket's, were destroyed or looted. When Henry also suppressed the monasteries, abbeys and hospitals that for centuries welcomed pilgrims were demolished, or turned into private houses. Old pilgrim routes became overgrown and long-established itineraries faded into obsolescence, existing only in a few rarefied documents such as the Gough Map.

Regardless of his most destructive efforts, Henry could not extinguish pilgrimage from our collective memory. All along my route I found its remnants. In the place names. In the customs and rituals unchanged for centuries. In those poignant park bench shrines. In the little kindnesses shown to a stranger on foot. Even in the tiny, chiselled symbols inside an isolated village church. In this age of turmoil and impermanence, when our lives can be so fragmented, I found this deeply reassuring.

The Old Way might be the pilgrimage route that history forgot, but nearly five centuries later it still lies there, just under our feet.

An account of the destruction of Roche Abbey

Written in 1591

In June 1538, Roche Abbey in South Yorkshire was surrendered to Henry VIII's commissioners, and the abbot and seventeen monks were made homeless. Thirty years later, one of these monks gave an account of the abbey's destruction to his nephew, Michael Sherbrook, the rector of nearby Wickersley.

Thereabout within the Abbey walls; nothing was spared but the ox-houses and swinecoates [pigsties], and such other houses of office that stood within the walls; which had more favour shown them than the very Church itself: which was done by the advice of Cromwell, as Fox reporteth in his Book of Acts and Monuments. It would have pitied any heart to see what tearing up of the lead there was, and plucking up of boards, and throwing down of the spares [rafters]; and when the lead was torn off and cast down into the Church, and the tombs in the Church all broken (for in most Abbeys were divers noble men and women, yea and in some Abbeys Kings, whose tombs were regarded no more than the tombs of all other inferior persons: for to what end should they stand, when the Church over them was not spared for their cause), and all things of price either spoiled, carped away, or defaced to the uttermost.

The persons that cast the lead into fodders, plucked up all the seats in the choir, wherein the monks sat when they said service, which were like to the seats in minsters, and burned them, and melted the lead therewithall: although there was wood aplenty within a flight shot of them: for the Abbey stood within the woods and the rocks of stone: in which rocks was pewter vessels found that was conveyed away and hid: so that it seemeth that every person bent himself to filch and spoil what he could: yea, even such persons were content to spoil them, that seemed not two days before to allow their religion, and do great reverence and worship at their Mattins, Masses and other service, and all other their doings: which is a strange thing to say, that they could this day think it to be the House of God, and the next day the House of the Devil.

The author entering Canterbury Cathedral, photographed by Will Parsons

Timeline

BC

c.145–65 | Formation of chalk during the Cretaceous period
million

c.500 | Mount Caburn, Chanctonbury and Cissbury Iron Age hillforts are built

AD

43–410 | Roman occupation of Britain

54 | Druidry is outlawed by Emperor Claudius

597 | St Augustine arrives in Canterbury

598 | St Augustine's Abbey, Canterbury, is founded

c.634 | Lyminge church is founded by St Ethelburga

c.650 | St Rumwold lives and dies

664 | Synod of Whitby

681 | St Cuthman is born

c.765 | Monastery is established at South Malling

c.950 | Botolphs church is built

1064 | Meeting between Harold Godwinson and Duke William of Normandy to discuss the succession to the English throne

1066 | Battle of Hastings and Norman Conquest

1070 | William orders Battle Abbey to be built; St Michael's Church, Southampton, built around this time c.1080   Lewes Priory is founded by William de Warenne and his wife, Gundrada

1086   *Domesday Book* is compiled

c.1120   Thomas Becket is born

1133   Southwick Priory is founded, initially sited in Portchester Castle

1154   Henry II becomes king of England; he appoints Becket as royal chancellor

1162   Becket takes holy orders and becomes Archbishop of Canterbury; he resigns as chancellor

1170   Thomas Becket is murdered in Canterbury Cathedral

1173   Becket is canonised as St Thomas Becket

1174   Henry II does penance at Becket's shrine; fire destroys part of Canterbury Cathedral

1197   God's House Southampton is founded

1215   Wilmington Priory is founded

1220   Becket's body is moved to new shrine in rebuilt Canterbury Cathedral

1222   Titchfield Abbey is founded

1238   Netley Abbey is founded

1264   Battle of Lewes

c.1280   Original Gough Map is produced

1287   The Great Storm redraws the south coast of England

1288   New Winchelsea is founded

c.1290   Richard of Southwick dies

1293   Joan de Vere dies; her tomb, originally at Lewes Priory, is now in Chichester Cathedral

TIMELINE

1320   William of Wykeham is born in Wickham

1329   Landgate is built in Rye

1338   French raid Southampton; Westgate is built

        Battle Abbey gatehouse and walls are begun

1348   Black Death arrives in England, carried by fleas on rodents

c.1360   Gough Map is recreated

1377   French attack Rye

1380   French raid Winchelsea and Appledore

1381   Peasants' Revolt

1387–1400   Chaucer writes *The Canterbury Tales*

1415   Henry V sails to France from Southampton, leading to the battle of Agincourt

1439   Henry V's flagship, the *Grace Dieu*, sinks in the Hamble

c.1440   *The Book of Margery Kempe* is dictated

1445   Henry VI marries Margaret of Anjou at Titchfield Abbey

c.1498   Wynkyn de Worde's *Informacion for Pylgrymes*

1521   Henry VIII is awarded title 'defender of the faith' by the Pope

1534   Henry VIII is declared Supreme Head of the Church in England

1536–9   Acts of Suppression (Dissolution of the Monasteries)

1538   Becket's shrine is destroyed during reign of Henry VIII and all images of Becket are ordered to be destroyed or covered up; St Richard of Chichester's tomb is destroyed; Camber Castle is begun

1541   Lady Margaret Pole, Countess of Salisbury, is executed

1546   Anne Askew is executed

1611   John Speed's map of Southampton

1720–1840   Acts of Enclosure

1804–9   Royal Military Canal is constructed as defence against a French invasion

1809   Richard Gough bequeathed the map that now bears his name to the Bodleian Library, Oxford

1904   Hilaire Belloc's *The Old Road* is published

1912   *Titanic* sails from Southampton

1932   Kinder Scout mass trespass, Derbyshire

1934   *The Book of Margery Kempe* is rediscovered

1935   First performance of T. S. Eliot's *Murder in the Cathedral*; Ramblers Association founded

1936   Jarrow March (also known as Jarrow Crusade)

1940   Southampton bombed in the Blitz

1941   Southwick House is requisitioned by the Royal Navy

1942   Eric Ravilious dies

1944   Operation Overlord (D-day landings) is planned at Southwick House

1954   A coffin containing the likely remains of King Harold is discovered at Bosham church

1956   Philip Larkin writes 'An Arundel Tomb'

1966   Pewter St Thomas ampule found in Cuckoo Lane, Southampton

1987   Great Storm on night of 15 October

TIMELINE

1993   High Weald becomes an Area of Outstanding Natural Beauty (AONB)

1994   Remains of Boxgrove Man/Woman are discovered

2000   Countryside and Rights of Way Act

2007   Steyning church is rededicated to St Andrew and St Cuthman

2010   South Downs are designated a National Park

2014   The British Pilgrimage Trust is founded

2018   Cuckmere Pilgrim Path is created

2020   Vera Lynn dies aged 103

       Start of Covid-19 pandemic and lockdowns

Acknowledgements

A solo walk is by definition a solitary undertaking, but pilgrims throughout history have relied on the support of family and friends, and random acts of kindness from strangers on the path. My walk along the Old Way was no exception. Indeed, it would never have transpired at all without Will Parsons, whose vision and dedication revived the Old Way after 500 years dormant, and whose sporadic company (with Holly and Felicity) added so much to my journey. Thank you, Will.

My gratitude extends to those along the path who appear in the book, particularly Rebecca Jennings for her hospitality and knowledge of the South Downs, as well as to those who don't, notably Ruth Lawrence, who offered lifts when buses proved sporadic, and Jackie Pelling for – literally – going the extra mile.

If an unaccompanied walk is (chiefly) autonomous, writing a book about it is anything but. Without the expertise of the following people, this would have been a markedly less scholarly effort: Stephen Moss, naturalist, author and supportive colleague at Bath Spa University; Dr Anne E. Bailey of Oxford University, medievalist and pilgrimage scholar; Tim Bridges, architectural historian and connoisseur of Sussex churches; William Connor, archivist and historian of Southampton (and elsewhere); Dr Amanda Tuke, botanist and plant ecologist; Dr Jennifer Jones, soil scientist at Liverpool John Moores University; Dr Corinna Riva of University College London, Etruscologist; Paul Gamble, Classicist; Dr Bozhil Hristov, Linguist; Sheila de Courcy, Researcher; Giles

Watson, Poet; John Strachan, Professor of English Literature at Bath Spa University; Laura Littlejohn, patient transcriber of copious voice recordings; Ian Cunningham, computer wizard; Venetia Kay and Philippa Rands, kind hosts in Cornwall as I finished this book.

With thanks to Guy Hayward and Dawn Champion of the British Pilgrimage Trust. You can find information on the Old Way and other pilgrim routes on the BPT website: www.britishpilgrimage.org. The BPT is also active on Twitter and Instagram: @pilgrimtrust.

To my agent, Sophie Lambert of C&W Agency, a thousand thanks. At Headline, Fiona Crosby, Sarah Emsley and Holly Purdham offered sterling help and advice, and Mark Handsley's copy-edits ironed out all those grammatical glitches that might otherwise have lingered in the text. Any remaining errors, factual or syntactical, are mine.

My final thanks go to Richard Bailey, domestic linchpin, history buff and neophyte shepherd.

PERMISSIONS

Chanctonbury Ring by Alec Buckels, reproduced with kind permission of Tim and Rupert Bridges.

The quotation on p. 155 is from *The Miracles of Saint James*, ed. and trans. by Thomas F. Coffey, Linda Kay Davidson and Maryjane Dunn. New York: Italica Press, 1996, p. 91. Copyright 1996 by Thomas F. Coffey, Linda Kay Davidson and Maryjane Dunn. Used by permission of Italica Press.